Dedication

Zora Arkus Duntov

He joined General Motors in 1953, the same year the Corvette was introduced. With a rich engineering and racing background, Zora Arkus-Duntov called the first Corvette a "sheep in wolf's clothing" and made it his personal mission to transform it into a world class performer. By 1957, Corvettes were ruling racetracks around the country and attaining the high-performance reputation that many say is the reason for its unprecedented thirty-year reign as *the* American sports car.

With respect and appreciation, this *Illustrated Corvette Buyer's Guide* is dedicated to Zora.

Michael Antonick

Illustrated **CORVETTE** BUYER'S GUIDE

Motorbooks International
Publishers & Wholesalers Inc.
Osceola, Wisconsin 54020, USA ®

First published in 1983 by Motorbooks International Publishers & Wholesalers Inc, PO Box 2, 729 Prospect Avenue, Osceola, WI 54020 USA

Printed and bound in the United States of America

Library of Congress Cataloging-in-Publication Data

Antonick, Mike.
Illustrated Corvette buyer's guide.

1. Corvette automobile. 2. Automobiles—Purchasing.
I. Title.
TL215.C6A58 1987 629.2'222 86-31070
ISBN 0-87938-240-6 (pbk.)

Cover photography by Michael Antonick

Motorbooks International books are also available at discounts in bulk quantity for industrial or sales-promotional use. For details write to Special Sales Manager at the Publisher's address

CREDITS AND ACKNOWLEDGEMENTS

My thanks to everyone who contributed in any way to the information and photos contained in this book. Special thanks to:

Noland Adams
John Amgwert
Pat Baker
Becky Bodnar
Dave Burroughs
Jim Downing
Ed Kenney
Gary Lisk
Bill Locke
Bob McDorman
Bill Munzer
Jeffrey Painter
Jon Solt
Chevrolet Motor Division

Corvette! America's Only—Michael Bruce Associates, Inc.
Corvette! America's Star Spangled Sports Car—Karl Ludvigsen / Automobile Quarterly
Corvette! The Sensuous American—Michael Bruce Associates, Inc.
The Corvette Black Book—Michael Bruce Associates, Inc.
Vette Vues—James Prather
The National Corvette Restorers Society

Mike Antonick

TABLE OF CONTENTS

INTRODUCTION

The Corvette is a uniquely American automobile phenomenon. Speak of Corvettes and someone within hearing range will join in as an expert. And if you find a person who hasn't owned a Corvette, he'll tell you he plans to own one, has always wanted one, has an uncle with five or a neighbor in the middle of a "body off" restoration. If Chevrolets are as American as apple pie, surely the Corvette must be the pie à la mode.

The Corvette has developed quite a following and reputation. Part of the reputation is the widespread belief in Corvettes as great investments. Owning a Corvette is the sure way to beat depreciation. Is it true?

A qualified yes. Historically, Corvettes have been excellent in value retention and appreciation. But there are exceptions.

Purchased new, a Corvette depreciates as any other car. Some salesmen would have you believe a new Corvette depreciates less than comparably priced American makes. Some Corvette models have, some haven't.

Anyone considering a new Corvette purchase who plans to keep it a few years or less should forget the investment angle. Operating expenses for the Corvette will be similar to other cars in the same price range. Corvette depreciation might well be less, but that will be offset by higher fuel, maintenance and insurance costs.

But what if you're planning to keep a new Corvette for a long time? Better yet, what if you're planning to get an older model? That's different.

Something interesting happens to Corvettes as they age. Depreciation stops and appreciation begins.

Mention "appreciation" and the economist in the crowd says cars are not great investments if a hard look is taken at the real rate-of-return. True enough, but cars aren't stocks and bonds. You can't drive a treasury note. Cars are instruments of utility or pleasure or both.

And they've become very expensive American habits, more so than most realize. In 1986, Hertz calculated the per mile operating costs for the average new car at over fifty cents. Fuel costs have seen dramatic swings since the early seventies, but the lion's share is still depreciation.

Shrewd Corvette owners have learned they can eliminate the depreciation factor from the operating cost equation and replace it with some appreciation which in some cases is enough to offset other costs. In effect, free driving.

Over the long run, would a smart Corvette purchase beat a solid investment in stocks, bonds or treasury notes? Probably not. Would a smart Corvette purchase beat most other automotive purchases? Yes.

At what point in its life cycle does a Corvette's value start increasing? There are no set rules. Every Corvette built between 1953 and 1967 is appreciating. Most built between 1968 and 1972 are appreciating. Some later models, up to and including 1978's, are appreciating.

As a group, the 1963 through 1967 models have been the hottest on the market in recent years. In the eleven-year period between 1975 and 1986, a *Vette Vues* survey of advertised prices indicated that both 1963 and 1967 models averaged over twenty-percent annual appreciation. That's enough to warm any CPA's heart.

For shock value, I'll tell you about some real appreciation. For a quarter-million dollars, you might be able to acquire one of the five Corvette Grand

Sports. Too stiff? $150,000 might be enough to acquire XP-819, the only experimental rear-engine Corvette Chevy ever let slip into private hands.

These are exceptions, cars most of us in the real world just talk about. They do illustrate that the Corvette market runs nearly as wide a price gamut as any of the so-called exotics, excluding $6 million Bugatti Royale madness.

The real world has thousands of older Corvettes available for purchase. Corvettes worth owning are never cheap, but I personally think even at today's prices many are bargains. Over the years I've observed that a really superb older Corvette was worth about the same as the current new model. It was true in 1962, 1972 and 1986. I think it will continue to be true.

Demand is the reason. More and more people recognize what these older Corvettes were . . . and are. They want one. It's important to understand the reasons the Corvette is perceived as being so desirable.

The construction of the car is one. For years Corvettes have been criticized by magazine people as having a chassis that was overbuilt and unnecessarily heavy. It's valid criticism because a lighter chassis with less-robust components would have been more fuel efficient. But from a prospective buyer's viewpoint, the rugged chassis construction of older Corvettes is purely advantageous.

Chevrolet mated a fiberglass body to that heavy chassis. Fiberglass doesn't rust, ever. But this doesn't mean rust is never a Corvette problem. Corvette frames rust, some so badly they have to be replaced.

The marriage of fiberglass body to metal frame meant the Corvette could never be of unit-body (body and frame welded together as a unit) construction. Unit-body versus separate body/chassis construction means little to a new car buyer, but body/chassis construction is a restorer's dream come true. After some disconnects and removal of body bolts, six average men can lift the entire body off a Corvette-chassis in an afternoon (the post-1984 models are a bit more complicated). Corvettes are built the way they are because of the fiberglass-to-metal-frame marriage, but Chevy engineers couldn't have created a more ideal car for restorers if that had been their top priority.

Another factor in the Corvette value story is what sort of car it is. The Corvette was born into Detroit's high performance era. In many ways it was the star of the show. As the industry swung from performance to economy, safety and pollution control, the Corvette remained a performer relative to competitors of the day. But relative to its own heritage, it lost ground.

An illustration: During 1981 I was at Chevrolet Engineering and spoke with engineers about the upcoming 1984 Corvette. The comment was made that with a skillful combination of engine tweaking and weight reductions, the new Corvette generation would achieve the straight-line acceleration levels of the 1963 models—not the fuel-injected 1963's—but those with carburetion.

The statement was made with a genuine degree of justifiable pride. After all, the 1984 and newer Corvette models are tremendous automobile achievements, especially in handling capability. But isn't it interesting that the 1963 was picked as the acceleration benchmark? Has there ever been another time in auto history when events so teamed-up against performance automobiles?

I never forgot that incident because it underscored clearly why older Corvettes have so much appeal and remain in demand. They were the premier performers in a performance age we're not likely to see again. Unlike cars that could make similar claims, the Corvettes were strongly built, available in adequate quantities to keep prices reasonable, and easily restored.

The government's role in auto performance during the seventies is important, too. New cars of today pollute less and are safer and more fuel efficient as the result of direct government regulation. Things like the seat-belt interlock systems of 1974 were fiascos, but the transportation world is a better place when all is weighed in.

Something had to give and performance was it. Corvette engineers deserve credit for maintaining a decent level of performance in the Corvette while coping with strangled engines, bloated bumper weights and all the rest. Give Uncle Sam credit for creating legendary Corvettes . . . the ones built before he got involved.

Another factor plays into the used Corvette value equation, but I'm pressed to know how to label it. It's a combination of World War II, the baby boom and lifestyle. Here's how it all ties together.

The contemporary sports car phenomenon is said to have started in this country when our servicemen returned from Europe with cars like the MG. But more important to the Corvette story is that when the servicemen returned to their wives and wives-to-be, they created the post World War II baby boom. The Corvette came along at the tail end of the boom and the two, the Corvette and the babies, grew up together. This was a golden era of auto production, an era when designs changed rapidly and kids sneaked around dealerships before introduction dates hoping for a glimpse of new models. For many of these young people, the Corvette represented the ultimate car dream.

This combination of events, Detroit's golden years, postwar babies, the Corvette's emergence as the performance dream car, is unique in auto history. No matter what era a young car-lover grew up in, there has always been some great car of the day to dream of. But cars usually get better as the years roll on. By the time those young people reached the point when they could afford the dream car of their youth, it no longer stacked up very well compared to newer offerings.

Not true for the Corvette; and this factor is the big one in the Corvette value story. People who would've done about anything to have a '61, or a split-window coupe, or a '67 roadster, grew up. When it was time to buy the car they'd dreamed of, the very same car looked and performed better than most available in new-car show rooms.

A personal example: I was in school when the 1963 Corvette was introduced. I walked into the local Chevy dealership cold. Thanks to the secrecy of the era, I hadn't seen a single photo of the new Corvettes. Some friends told me the new "Vettes" were slick, but I didn't pay any attention. Corvettes had never appealed to me all that much.

The first 1963 I saw, a Daytona blue, fuel-injected split-window coupe, stunned me. I walked around it in awe for an hour. No new car has ever done what that one did to me. My first Corvette came five years later, a well-worn 1963 convertible. More years passed before I could afford a new one, but guess what I bought. An immaculate 1963 coupe. Daytona blue. Fuel injected. Having been around Corvettes for several years, I assure you this is not a unique story.

What matters most is that Corvettes are great cars. If they weren't, the mystique, baby boom, fiberglass bodies . . . all of it would be meaningless if it turned out Corvettes weren't worth owning.

An entire aftermarket business of tremendous size exists for Corvette parts and related merchandise. It is far easier to maintain or restore any model Corvette today than it was fifteen years ago. In years past, I bought entire Corvettes just to switch interior components that weren't available. Today there are hundreds of

Corvette suppliers who offer a range of products to satisfy practically any need. No sooner does GM discontinue a Corvette part than some enterprising enthusiast has a reproduction available.

The parts availability in the Corvette aftermarket greatly reduces financial risk for a first-time buyer. A Corvette in your driveway may not impress the neighbors as much as a Lampredi V-12 Ferrari, but the risk factors aren't even in the same league. Pick a Ferrari with a sour motor and the repair bills could cost more than you pay for a gem of a Corvette . . . the whole car!

Don't think you can't make a mistake buying a Corvette. The consequences of making an error just aren't likely to be as painful as with other makes. Provided you don't buy a bogus Corvette, paying too much for it is like paying too much for good real estate. Eventually you'll be all right. It just takes longer.

There's no need to go through the pain of a poor purchase and that's what the *Illustrated Corvette Buyer's Guide* is all about. It's written with the assumption that you're not a Corvette expert and its purpose is twofold: to help you decide which Corvette model is best for you, and to help you select a good example.

Like any major purchase decision, you should research the subject thoroughly. Interest in Corvettes has led to several excellent Corvette books. There are also monthly Corvette magazines loaded with ads for Corvettes and parts that will give you a good feel for the market.

Where should your search for the right car begin? The common first choice is a local newspaper. For someone starting to look, it isn't the best choice. Nor is a monthly Corvette magazine. Anyone just beginning should expose himself to a lot of examples. Looking at cars advertised in the media takes too much time. Many people who try to find their first Corvette this way either jump into a purchase too quickly and get the wrong car, or they get so frustrated looking they give up.

I recommend going to a Corvette show. Corvette shows are unique to the Corvette hobby. There are hundreds held each year, ranging from small local events to major ones that draw over 10,000 people from all over the country. Shows are usually built around a concours competition, but the real attractions are the parts vendors and the buying and selling of Corvettes between individuals. A couple of the shows even conduct all-Corvette auctions. These are great for a first-time buyer as learning experiences, but I wouldn't recommend purchasing at an auction until you're very comfortable with your expertise level.

Check with some local Corvette enthusiasts to find out which shows in your area are worthwhile. Major ones include Knoxville, Tennessee, in mid-March; Bloomington, Illinois, in June; and Corvettes at Carlisle, at Carlisle, Pennsylvania, in August. On the West Coast, the big swap meet held four times per year at the Los Angeles County Fairgrounds in Pomona is always well-stocked with Corvettes for sale.

Go to just one good Corvette show and you'll see more Corvettes in a day than years of newspaper searching will yield.

Should you buy a Corvette at a show? Possibly, but the best Corvettes for sale are often not found at shows, or auctions, nor advertising in newspapers or magazines. They're sold by word of mouth. When someone has a topnotch Corvette for sale he need only mention it to a few people. The word spreads.

Finding a car by word of mouth is easier said than done for someone just entering the market. But it's not as hard as it sounds. Contacts you make with a local Corvette club, regardless of whether you join, can pay off. So can the right word placed with a few people at your local Chevy dealership. Once you've gone to a few shows and have a clearer idea of what you're after and the right questions to ask, you should definitely search monthly magazines like *Vette Vues, Hemmings Motor News* and *Cars & Parts*. The car you call about might not be the right one but the conversation could lead to it. Expose yourself.

More important than *where* you find a Corvette is the scrutiny you give it before buying. Taking along a knowledgeable Corvette buff really pays off. What you have to avoid at all costs is unknowingly buying a bogus Corvette. Bogus?

Simply put, a bogus Corvette is not what it appears. It's a '64 coupe that's been altered to look like a more valuable '63 split-window. Or it's a '68 with a disguised '76 Camaro engine. Or it's four wrecks pieced into one. The caliber of the seller can be an indication, but not necessarily. He may have been stuck by someone else and is trying to unload.

A bogus Corvette is a fake, and there are lots of them. For example, real fuel-injected Corvettes of the variety built between 1957 and 1965 are rare and valuable. There are probably twice as many fuel-injected Corvettes in existence today than GM ever built.

Is originality such a big deal? So what if an engine or a few components have worn out and been replaced? As long as everything works properly, what's the difference?

The difference is in the Corvette's value. Originality is tremendously important to Corvette enthusiasts. It is to any auto enthusiast group, but Corvette buffs take it to extremes.

I'm not sure why. Part of it may be a backlash to all the modifications done to Corvettes during the hot rod era. A lot of Corvettes have been abused. If an older Corvette survived with all components intact, it's a good indication that it's been reasonably well treated. Also, Corvettes have been a favorite of thieves for years. Most often they're stripped and the parts wind up on cars from one end of the country to the other.

There's something unsettling about all this to Corvette enthusiasts which makes them insist that a Corvette be as close as possible to the way it left the factory. Don't take originality lightly. It's a serious consideration and greatly affects a Corvette's value.

Most advertisements for Corvettes contain a statement like "all numbers match." Many people who advertise this way don't know themselves what numbers they're referring to, but figure they'd better say they're correct since everyone else does. The *Illustrated Corvette Buyer's Guide* will explain the "numbers" so that you'll be able to determine with reasonable assurance that the Corvette you're considering for purchase is what it's represented to be.

Even if all numbers appear correct, you can't be absolutely certain the car is correct—the rewards for faking a Corvette can be high. Faking a Corvette properly takes skill and expense and normally occurs only on models where it's worthwhile. If you're looking for a very special and expensive Corvette, like a '63 fuel-injected coupe, do your homework well before making the purchase decision.

Many people looking for a used car take their "mechanic" along. If you're after a Corvette and your mechanic isn't a Corvette specialist, his usefulness to you is limited. He can tell you some things about the car's general operating condition, but this is only part of what you need to know. Take along someone who can also help you determine the car's correctness in terms of originality.

Does it matter if a Corvette has been painted a different color than originally painted by the factory? Yes, especially if it's a '63 or later model, because the correct color is coded into trim plates on the car. As a general rule, a repaint of the wrong color devalues a Corvette by the amount it would cost to correct it. Unless you do your own work, you'll never get by for under $1,500.

Body damage is another area of importance. Some people place great value on a Corvette that has had minimal bodywork. I'm one of them. It's not easy to find exactly what you want in an older Corvette—and find it with no body damage to boot—but I'd sacrifice a few things to get a good body. Corvettes with extensive damage, particularly front end, never seem to look right again. This is especially true of '63 and later models with hidden headlights. Invariably, repaired Corvettes wind up with just enough misfitting components to give the car a sort of goofy, distorted look.

One of the first things to do when inspecting a Corvette is to get it on a big level parking lot and walk around it awhile. If it's been whacked, it'll show up in bad panel alignments, cocked bumpers . . . a kind of disheveled look.

But Corvettes weren't flawlessly built by General Motors; and some body flaws occur naturally with age. To an untrained eye, some things that look like signs of a crash aren't. This is another good reason to get to a show and view as many Corvettes as possible. You'll learn that stress-cracking of paint due to the flexing of the fiberglass body is normal. But if you look at enough examples of the model you're interested in, you'll also know that the cracks occur in predictable areas. Finding one with cracks where they don't normally occur is a sign of trouble.

Though the main body shell of 1953-82 Corvettes looks like a single piece of fiberglass, it isn't. It is made up of many panels, much like a metal car, that are bonded together. At the point the panels bond, a groove is created. The factory fills and sands these grooves before painting, but it is common for seams to separate slightly or for the filler material to shrink a little. Barely visible seam lines on a Corvette with a few years' use are to be expected and don't reduce its value at all, unless it's being presented and priced as a concours specimen.

If a series of little dimples around the seams are seen, watch out. The car has been in an accident because the dimples are filled holes created by screws or rivets that temporarily held the panels in position during a repair. Investigate thoroughly. Possibly it was just a minor scrape that only popped the panels loose. Or the damage may have been serious enough to require complete panel replacements.

Starting with the 1984 model, engineers eliminated all visible seams by hiding them behind the side-body rub strip, or just casting large panels like the one-piece hood. Damage to these models can't be passed off as seam flaws.

I don't wish to overemphasize the repair aspect. You can find Corvettes with absolutely no body damage, but you may rule out some perfectly fine examples in the process. The important thing is to remove as much mystery as possible before you buy. Nothing is more sickening than buying what you thought was a jewel, only to discover the following morning the whole nose has been replaced from the wheel wells forward. I hate to admit it, but I've done just that.

As a matter of courtesy, don't demand to drive a Corvette that's for sale unless you have some interest in it. One of the bad things about being on the selling side of the transaction is the number of joy-riders who show up with no intention of purchasing.

If all stacks up correctly and you've found a genuine candidate, by all means give it a thorough shakedown. Don't abuse it. The owner will likely demand to ride along and I've heard of some who refused to sell to someone who acted like the village idiot on the test drive.

Start by giving the Corvette the same scrutiny you would any used car. Ailments often show up as sounds so listen carefully. If equipped with manual transmission, don't "speed shift," but do shift briskly through all gears. Downshift through the gears at reasonable rpm. Double-clutching the downshifts is fine once you own it, but not when you're test driving, as this could hide marginal synchronizers.

Corvettes built between 1963 and 1982 have six universal joints in the drive line. They're heavy-duty units, but six means that at any given time it isn't unusual for one to be acting up. Minor consideration, but just don't confuse a bad U-joint with a growling differential making its last stand.

Another common failure point in 1963 through 1982 Corvettes is the rear wheel bearing and spindle setup. If one is going out it won't be any secret. These cost more to repair than you'd anticipate, but still are relatively minor considerations. Negotiate a hundred or two off the asking price.

I can't describe to you how the model Corvette you want should feel and sound when you drive it. You'll have to develop the experience yourself. I'll tell you this: I've driven a few '63 Corvettes that were breathtakingly exciting. Exaggerating very little, I've also driven some that felt and sounded like dump trucks — breathtaking in their own bizarre way, but not worth owning. Many Corvettes have been terribly abused. Others have been subjected to amateur restorations. There is a world of difference in used Corvettes and in the way they drive.

Obviously, the ideal used Corvette is a well-maintained, low-mileage original purchased from its only owner with a documented history from the date of purchase. They're around but scarce and expensive.

But don't get too hung up on miles. The nicest driving Corvette I've ever experienced is one I still have, a '67 with just over 15,000 miles. The next best is a friend's nearly identical '67 with over 100,000 miles. An abused Corvette can be shot after a few thousand miles. A cared-for Corvette will drive well indefinitely.

I think the single most important mistake a first-time Corvette buyer can make is to pay too much for a Corvette that needs considerable work. Someone unfamiliar with the Corvette parts aftermarket will underestimate refurbishing costs every time. Unless you're itching to do your own complete restoration, my advice is to pay the additional price for a solid, complete and correct car. It's been my observation for years that excellent Corvettes seldom sell for what they're really worth, but junkers sell for too much.

The next chapters of the *Illustrated Corvette Buyer's Guide* deal with individual Corvette models and will help you narrow your choices before the search begins. As you read these chapters, another of the Corvette's great virtues becomes apparent: because of the range of engines and options, Corvettes can be about any kind of car you want. In the mid-sixties alone, they ranged from air-conditioned, 250-horsepower turnpike cruisers, to street-scorching, 435-horsepower whiplash specials. And everything in between.

INVESTMENT RATING

★★★★★ The best investments. Already expensive, but continued high appreciation can be expected. The finest examples are most often sold or traded between Corvette enthusiasts without advertising.

★★★★ Excellent investments. More affordable than five-star-rated Corvettes, but still expensive with high appreciation anticipated. These are often sold or traded among enthusiasts, but they can also be located at Corvette shows and meets, and are often advertised in Corvette-only publications.

★★★ Very good investments. These are less expensive than four- or five-star-rated Corvettes and will appreciate at lower rates, but are still solid values. Because of their lower cost and a correspondingly larger market, cars in this category are particularly attractive to first-time buyers.

★★ Good investments. These are Corvettes which are too new to be in the appreciation cycle, or older models which haven't developed a strong appreciation history. There are possible "sleepers" in this category, which could develop into tomorrow's three- or four-star models.

★ Marginal investments. Corvettes don't belong in this category unless they've been seriously damaged, substantially modified, or have had major components (i.e., engine) changed.

The star rating system above requires interpretation for Corvettes. With just a few exceptions, annual Corvette production has always far exceeded that of "exotic" sports cars. Corvettes are not scarce, but some Corvettes with special equipment are.

Some of the chapters that follow group several Corvette model years. The groups are star-rated according to their overall strength and popularity. Within each group—each year for that matter—there are Corvettes which both exceed and fall short of the group rating and the more significant ones are given separate ratings where appropriate. For example, Chapter Six covers 1963 and 1964 models, which are very similar, and as a group the two years merit a four-star rating. However, a very original 1963 coupe with desirable options like fuel injection and knock-off wheels would definitely qualify as a five-star investment. In all cases, the ratings require some judgment and common sense application by the prospective buyer.

The one-star rating has not been given to any group because it is a condition rating reserved for problem cars. Any Corvette in any category could be one-star rated. Conversely, very special Corvettes exist in each group which deserve five stars regardless of the group's rating.

The single most important factor in determining an individual Corvette's value is its originality. Corvette enthusiasts believe that the ideal Corvettes are those in the condition they were in when built. This concept places great value on highly documented cars with original equipment. Restored Corvettes can be nearly as valuable, but must be correctly restored to factory specifications. Custom or modified Corvettes, while interesting in their own right, should not be a part of anyone's investment strategy.

Good luck with your Corvette search and purchase. It'll be worth it.

CHAPTER 1

1953 CORVETTE

Serial Nos. E53F001001 - E53F001300

Life began for the Corvette in 1951. The initial seed was planted by Harley Earl, the legendary creator of GM's Art and Color Section, which was the predecessor of auto industry styling departments around the world.

Like many great ideas, the Corvette was almost an accident. From 1949 to 1961, General Motors operated its famous Motorama shows, lavish showcases for presentation of each year's new offerings plus a few "dream" cars to pull the crowds in.

In 1951, Earl commissioned a young stylist, Bob McLean, to draw up a two-seater "sports car" for the 1953 Motorama. McLean created the Corvette, Chevy Chief Engineer Ed Cole saw and loved it; and the rest is history.

But it wasn't a smooth history, at least not early on. Cole begged for and got permission to bring the Corvette into the Chevrolet camp and to display it as a running dream car in the 1953 Motorama. If public response justified it, consideration would be given to putting a derivative into production.

Cole decided instead to build the Motorama Corvette as a genuine preproduction prototype. The Corvette went from styling clay model to running prototype in seven months, surely a record of some sort. Cole was gambling that he would get permission to put the Corvette into production and he wanted to be ready. The Corvette was finished in time, barely, for the January kickoff of the 1953 Motorama at the Waldorf Astoria in New York City.

Cole had guessed correctly. The Corvette was a smashing crowd success and Cole got the permission he'd anticipated to rush the Corvette into production.

Rush is hardly the adequate description of the Corvette's blazing journey from idea to reality. In June 1952, it was a clay model. In January 1953, it was a running preproduction prototype. By the end of 1953, Chevrolet managed to introduce the car as a 1953 model and to build 300 units!

The 1953 is the rarest of all Corvette years. About 200 of the 300 built are still known to exist, but the first two off the line have never been accounted for. Officially, they were engineering test vehicles and were destroyed, but no witnesses or documentation has ever surfaced. Find one of these and you'll have found one of the most valuable cars in existence.

All 1953 Corvettes were polo white with sportsman red interiors and had black canvas convertible tops. All were pretty much hand-built in Flint, Michigan, in the back of the customer delivery garage, an old building on Van Slyke Avenue. Chevrolet sensed tremendous demand for the Corvette and readied a plant in St. Louis to build nearly a thousand per month starting with the 1954 model.

On June 30, 1953, the first Corvette was driven off the assembly line in Flint, Michigan. Officially, the first and second Corvettes built were destroyed as test vehicles, but neither a witness nor documentation has ever surfaced. Enthusiasts still dream today of finding Corvette serial number one. Whoever does will have found the most valuable Corvette ever. Chevrolet photo.

The original Motorama Corvette shown here was remarkably similar to the production version that followed. The Chevrolet script above the grille and the air scoops on the front fenders ahead of the windshield were deleted from the production cars. The side body trim was also changed. The photo showing the Chevrolet sedan behind the Motorama Corvette illustrates that the Corvette, with a wheelbase of 102 inches, was not a small automobile. Chevrolet photos.

Visually, the 1953 is a virtual twin to the 1954 and 1955 Corvettes. But because of its scarcity, its hand-built characteristics in the humble Flint facility, and most of all because it started it all, the 1953 is in a category by itself when it comes to ownership.

Contrary to popular belief, 1953 Corvettes are available. The days of finding one in an unknowing farmer's barn for $800 (if those days ever existed) passed twenty years ago. But if you have the financial means, you can buy one. Expect to pay at least double, perhaps triple, the price of a 1954 in comparable condition.

Anyone serious about purchasing a 1953 should plan to join the National Corvette Restorers Society (NCRS) and to attend some of their events. The NCRS is dedicated to the restoration and preservation of 1953 through 1972 Corvettes. In its earlier days, the NCRS limited its membership to owners of 1953 through 1962 models, the so-called classics, and the organization is still top-heavy with these members. Most of the good 1953's are owned by NCRS members, which means attending their events will allow you to view early Corvettes and get firsthand information of those for sale. Joining the NCRS is excellent advice for someone searching for any 1972 or older model.

They may look alike, but the 1953 was not a 1954. In fact, because of the evolutionary way they were hand-produced, an early 1953 was a lot different than a late 1953. So not only do you need to know the differences between the two years, you should also master the 1953 model running changes.

Things unique to the 1953 model included a black oilcloth window storage bag, a black canvas top, special valve cover, one-piece carburetor connecting linkage and a smaller trunk mat. Short exhaust extensions were used on all 1953's and early 1954's, then were extended to eliminate a tendency of early Corvettes to suck exhaust fumes into the cockpit when a vent window was open.

All 1953 and 1954 Corvettes used a Blue Flame six-cylinder engine, a tweaked version of a motor that had been in the Chevrolet stable for years, but the engines installed in the first two Corvette years have different serial coding and some internal running changes.

Very early 1953 models left the factory with Chevy Bel Air "dome" wheel covers before the Corvette covers arrived. The Corvette wheel cover for the rest of 1953 through 1955 was essentially the same design except that a few vendor prototype caps (maybe a hundred) got mixed in with 1953 production. The difference was that the rare caps had the spinner ornaments mounted perpendicular to the center bow-tie emblem. The rest were parallel. The spinners themselves were plated brass forgings at first, then zinc die castings.

Chevrolet didn't offer any 1953 Corvettes with wire wheels, but some dealers added them, hence the "My uncle bought it new and it came with . . ." dilemma. The same is true for hardtops.

When you get right down to it, there's very little leeway in what a 1953 should or shouldn't have. Though listed as options, every 1953 had a radio and heater. All had whitewalls. None had tinted glass, air conditioning, power steering or power brakes. There were no color and trim plates, but it didn't matter. Every 1953 was painted and trimmed to match the Motorama car . . . polo white exterior with sportsman red interior. Period.

With every other Corvette model year, the buyer has some choice of colors and options to weigh into the purchase decision. With the 1953, originality and condition are the value factors.

If you're considering a 1953, it's important to take special note of any missing parts. Some engine components were shared with the passenger car version of the engine. But others, like the valve cover, were unique to the Corvette. The 1953 Corvette valve cover was a highly modified passenger car type (front section flattened to clear hood), which bolted to the head with two studs attached to the top of the rocker arm assembly. Nineteen fifty-three Corvette valve cover decals were also unique. The decals had the words Blue Flame on the passenger side, and Special on the driver side. There's also a lightning bolt decal on the driver side of the cover.

Body parts like the grille, grille oval, bumpers, taillights and especially the side window frames, are expensive to find and purchase. Make a careful list of what parts the car you're interested in needs, and get an idea of their cost before closing the deal. What at first appeared to be an excellent buy may be washed out by the steep cost of parts for the first Corvette series.

Can the 1953 be a good investment? Definitely. The one thing keeping most Corvettes out of the mega-buck collector category is that, compared to foreign exotics, a lot of Corvettes were built and a lot survive thanks to the fiberglass body and generally rugged construction. But production of 300 cars over thirty years ago is low by any measure. The mere scarcity of the 1953 Corvette will keep its appreciation strong.

Is the 1953 a practical year to own? Aside from its value and the special constraints that imposes, definitely yes again. The 1953 does suffer from some problems that nearly sank the entire Corvette boat right after launch—things like a leaky top, less-than-breathtaking performance from its six-cylinder/Powerglide combination and finicky side-mounted carbs—but over the years it has proven to be very durable and generally trouble-free. As an everyday driver, most people would opt for a 1956 or later. A 1954 looks the same as a 1953 to most people at a fraction of the initial cost. But as an investment, the 1953 stands alone.

1953 Corvette

BASE ENGINE	
Type:	Chevrolet ohv inline 6
Bore x stroke, inches:	3.56x3.96
Displacement, inches:	235.5
Compression ratio:	8.0:1
Carburetion:	Three Carter single-throats
Horsepower:	150 @ 4200
Distributor:	Single point breaker
Other engines offered:	None
CHASSIS AND DRIVETRAIN	
Clutch:	n/a
Transmission:	Two-speed automatic
Front suspension:	Coil springs, tube-type shock absorbers, stabilizer bar
Rear suspension:	Leaf springs, tube-type shock absorbers, rigid axle
Axle ratio:	3.55:1
Frame:	Steel box sections, welded
GENERAL:	
Wheelbase, inches:	102
Track, front, inches:	57.0
rear, inches:	58.8
Brakes:	Drum
Tire size, front and rear:	6.70-15
Wheels:	Steel
Body material:	Fiberglass
Assembly plant:	Flint, Michigan

Shortly after the Corvette was introduced in 1953, Chrysler engineers borrowed one from a dealer and photographed it extensively. The photos are valuable to restorers today because they show a very early Corvette completely untouched. These exterior views show ill-fitting panels (note hood), short exhaust tips common to all 1953's and the rare hubcaps with spinners perpendicular to the bow-tie emblem. Chrysler photos.

1953 Corvette Colors/Options

Color Code	Body Color	Soft Top Color
None	Polo White	Black

INTERIOR COLOR: Red

Order #	Item Description	Sticker Price
2934	Base Corvette Convertible	$3498.00
101A	Heater	91.40
101B	Signal Seeking AM Radio	145.15

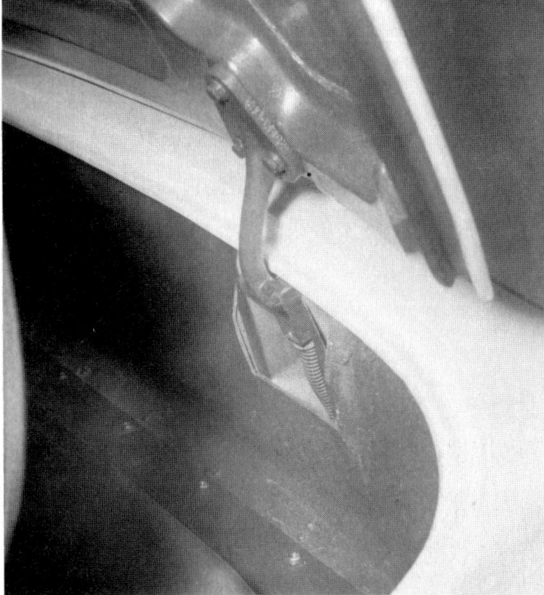

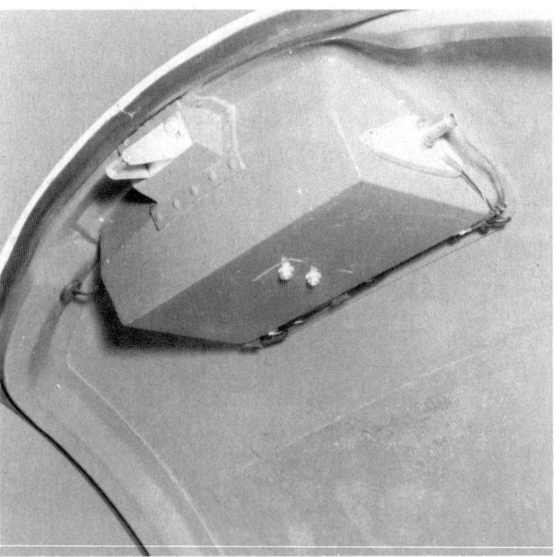

These photos from the Chrysler series show the roughness which was characteristic of early Corvette production. Most restorers today feel it is wrong to correct the roughness for cosmetic appearance. Early Corvettes that have been "over-restored" are usually less valuable than those restored to a state typical of factory build. Chrysler photos.

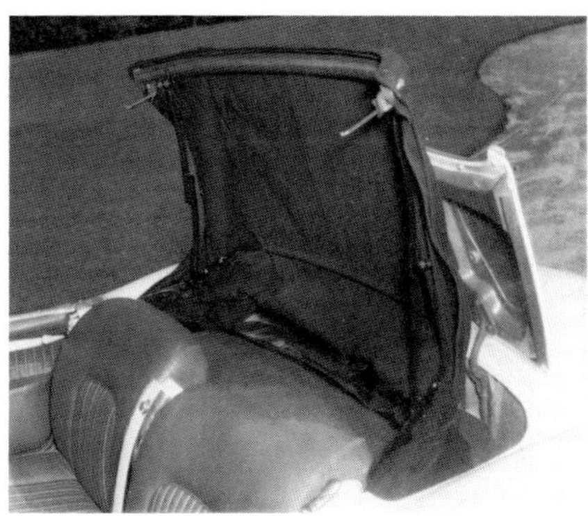

The side windows of the 1953 Corvette were plastic and had to be removed for storage in black oilcloth bags in the trunk. The soft top folded manually into a storage compartment behind the seats. These features were consistent with European sports cars of the period, but didn't find favor among the country club set "chosen" by Chevrolet to buy the 1953 Corvettes. Chrysler photos.

All 1953 Corvettes had Powerglide automatic transmissions with an unusual floor-mounted selector lever. Some criticized the instrument panel of the first generation of Corvettes for the central placement of engine-monitoring instruments, a shortcoming not corrected until the 1958 model. But to its credit, even the 1953 Corvette came with complete instrumentation including tachometer, oil pressure, battery, water temperature and fuel gauges, and a clock. Chrysler photo.

It may not have been exotic, but the Blue Flame six-cylinder engine installed in the first Corvette generation was certainly durable. This engine, a modified version of one that had been in Chevrolet's stable for years, required side-draft carburetors and a modified valve cover to clear the Corvette's low hood. Chrysler and Chevrolet photos.

In the euphoria surrounding the introduction of the Corvette, Chevrolet had visions of producing an entire family of vehicles based on the Corvette, including a station wagon and sport coupe. Disappointing sales canceled those projects and almost canceled the Corvette itself. Chevrolet photo.

CHAPTER 2

1954-1955 CORVETTE

(1955 V-8)

Serial Nos. 1954: E54S001001 - E54S004640
1955: VE55S001001 - VE55S001700*
(*no "V" prefix for six-cylinder 1955 models)

As planned, Chevrolet shifted production of the Corvette from Flint, Michigan, to a newly prepared facility in St. Louis, Missouri, for the 1954 model. As the 1953 was being mostly hand-built in Flint, tooling designed for higher volume was phased in. For 1954, Chevrolet was all set to roll with the Corvette. The planned 10,000-plus production for 1954 was small compared to GM's other car lines, but still a far cry from the 300 Corvettes made in Flint during the first year.

Chevrolet was ready, but the public wasn't. More accurately, the public had changed its mind. In a classic marketing misfire right up there with the Edsel, Chevrolet had decided to sell its 300 1953 Corvettes to special customers of its choosing, well-heeled status people. This highly discriminating policy would never fly today, but Chevy reasoned then that if high rollers owned the first Corvettes, there'd be a sort of image ruboff.

The problem was that the Corvette rubbed the country club set the wrong way. Remember, the Corvette wasn't cheap. It was a few dollars more than a Cadillac and double a bare-bones Chevy coupe. For Caddy dollars, these folks expected their Corvettes to be two-seat powderpuffs. Imagine their surprise the first time they tried to roll the windows down. They didn't roll down, they unbolted and stored in the trunk. And they leaked, as did the top.

Maybe marketing the Corvette directly to the sports car crowd wouldn't have worked either. Regardless, by the time Chevy was rarin' to go in St. Louis, the market had vanished.

Of the only 3,640 1954 Corvettes built in St. Louis, over 1,100 remained unsold at year's end. Faced with this, Chevrolet slashed 1955 Corvette production to the bone—a mere 700 cars. In so doing, it created the second scarcest model year Corvette.

The Corvette was in real trouble and Chevrolet knew it. By 1954, the problems were clear, but solving them would take some time. In the meantime, Chevy had to resort to the expedient.

One obvious need was for some colors. The white/red combination, which continued to dominate, and a new pennant blue/shoreline beige package accounted for ninety-five percent of 1954 production. A beautiful red/red combination crept in for about three percent. A few black/red cars were also definitely built, but no others have been absolutely confirmed. Some enthusiasts maintain that metallic green and metallic bronze were used in 1954 and cite memos

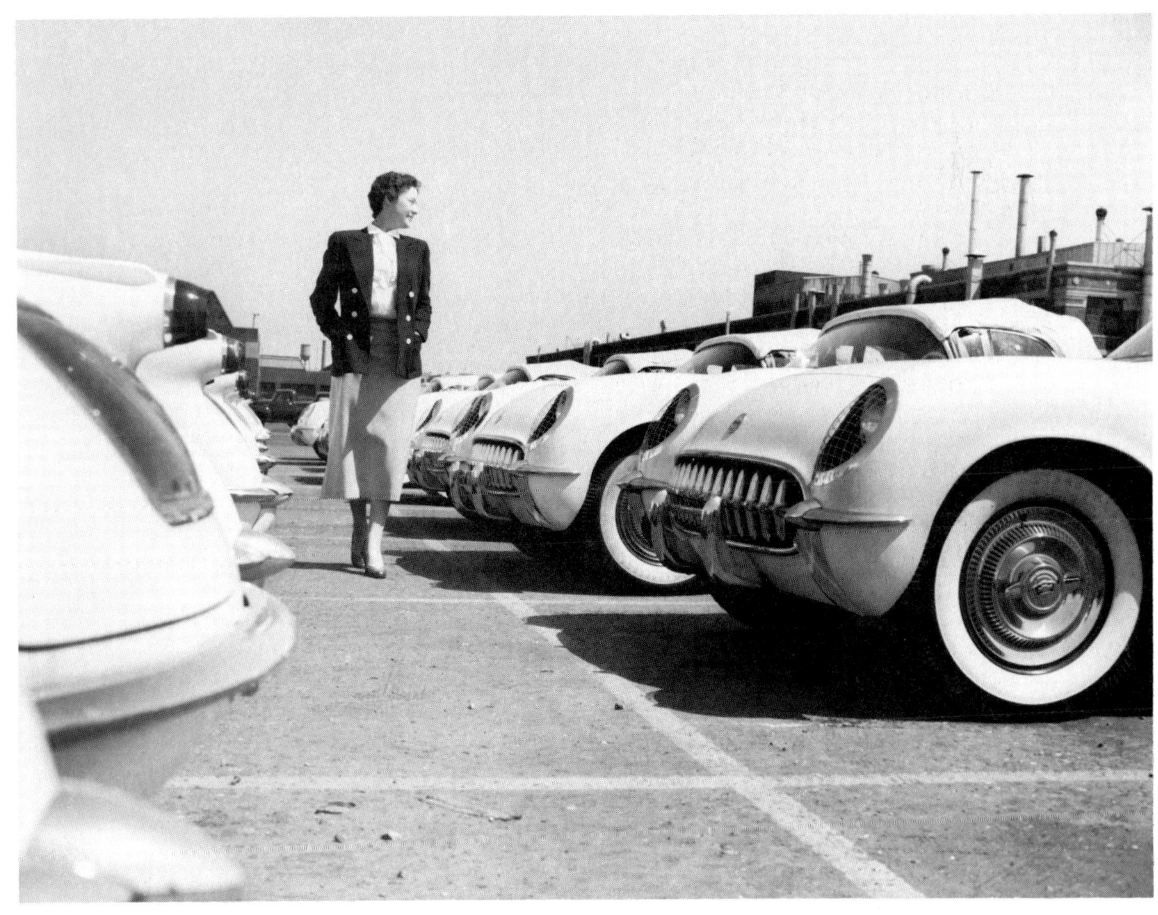

This photo shows 1954 models in the holding yard outside the new Corvette plant in St. Louis. The plant was designed to produce at least 10,000 Corvettes annually, but only 3,640 were built in 1954 and many of those were unsold at year's end. The Corvette was in trouble. Chevrolet photo.

from paint suppliers to GM as evidence. But no color/trim tags were attached to 1954 or 1955 models, so positive confirmation isn't possible. Since original colors were not color coded to individual cars, some enthusiasts today accept a paint change to another correct color as not particularly sinful.

All the 1954 models had the Powerglide automatic transmission and the six-cylinder Blue Flame engine. Horsepower during 1954 production was increased from 150 to 155. All 1954 models had the 6-volt electrical system common to the 1953. A 1954 engine looked much like a 1953, but there were differences. The serial numbers were different, and the valve cover was different. Where the 1953 Corvette cover attached with two central studs, the 1954 type attached with four bolts around the outside lip. The 1954 Corvette valve cover decals had Blue Flame and 150 reading from the passenger car side, and the 1954 decal lettering was larger than that of the 1953.

To alleviate complaints about power, Chevrolet wedged its hot new V-8 into the Corvette in 1955 and made a manual transmission available later in the year. Most 1955's were V-8-powered but a handful of sixes were built. Interestingly, the V-8's got 12-volt electrical systems, but the six-cylinder models got the old 6-volt electrics. Nobody has ever found a six-cylinder 1955 with anything but a Powerglide transmission. Also, six-cylinder 1955's did not have the frame relief (unique to the 1955) required for V-8 fuel pump clearance.

The six-cylinder engine and Powerglide automatic transmission installed in all 1954 and a few 1955 Corvettes remained the same as in 1953 except for subtle differences. Internally, a camshaft modification during 1954 production increased engine horsepower from 150 to 155. Photos by Bill Locke during the restoration of his 1954 model.

Robust chassis construction of the Corvette is evident in this photo of Bill Locke's 1954. Note the different-style valve cover used on 1954 and 1955 six-cylinder models. The individual bullet air cleaners were used on all Corvettes through serial number E54S003906. Later six-cylinders had an integrated dual-pot apparatus. Bill Locke photo.

The interior of 1954 and 1955 models remained similar to the 1953. Differences included the addition of Conelrad national defense markings to the radio face and a change from two interior hood releases to one early in 1954 production. Tonneau cover snaps are often seen on Corvettes of this period but they were owner additions, since Chevrolet has never offered a tonneau cover option for the Corvette. Author photo.

1954 Corvette Colors/Options

Color Code	Body Color	Soft Top Color
None	Polo White	Beige
None	Pennant Blue	Beige
None	Sportsman Red	Beige
None	Black	Beige

INTERIOR COLORS: Red, Beige

Order #	Item Description	Sticker Price
2934	Base Corvette Convertible	2774.00
100Q	Directional Signal, Polo White	16.75
100R	Directional Signal, Pennant Blue	16.75
101A	Heater	91.40
102A	Signal Seeking AM Radio	145.15
290B	Whitewall Tires, 6.70x15	26.90
313M	Powerglide Automatic Transmission	178.35
420A	Parking Brake Alarm	5.65
421A	Courtesy Light	4.05
422A	Windshield Washer	11.85

1955 Corvette Colors/Options

Color Code	Body Color	Soft Top Color
None	Polo White	White-Beige
None	Harvest Gold	Dark Green
None	Gypsy Red	Beige
None	Corvette Copper	White
None	Pennant Blue	Beige

INTERIOR COLORS: Red, Yellow, Light Beige, Dark Beige

Order #	Item Description	Sticker Price
2934-6	Base Corvette Convertible—6 Cylinder	2774.00
2934-8	Base Corvette Convertible—8 Cylinder	2909.00
100Q	Directional Signal, Polo White	16.75
100R	Directional Signal, Pennant Blue	16.75
101A	Heater	91.40
102A	Signal Seeking AM Radio	145.15
290B	Whitewall Tires, 6.70x15	26.90
313M/N	Powerglide Automatic Transmission	178.35
420A	Parking Brake Alarm	5.65
421A	Courtesy Light	4.05
422A	Windshield Washer	11.85

Corvette buffs argue about exterior colors for 1955 and the picture is even more confusing than 1954. Chevrolet definitely added a Corvette copper with beige interior and a harvest gold (really a yellow) with green and yellow interior. Repeat, green and yellow. GM was willing to try anything!

A red exterior was again available in 1955 but it was combined with a light beige interior instead of red as before. The soft top of the 1954 was canvas like the 1953 except that 1954's were tan. In 1955, soft tops were both canvas and vinyl. And new top colors appeared including white and dark green. Air conditioning, power windows and power steering were not available.

As investments, both the 1954 and 1955 Corvettes have been excellent. Because of the lower number built, and the tendency to abuse the V-8 engine package, good 1955's are much harder to find and are considerably more valuable. Though the Blue Flame six-cylinder was very durable, the Chevrolet V-8 is surely one of history's great motors. It was instrumental in the Corvette's later success, and installed in a 1955 yielded a quick, responsive package combined with the Corvette's original body style. It's a very desirable automobile.

On the other hand, the 1954 model offers the prospective owner the chance to own a genuine classic Corvette for a relatively modest cost, due to the quantity built and the uncommonly high survival rate.

Speaking of survival, you may be wondering how the Corvette managed to survive 1955 when a facility designed to pump out 10,000 cars made a paltry 700. There *was* some corporate ego at stake since Ford introduced its highly successful Thunderbird in 1955; but history tends to give credit for the Corvette's survival to two men: Ed Cole and Zora Arkus-Duntov.

Cole simply never wavered in his love of the Corvette and his belief that it was good for Chevrolet, General Motors and America. He wouldn't take no for an answer.

Duntov came to Chevrolet in 1953 at the age of forty-three after a career mostly in Europe as an engineer and racer. He wasn't hired to transform the Corvette, but he did. He sensed immediately that the Corvette's very life hinged on making it do what it looked like it should. In a word, he made it *go*.

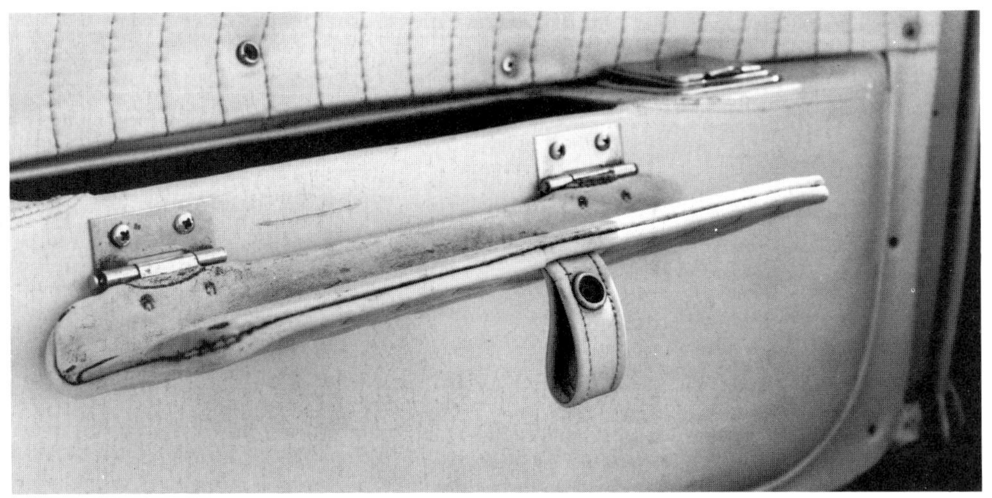

All 1953-55 Corvettes had this handy flip-up armrest cover, which exposed a large storage bin inside the inner door. Author photo.

The 1955 Corvette was a near duplicate of the previous two models, but performance was enhanced by the addition of the V-8 engine and manual transmission. Chevrolet also added several new colors to enhance sales. Despite these efforts, a mere 700 1955 Corvettes were built. Author photo.

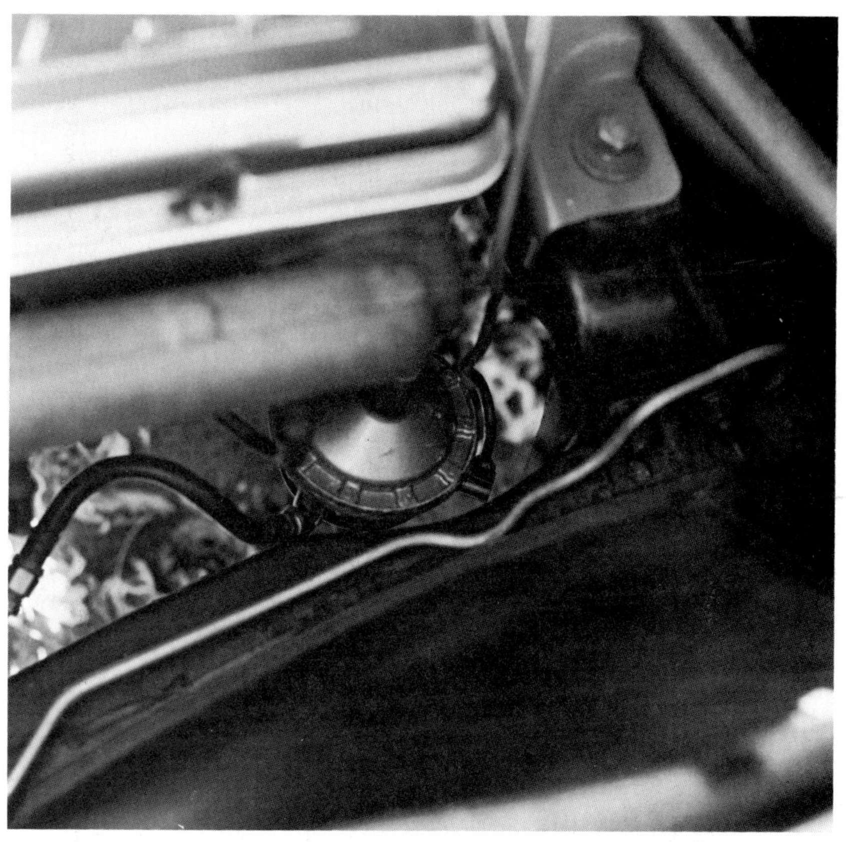

The first Corvettes were designed around the six-cylinder engine, so it was necessary for engineers to create a relief in the frame to clear the fuel pump of the V-8. The few 1955's uncovered with six-cylinder engines do not have the relief. Author photo.

1954-1955 Corvette

BASE ENGINE

Type: . . . . Chevrolet ohv inline 6
Bore x stroke, inches: 3.56x3.96
Displacement, inches: 235.5
Compression ratio: 8.0:1
Carburetion: . . . . Three Carter single-throats
Horsepower: 150, 155*
Distributor: . . . . Single point breaker
Other engines offered:...*In 1954, only the 6-cylinder was used. Horsepower increased during the year from 150 to 155. In 1955, both the six and a V-8 were considered "base" engines. All but a few 1955 Corvettes had the V-8 engine.

CHASSIS AND DRIVETRAIN

Clutch: . . . . Single dry-plate (1955)
Transmission:...Two-speed automatic (standard 1954, optional 1955). Three-speed manual standard in 1955.
Front suspension:...Coil springs, tube-type shock absorbers, stabilizer bar
Rear suspension:...Leaf springs, tube-type shock absorbers, rigid axle
Axle ratio: 3.55:1
Frame: . . . . Steel box sections, welded

GENERAL:

Wheelbase, inches: 102
Track, front, inches: 57.0
rear, inches: 58.8
Brakes: . . . . Drum
Tire size, front and rear: 6.70-15
Wheels: . . . . Steel
Body material: . . . . Fiberglass
Assembly plant: . . . . St. Louis, Missouri

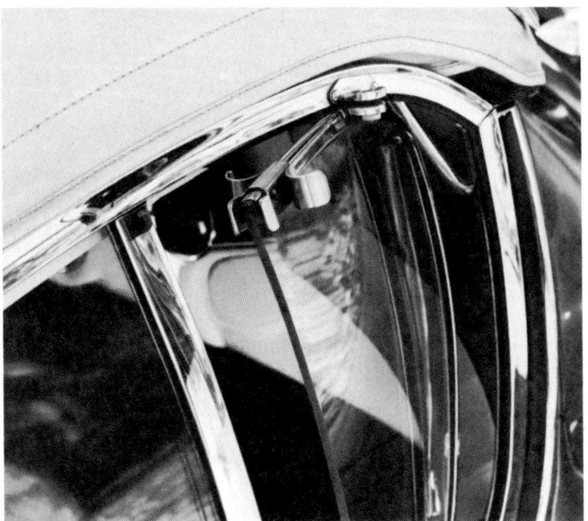

The 1955 Corvette with V-8 engine was identified by a gold "V" incorporated into the Chevrolet side script. The vent window closure clip was used on all 1955 models and late 1954's. Author photos.

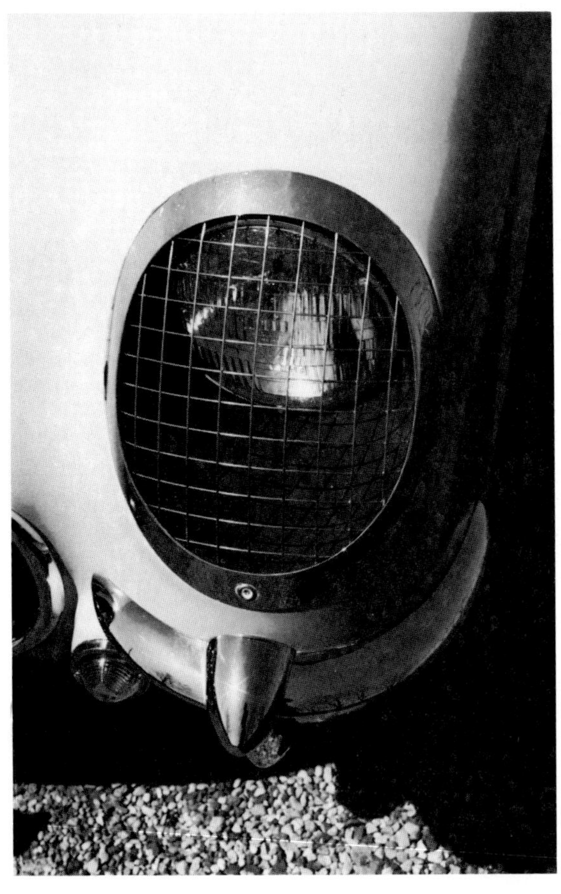

The most distinctive feature of 1953 through 1955 Corvettes was the beautifully detailed "fence mask" headlight stone guard. Protection offered by the bumpers of early Corvettes was negligible. Author photo.

Although only 700 1955 Corvettes were sold, the installation of the V-8 engine signaled the start of the Corvette's transformation into a true high-performance sports car. Good examples of 1955 Corvettes are hard to find because of the low number built and because the V-8 invited abuse. These are excellent investment choices. Chevrolet photo.

CHAPTER 3

1956-1957 CORVETTE

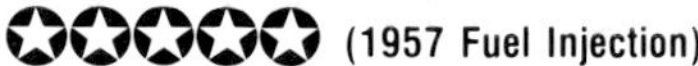 **(1957 Fuel Injection)**

Serial Nos. 1956: E56S001001 - E56S004467
1957: E57S100001 - E57S106339

The Corvette was born in 1953 but it grew up in 1956. Chevrolet learned the hard way that as an American car company building an American sports car for American consumption, it was on uncharted ground. Foreign sports cars got away with four- and six-cylinder engines, so what was wrong with putting a Blue Flame six in the Corvette? Foreign sports cars had leaky tops and side curtains instead of windows, so why not the Corvette?

What Chevrolet hadn't realized was that the Corvette was an American sports car, not a foreign one. It would have to cultivate and define its own market. To do so, it would have to be exciting both to look at and to drive. In 1956, Chevrolet started the ball rolling in incredible fashion.

The body for the 1956-57 Corvette was extensively redesigned. The chassis and dash were carryovers from the previous year, but the fiberglass was all new . . . and gorgeous. In one of the styling coups of all time, Chevy's stylists created a masterpiece. These Corvettes were lithe, sculptured works of automotive art, devoid almost entirely of the unnecessary frills and accouterments so common to the era. Other than fake air scoops atop the front fenders, scoops planned to be functional up to the last minute, there was nothing on these cars that didn't belong.

In the first three years of Corvette production, Chevrolet gave the impression that it was confused itself about what the Corvette was and where it was going. Cars were painted colors that officially didn't exist, colors listed as available weren't, 6- and 12-volt electrical systems were used during the same year . . . all of this makes for great conversations and arguments thirty years later among enthusiasts, but it was hardly the kind of organized effort you'd expect from the largest auto producer in the world. But in 1956, Chevrolet got its Corvette act together.

The creature comfort failings of the early Corvettes were corrected. The soft tops fit better, a power unit for raising and lowering the top became optional, a snug factory hardtop was offered and, best of all, the windows were real glass and rolled down. Even power assists for the windows could be ordered.

Six exterior colors were available in 1956 and there's little argument about their use. The V-8 265-cubic-inch engine was the only displacement used, but carburetor and camshaft options yielded horsepower ratings of 225 and 240 in addition to the base 210. A three-speed manual transmission became standard equipment with the Powerglide automatic optional. For the first time in Corvette production, optional differential ratios could be selected.

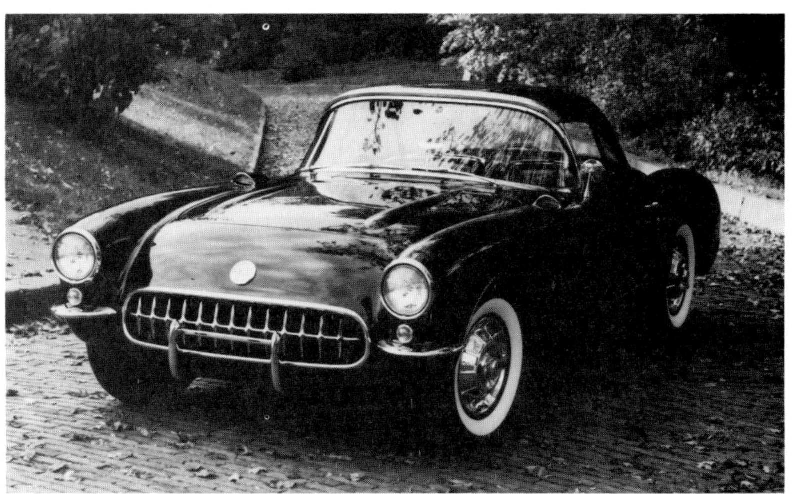

The styling of the 1956 and 1957 Corvettes was virtually identical and is still considered a masterpiece of sports car design. In all of Corvette history, those two models were the most responsible for charting the Corvette's destiny. Author photos.

The transformation the Corvette went through from 1953 to 1957 was almost unbelievable. As introduced in 1953 with six-cylinder engine and automatic transmission, it had no racing credentials. By 1957, it was almost unbeatable. These photos show the SR-2 (Sebring Racer), one of two built by Chevrolet specifically for racing. Dick Thompson is shown at Marlboro Motor Raceway carrying the checkered flag after he won the C modified and Formula Three event. He set a course record the same day and ultimately went on to win the SCCA championship for Class B production in his 1957 Corvette. Both SR-2 racers are in private hands today. Chevrolet photos.

In 1956, Chevrolet was starting to brew its performance potion. The engines were hot, the optional ones having dual four-barrel carburetion and dual point distributors. The 240-horsepower 1956 Corvette was a far cry from the Blue Flame 150-horsepower model. The 1956 Corvette set the automotive world right on its ear. In three short years, Chevrolet had transformed the Corvette from a cute little car in a nebulous market slot into one of the great sports cars of all time. Then it made it better in 1957.

The two years were lookalikes. From the outside about the only indicator was the rearview mirror visible through the windshield; the 1956 adjusted with a thumbscrew, the 1957 required a wrench. The colors were all the same except that silver was added to the 1957 choices.

What happened to the 1957 Corvette to make the year so special was the addition of two options, fuel injection and four-speed transmission. This was the icing that eliminated every trace of doubt about the Corvette's performance credibility and about Chevrolet's intentions.

Displacement of the V-8 was increased to 283 cubic inches in the 1957 Corvette, and the strongest version of the fuel-injected motor developed 283 horsepower, a number-matching feat that Chevrolet's advertising group made sure no one overlooked. Engines of this strength and other "off-the-shelf" performance items made available in 1956 and 1957 meant that Corvettes in near race form could be purchased right off the show room floor.

Corvettes with the V-8 went racing a little in 1955 with little success. They tried again in 1956 with considerable success. In 1957, they cleaned up. Dick Thompson and Gaston Audrey blew out the competition at the twelve-hour Sebring race in March 1957, for a class victory. Earlier in the year on the Daytona sand, Corvettes places first, second and third in both the flying mile and acceleration runs. To cap it off, Thompson won the 1957 Sports Car Club of America (SCCA) championship for class B production cars in his Corvette.

All of this heritage adds up to two Corvette years that are very desirable. The 1957, because of the justified hoopla surrounding the introduction of fuel injection and four-speed transmissions, commands the higher prices. But only 1,040 of the 6,339 1957's built were equipped with fuel injection. A few fuel-injection units made it onto early cars, but most appeared after serial number E57S102000, the 2,000th 1957 made.

The four-speed transmission became available on May 1, 1957, which approximately equates to 1957 serial number E57S103750, the 3,750th built.

Chevrolet built 3,467 1956 models, less than in 1954. The 1956 is thus quite rare since only in 1953 and 1955 were fewer built. And the 1956 was a rip-snorter, a car that tended to wind up on drag strips and racetracks. Its survival rate is much lower than earlier models.

Both the 1956 and 1957 models ride somewhat harshly. Handling was excellent for its day, but feels dated now. Many owners insist on using original-style tires for appearance, but these are terrible in cornering ability by today's standards. Neither year had power steering, brakes or air conditioning available. Both models are fairly noisy and loose-feeling and the seating support leaves something to be desired for cross-country jaunts. But for short blasts, they're unbeatable. They deliver spine-chilling performance wrapped in a stylish design that still turns every head within blocks.

Parts unique to the 1956 and 1957 models, things like taillights and bumpers, are relatively rare and expensive. Be sure to consider the cost of replacing missing parts for any Corvette of this vintage you're interested in buying.

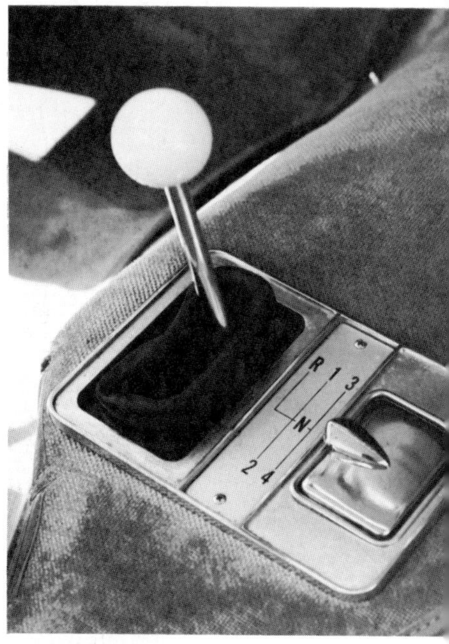

The 1956 Corvette had a dual four-barrel carburetor package available, but it was the introduction of fuel injection and four-speed transmission in 1957 that really made the motoring world take notice. All 1956 and 1957 Corvettes are excellent investments, but the 1957 with the fuel injection and four-speed transmission options is particularly sought after. Author photos.

The massive grille teeth date the 1956 and 1957 Corvettes to the era, but the single headlight treatment and flowing body forms contribute to an overall design that many feel is the best of the pre-Sting Ray models. Author photo.

The hubcap shown was introduced in 1956 and was used through early 1958. A similar hubcap was used through the end of 1962 production but the later units had holes added to simulate brake-cooling slots. The non-hole version shown is more rare. Author photo.

1956 Corvette Colors/Options

Color Code	Body Color	Soft Top Color
None	Onyx Black	Black/White
None	Aztec Copper	Beige/White
None	Cascade Green	White/Beige
None	Arctic Blue	White/Beige
None	Venetian Red	White/Beige
None	Polo White	Black/White

INTERIOR COLORS: Red, Beige

Order #	Item Description	Sticker Price
2934	Base Corvette Convertible	2900.00
101	Heater	115.00
102	Signal Seeking AM Radio	185.00
107	Parking Brake Signal	5.00
108	Courtesy Lights	8.00
109	Windshield Washer	11.00
290	Whitewall Tires, 6.70x15	30.00
313	Powerglide Automatic Transmission	175.00
419	Auxiliary Hardtop	200.00
426	Electric Power Windows	60.00
449	Special High-Lift Camshaft	175.00
469	Dual Four Barrel Carburetor Equipment	160.00
473	Hydraulic Folding Top Mechanism	100.00

1957 Corvette Colors/Options

Color Code	Body Color	Soft Top Color
None	Onyx Black	Black/White/Beige
None	Aztec Copper	Beige/White
None	Cascade Green	Black/White/Beige
None	Arctic Blue	Black/White/Beige
None	Venetian Red	Black/White/Beige
None	Polo White	Black/White/Beige
None	Inca Silver	Black/White

INTERIOR COLORS: Red, Beige

Order #	Item Description	Sticker Price
2934	Base Corvette Convertible	3176.32
101	Heater	110.00
102	Signal Seeking AM Radio	185.00
107	Parking Brake Alarm	5.00
108	Courtesy Lights	8.00
109	Windshield Washer	11.00
276	5-15x5.5'' Wheels	14.00
290	Whitewall Tires, 6.70x15	30.00
313	Powerglide Automatic Transmission	175.00
419	Auxiliary Hardtop	200.00
426	Power Windows	55.00
440	Additional Cove Color	18.00
469A	Optional 245 HP, 283 CI Engine (2x4 Carb)	140.00
469B	Optional 270 HP, 283 CI engine (2x4 Carb)	170.00
579A	Optional 250 HP, 283 CI Engine (Fuel Inj)	450.00
579B	Optional 283 HP, 283 CI Engine (Fuel Inj)	450.00
579E	Optional 283 HP, 283 CI Engine (Fuel Inj)	675.00
473	Power Operated Folding Top Mechanism	130.00
677	Positraction Axle, 3.70:1 Ratio	45.00
678	Positraction Axle, 4.11:1 Ratio	45.00
679	Positraction Axle, 4.56:1 Ratio	45.00
684	Heavy Duty Racing Suspension	725.00
685	4-Speed Transmission	175.00

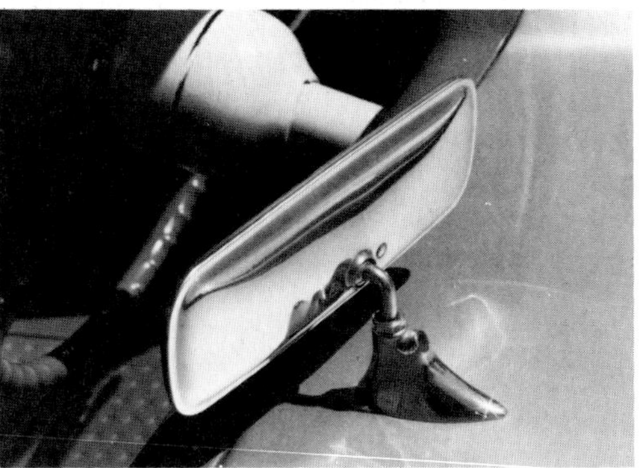

One of the few ways to differentiate between a 1956 and 1957 model without opening the hood is to compare the inside rearview mirrors. The 1956 at left adjusts with a thumbscrew. The 1957 requires a wrench to loosen a locknut. Author photos.

Fuel-injected models are more responsive and quicker, and are much more expensive. In the past, some owners became disenchanted with the ability of local dealers to service their fuel injection and had the units removed and replaced with carburetors. Rebuilding these fuel-injection systems properly does require expertise and may mean that you'll have to unbolt the unit and ship it to a specialist. But once set up properly, they are reliable and require minimal maintenance.

Both the 1956 and 1957 Corvettes are fine investments. The only negative factor is that prices have already been bid up quite high because enthusiasts sized up these models long ago. Simply put, many believe these to be among history's best all-time sports cars. Without question, the Corvette was grossly underpriced in its day. The logical comparison cars, the Mercedes, Jaguar and Ferrari, were much more expensive. The Corvette was so cheap a lot of people initially discounted it as a serious competitor. It was hard for them to believe the Corvette could have come so far so quickly.

Enthusiasts who want to drive a vintage Corvette daily appreciate the externally opening trunk common to all Corvettes up to the 1962 model. Many also prefer the spare tire location, which is reached by lifting the trunk mat. Post-1962 models have spares located under the car and often requires one to lie on the ground to extract the tire. Author photo.

Unique to the 1956 and 1957 models was an unusual waffle-pattern interior vinyl. Removable hardtops were available for the first time as a factory option in 1956 and the waffle-pattern vinyl was used on the inner top surface as well. Author photos.

The dash of the 1956 and 1957 was similar to the earlier Corvettes and still had all instruments except the speedometer strung out across the center dash area. But the 1956 Corvette had roll-up windows and even offered power-assisted windows as an option. (Note the power window button just forward of the door opening knob.) Author photo.

In the age of massive chrome adornments, the 1956 and 1957 Corvettes somehow managed to emerge with exquisite detailing. Emblems and scripts were understated and items like the exhaust exit and taillight were beautifully executed. Author photos.

1956-1957 Corvette

BASE ENGINE

Type: Chevrolet ohv V-8
Bore x stroke, inches: 3.75x3.00 (1956), 3.875x3.00 (1957)
Displacement, inches: 265 (1956), 283 (1957)
Compression ratio: 9.25:1 (1956), 9.5:1 (1957)
Carburetion: Single four-barrel carburetor
Horsepower: 210 (1956), 220 (1957)
Distributor: Single point breaker
Other engines offered: Higher horsepower variations were available in both 1956 and 1957. See option charts.

CHASSIS AND DRIVETRAIN

Clutch: Single dry-plate
Transmission: Three-speed manual
Front suspension: Coil springs, tube-type shock absorbers, stabilizer bar
Rear suspension: Leaf springs, tube-type shock absorbers, rigid axle
Axle ratio: 3.70:1
Frame: Steel box sections, welded

GENERAL:

Wheelbase, inches: 102
Track, front, inches: 57.0
rear, inches: 58.8
Brakes: Drum
Tire size, front and rear: 6.70-15
Wheels: Steel
Body material: Fiberglass
Assembly plant: St. Louis, Missouri

CHAPTER 4

1958-1960 CORVETTE

Serial Nos. 1958: J58S100001 - J58S109168
1959: J59S100001 - J59S109670
1960: 00867S100001 - 00867S110261

There was one problem with building what might have been the world's best production sports car before 1958. How do you make it better?

In 1958 Chevrolet decided to make the Corvette more, well . . . contemporary. Nineteen fifty-eight started what many people now believe was Detroit's worst design era. Great cars, mind you, but dripping with chrome, tailfins and any number of other excesses.

The Corvette managed to avoid tailfins but not much else. The 1956 and 1957 Corvettes were among the cleanest designs ever, but the 1958 turned out just the opposite. It got quad headlights, eighteen fake louvers across the hood, spears down the trunk and lots of chrome. Worst of all, it started a two-decade Corvette weight-gaining trend. The 1958 was the first Corvette to exceed 3,000 pounds.

But there is another side. The 1958 was the tightest, strongest, fastest Corvette yet. Five engines were offered: a standard single four-barrel at 230 horsepower, two dual-carburetor versions at 245 and 270 horsepower, and two fuel-injected versions at 250 and 290 horsepower. The dash was new and grouped all engine-monitoring instruments in front of the driver, a failing of earlier Corvette interiors. General Motors joined the Automobile Manufacturers Association (AMA) ban on racing in 1957, but you'd never know it looking at the 1958 option list.

The 1959 and 1960 models are very similar to each other and both are similar to the 1958, other than being considerably cleaner. Stylists got roasted for the excesses of the 1958 model, so the hood louvers and trunk spears were gone by 1959. Interior vinyl *looked* like interior vinyl in the 1959 and 1960, whereas the 1958 had an unusual pebble grain. Nineteen fifty-nine was the first year for a genuine black interior in a Corvette, though the 1958 had a dark gray unique to the year that can be mistaken for faded black.

The 1959 got a reverse lockout T-shift handle for four-speeds, another Corvette first. The engines were much the same for all years except the top of the line fuel-injected version grew to 315 horsepower in 1960. All three years had seat belts standard; they were dealer-installed in 1956-57 and not generally available before that.

The 1958-60 Corvettes have never really "caught on" and, considering what lies under their criticized exteriors, they're bargains. The 1958 belongs in a

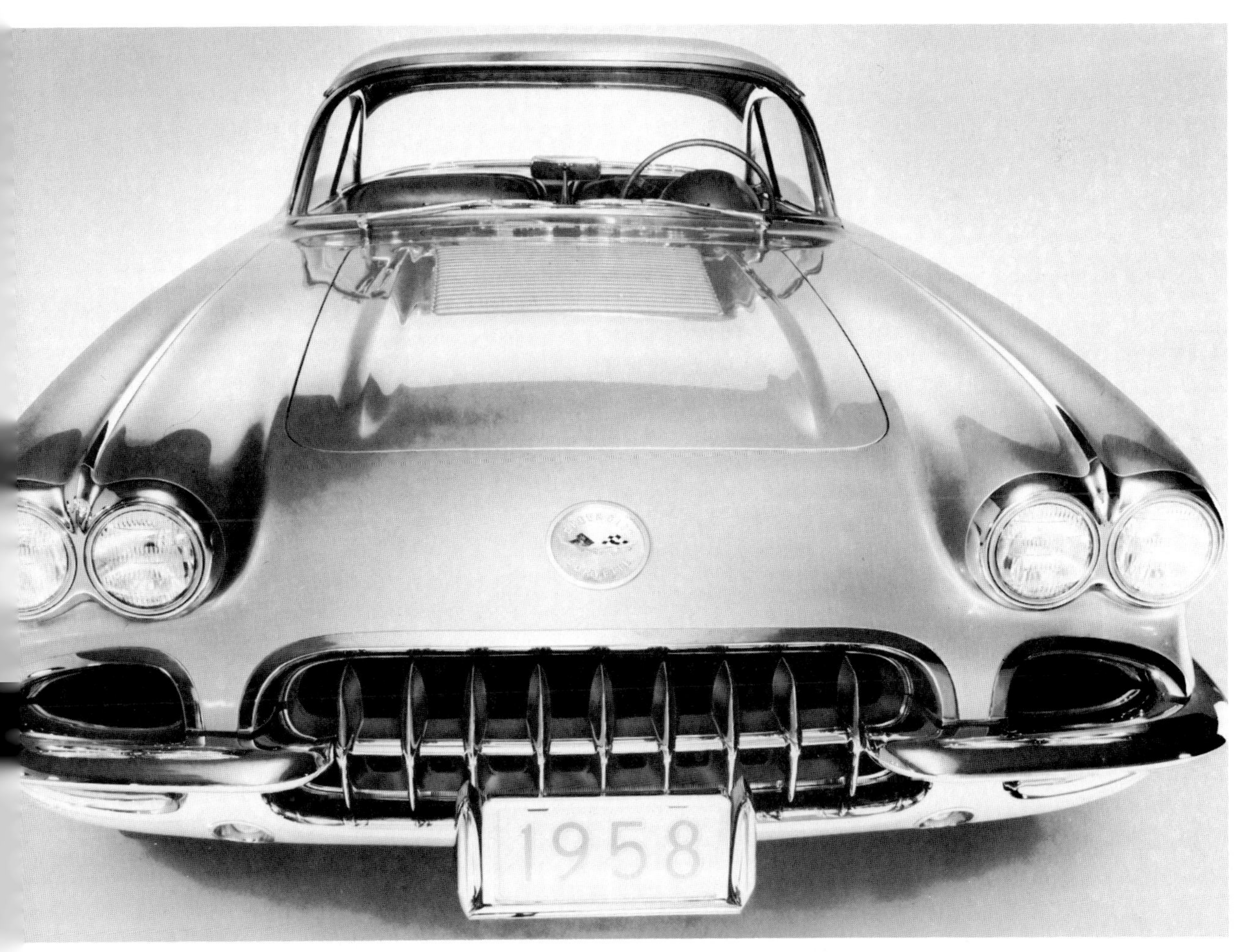

There was no mistaking the 1958 Corvette. Chevrolet photo.

Although the 1958 Corvette outsold any previous year, the model was criticized because of design excesses and for starting a weight-gaining Corvette trend. Nonetheless, there are some who predict the 1958 will become a great collector car because of the controversy that has always surrounded it. It remains to be seen. Author photos.

category by itself, definitely a love-it or hate-it car. In the view of some, the controversy surrounding the car since its introduction just adds to its charm. For others, the cleaner 1959 and 1960 models, the last "classic" Corvettes with consistent round fender shapes front and rear, are the most desirable.

High-performance Corvettes always score well with collectors looking at the investment angle, but this isn't a critical consideration for this series of Corvettes. The Corvette's option list, as well as color and trim choices, was getting better than ever. By 1960 there were some terrific combinations and it became clear that Chevrolet was going to let customers tailor the Corvette to their own liking, in true American auto industry tradition. Turquoise convertible top? You could get it in 1959.

The Powerglide automatic transmission and power windows were available in these models, but power steering, power brakes and air conditioning were not. Like the Corvettes before them, the 1958-1960 Corvettes tend to feel harsh and heavy compared to contemporary sports cars, particularly if fitted with original style tires.

Corvette production was growing but still modest by most standards. In 1958, 9,168 were made. It increased to 9,670 in 1959 and to 10,261 in 1960. For someone who likes Corvettes of this period, there are no real disadvantages of ownership of any of these models other than an appreciation rate that historically has not kept pace with the rest of the Corvette fleet. For the gambler, the 1958 is the closest thing to a "sleeper" of all classic Corvette years.

In its advertising, Chevrolet pointed out that the "new assist bar aids passenger." Chevrolet photo.

1958 Corvette Colors/Options

Color Code	Body Color	Soft Top Color
None	Charcoal	Black/White
None	Snowcrest White	Black/White/Beige
None	Silver Blue	White/Beige
None	Regal Turquoise	Black/White
None	Panama Yellow	Black/White
None	Signet Red	Black/White

INTERIOR COLORS: Charcoal, Blue-Green, Red

Order #	Item Description	Sticker Price
867	Base Corvette Convertible	3591.00
101	Heater	96.85
102	Signal Seeking AM Radio	144.45
107	Parking Brake Alarm	5.40
108	Courtesy Lights	6.50
109	Windshield Washer	16.15
276	5 15x5.5'' Wheels	NC
290	Whitewall Tires, 6.70x15	31.55
313	Powerglide Automatic Transmission	188.30
419	Auxiliary Hardtop	215.20
426	Electric Power Windows	59.20
440	Additional Cove Color	16.15
469	Optional 245 HP, 283 CI Engine (2x4 Carb)	150.65
469C	Optional 270 HP, 283 CI Engine (2x4 Carb)	182.95
579	Optional 250 HP, 283 CI Engine (Fuel Inj)	484.20
579D	Optional 290 HP, 283 CI Engine (Fuel Inj)	484.20
473	Power Operated Folding Top Mechanism	139.90
677	Positraction Axle, 3.70:1 Ratio	48.45
678	Positraction Axle, 4.11:1 Ratio	48.45
679	Positraction Axle, 4.56:1 Ratio	48.45
684	Heavy Duty Brakes and Suspension	780.10
685	4-Speed Transmission	215.20

The dual headlights and massive bumpers got their share of criticism, but it was the "washboard" hood and chrome trunk spears that seemed to rankle enthusiasts most. These features were unique to the 1958 Corvette as both were dropped the following year. Author photos.

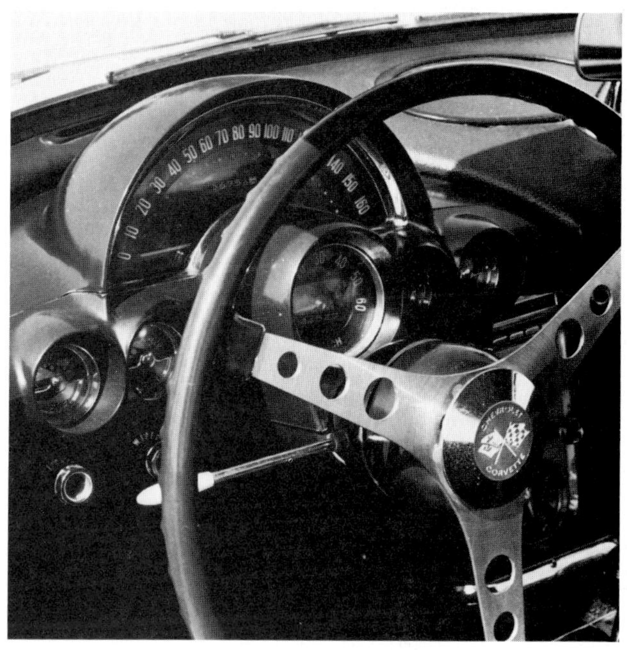

Corvette designers heard the criticism of earlier Corvette instrument layouts and redesigned the 1958 dash with all instruments except the clock right in front of the driver. Author photo.

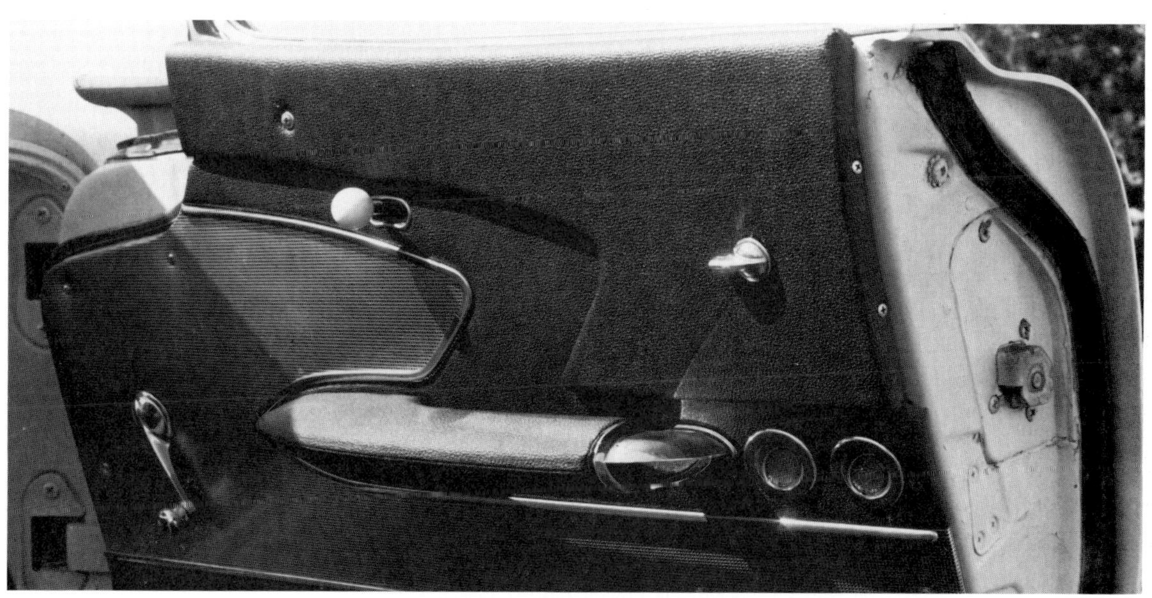

The 1958 inner door panel was a complicated affair, but did include reflector buttons, a Corvette first. Note also the pebble grain, unique to the 1958 model. Author photo.

1959 Corvette Colors/Options

Color Code	Body Color	Soft Top Color
None	Tuxedo Black	Black/White
None	Classic Cream	Black/White
None	Frost Blue	White/Blue
None	Crown Sapphire	White/Turquoise
None	Roman Red	Black/White
None	Snowcrest White	Black/White/Tan/Blue
None	Inca Silver	Black/White

INTERIOR COLORS: Black, Blue, Red, Turquoise

Order #	Item Description	Sticker Price
867	Base Corvette Convertible	3875.00
—	Additional Cove Color	16.15
101	Heater	102.25
102	Signal Seeking AM Radio	149.80
107	Parking Brake Alarm	5.40
108	Courtesy Light	6.50
109	Windshield Washers	16.15
261	Sunshades	10.80
276	5 15x5.5'' Wheels	nc
290	Whitewall Tires, 6.70x15	31.55
313	Powerglide Automatic Transmission	199.10
419	Auxiliary Hardtop	236.75
426	Electric Power Windows	59.20
269	Optional 245 HP, 283 CI Engine (2x4 Carb)	150.65
469C	Optional 270 HP, 283 CI Engine (2x4 Carb)	182.95
579	Optional 250 HP, 283 CI Engine (Fuel Inj)	484.20
579D	Optional 290 HP, 283 CI Engine (Fuel Inj)	484.20
473	Power Operated Folding Top Mechanism	139.90
675	Positraction Axle, Optional Ratio	48.45
684	Heavy Duty Brakes and Suspension	425.05
685	4-Speed Transmission	188.30
686	Metallic Brakes	26.90

1960 Corvette Colors/Options

Color Code	Body Color	Soft Top Color
None	Tuxedo Black	Black/White/Blue
None	Tasco Turquoise	Black/White/Blue
None	Horizon Blue	Black/White/Blue
None	Honduras Maroon	Black
None	Roman Red	Black/White
None	Ermine White	Black/White/Blue
None	Sateen Silver	Black/White/Blue
None	Cascade Green	Black/White/Blue

INTERIOR COLORS: Black, Blue, Red, Turquoise

Order #	Item Description	Sticker Price
867	Base Corvette Convertible	3872.00
—	Additional Cove Color	16.15
101	Heater	102.25
102	Signal Seeking AM Radio	137.75
107	Parking Brake Alarm	5.40
108	Courtesy Light	6.50
109	Windshield Washers	16.15
121	Temperature Controlled Radiator Fan	21.55
261	Sunshades	10.80
276	5 15x5.5'' Wheels	nc
290	Whitewall Tires, 6.70x15.4-ply	31.55
313	Powerglide Automatic Transmission	199.10
419	Auxiliary Hardtop	236.75
426	Electric Power Windows	59.20
469	Optional 245 HP, 283 CI Engine (2x4 Carb)	150.65
469C	Optional 270 HP, 283 CI Engine (2x4 Carb)	182.95
579	Optional 275 HP, 283 CI Engine (Fuel Inj)	484.20
579D	Optional 315 HP, 283 CI Engine (Fuel Inj)	484.20
473	Power Operated Folding Top Mechanism	139.90
675	Positraction Axle, Optional Ratio	43.05
685	4-Speed Transmission	188.30
686	Metallic Brakes	26.90
687	Heavy Duty Brakes and Suspension	333.60
1408	5 6.70x15 Nylon Tires	15.75
1625A	24 Gallon Fuel Tank	161.40

The 1958 four-speed shifter at left was the same as the 1957, but in 1959 (right) the reverse lock-out "T" bar was incorporated. The chrome shift knob shown in the 1958 is owner-added. Original equipment was a white plastic knob. Author photos.

The 1959 and 1960 models were virtually indistinguishable and both bear strong resemblance to the 1958 model. These Corvettes were excellent performers but their styling has kept prices reasonable. Some are excellent values today. Chevrolet photo.

Both 1959 and 1960 Corvettes had clean hoods and trunks, surely a response to criticism of the 1958 models. Note the slotted hubcap design, which was common to all Corvettes in the 1958 through 1960 period except for early 1958's which did not have the slots. Author photos.

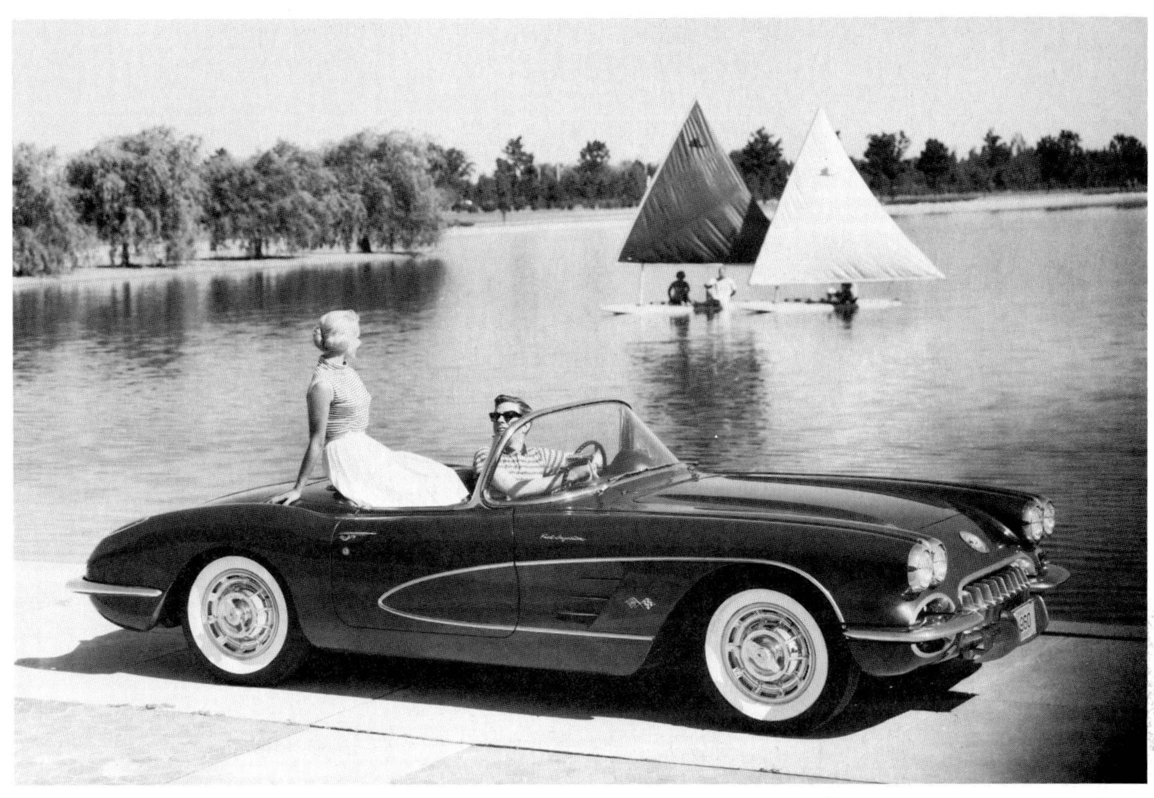

Corvettes and women always seemed to go together nicely, a fact not lost upon those responsible for Chevrolet advertising. 1960 shown. Chevrolet photo.

1958-1959-1960 Corvette

BASE ENGINE
Type: .... Chevrolet ohv V-8
Bore x stroke, inches: .... 3.875 x 3.00
Displacement, inches: 283
Compression ratio: 9.5:1
Carburetion: .... Single four-barrel carburetor
Horsepower: 230
Distributor: .... Single point breaker
Other engines offered:...Higher horsepower variations were available in 1958, 1959 and 1960. See option charts.

CHASSIS AND DRIVETRAIN
Clutch: .... Single dry-plate
Transmission: .... Three-speed manual
Front suspension:...Coil springs, tube-type shock absorbers, stabilizer bar
Rear suspension:...Leaf springs, tube-type shock absorbers, rigid axle
Axle ratio: 3.70:1
Frame: .... Steel box sections, welded

GENERAL:
Wheelbase, inches: 102
Track, front, inches: 57.0
rear, inches: 58.8
Brakes: .... Drum
Tire size, front and rear: 6.70-15
Wheels: .... Steel
Body material: .... Fiberglass
Assembly plant: .... St. Louis, Missouri

CHAPTER 5

1961-1962 Corvette

Serial Nos. 1961: 10867S100001 - 10867S110939
1962: 20867S100001 - 20867S114531

"Classic" is a term used by Corvette enthusiasts to denote Corvettes built up to and including the 1962 model. All of these share two main characteristics cherished by classic loyalists: All have external trunks and all have solid rear axles (as compared to the independent rear suspensions common to all 1963 and later Corvettes).

The trunk aspect permits things like golf clubs and other necessities to be loaded from the rear of the car and locked out of sight. This is a feature Corvettes were never to see again, unless the definition of trunk is stretched to include the opening rear window started by the 1982 Collector Edition.

The solid rear axle is not state-of-the-art design but, characteristic of the period, it is very durable and it imparts a "feel" to classic Corvettes which later models just don't have. Some like the feel, some don't. Those who do, think the feel plus the high "elbow out the window" seating of the classics add up to an unbeatable sports car driving environment.

For those who love classic Corvettes, the 1961 and 1962 models have a lot going for them. They're the last of the breed and definitely the best in some ways. The overall quality of construction of the 1961-62 Corvettes was as good as any in Corvette history, especially if you limit consideration to those built in St. Louis. Production jumped dramatically in following years and took its inevitable toll in quality.

As performers, the cars were fierce, the best yet in the Corvette's evolution. A little history lesson is required to understand why.

General Motors joined other manufacturers in banning factory participation in auto racing in 1957. Zora Arkus-Duntov, unofficially the Corvette's chief engineer by then, was always a believer in building two versions of a sports car—one to go racing and another to sell to the public. With his racing wings clipped, Duntov had to try building one Corvette that could satisfy both camps. The result was a production Corvette for racers that was a little less than they needed, but a production Corvette for consumers that was more than they ever expected.

This effect started showing up in the 1959 model but really began to be strongly felt in the 1961. All 1961 Corvettes got aluminum radiators, previously standard only with hot "Duntov" cam engines. The 1961 also got a temperature-controlled fan behind the radiator that didn't drain power unless necessary. The four-speed transmission case was changed to aluminum in 1961 and even the Powerglide case got the aluminum treatment for 1962.

1961 Corvette. Chevrolet photos.

The 1961 Corvette was the last available with a contrasting color in the side cove area. Stylists toned down the front end by painting the headlight bezels body color (previously chrome) and replacing the grille teeth with fine mesh. The rear was all-new, borrowed from the Sting Ray design still two years away. Chevrolet photos.

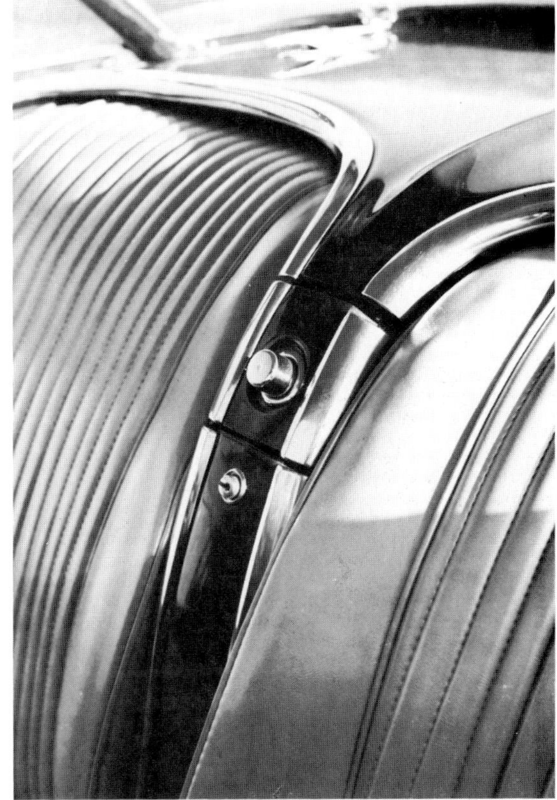

The 1961 and 1962 Corvettes continued with features started by the 1956 model, including a lockable storage area between the seats and optional power windows. The restored 1962 Corvette pictured has genuine stitching in its seats and door panels, but the originals had simulated stitches. Author photos.

1961 Corvette Colors/Options

Color Code	Body Color	Soft Top Color
None	Tuxedo Black	Black/White
None	Ermine White	Black/White
None	Roman Red	Black/White
None	Sateen Silver	Black/White
None	Jewel Blue	Black/White
None	Fawn Beige	Black/White
None	Honduras Maroon	Black/White

INTERIOR COLORS: Black, Red, Fawn, Blue

Order #	Item Description	Sticker Price
867	Base Corvette Convertible	3934.00
—	Additional Cove Color	16.15
101	Heater	102.25
102	Signal Seeking AM Radio	137.75
276	5 15x5.5'' Wheels	nc
290	Whitewall Tires, 6.70x15	31.55
313	Powerglide Automatic Transmission	199.10
419	Auxiliary Hardtop	236.75
426	Electric Power Windows	59.20
441	Direct Flow Exhaust System	nc
469	Optional 245 HP, 283 CI Engine (2x4 Carb)	150.65
468	Optional 270 HP, 283 CI Engine (2x4 Carb)	182.95
353	Optional 275 HP, 283 CI Engine (Fuel Inj)	484.20
354	Optional 315 HP, 283 CI Engine (Fuel Inj)	484.20
473	Power Operated Folding Top Mechanism	161.40
675	Positraction Axle, Optional Ratio	43.05
685	4-Speed Transmission	188.30
686	Metallic Brakes	37.70
687	Heavy Duty Brakes and Suspension	333.60
1408	5 6.70x15 Nylon Tires	15.75
1625	24 Gallon Fuel Tank	161.40

The chassis of the 1961-62 was the same as in previous years, but the fiberglass body was reworked. Quad headlights remained, but the big grille teeth were replaced by a tasteful mesh. The 1961 still had the side cove outlined by a bright molding (started in 1956) and the area inside the cove could be ordered in a color contrasting the body color. But in 1962 the bright molding was replaced with a highlight lip. Two-tones were gone from the Corvette scene until the silver anniversary paint scheme arrived in 1978.

The rear end styling of the 1961-62 was changed extensively and drew mixed reviews. The design was obviously grafted from the new Sting Ray scheduled for 1963 introduction. It incorporated a four-taillight set up; now a Corvette trademark, but a first for the Corvette in 1961.

Viewed on its own, the rear end styling is very nice. The controversy centered on the mismatched look, front to rear. The front was a carryover of the old Corvette rounded look, but the rear was a preview of the crisper "beltline" styling of the Sting Rays to come. Two concepts or not, stylists pulled it off quite well and these Corvettes look fine today. And the restyled rear added twenty percent to the trunk volume.

All engines in 1961 continued to be based on Chevy's 283-cubic-inch V-8. But in 1962, displacement went up to 327 cubic inches. In fact, even though the 1963 Corvette made its debut as an all-new model, the engines were exact carryovers from 1962. As was the case with all Corvettes built up to and including the 1962 model, power steering, power brakes and air conditioning were not available.

Both the 1961 and 1962 Corvettes are excellent investments. Each does have its advantages. They both can lay claim to being the hottest performer in the classic era, a slight edge going to the 1962 with its larger-displacement engines. With its wide whitewalls and two-tone paint treatment, the 1961 is more reminiscent of earlier Corvettes. The whitewalls were thinner in 1962 and this, plus the single body color, makes it more the harbinger of things to come while still maintaining all the attributes classic Corvette lovers love. It's a draw.

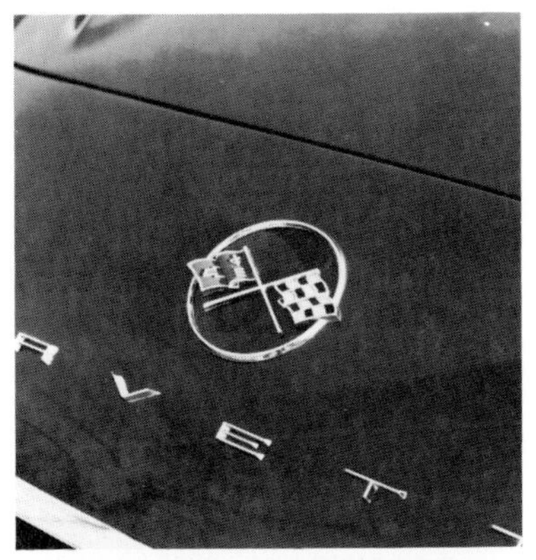

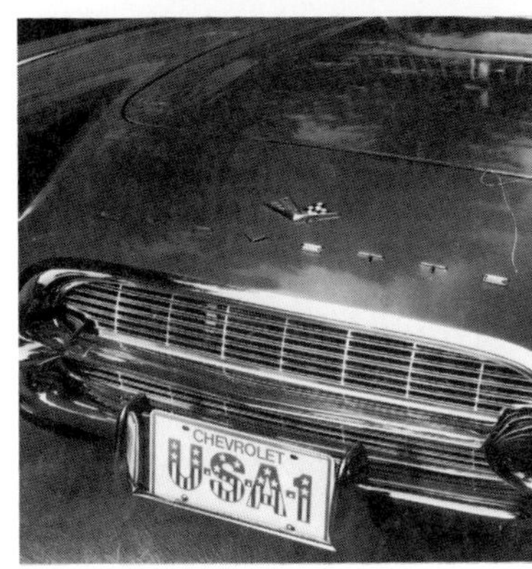

There were subtle emblem changes between 1961 and 1962. The nose emblem of the 1961 was a crossed flag over a "V," but the 1962 was a crossed flag inside a circle. The rear emblems were similar except that the 1961 had a spun silver background and the 1962 background was black. Author photos.

1962 Corvette Colors/Options

Color Code	Body Color	Soft Top Color
None	Tuxedo Black	Black/White
None	Fawn Beige	Black/White
None	Roman Red	Black/White
None	Ermine White	Black/White
None	Almond Beige	Black/White
None	Sateen Silver	Black/White
None	Honduras Maroon	Black/White

INTERIOR COLORS: Black, Red, Fawn

Order #	Item Description	Sticker Price
867	Base Corvette Convertible	4038.00
102	Signal Seeking AM Radio	137.75
276	5 15x5.5'' Wheels	nc
313	Powerglide Automatic Transmission	199.10
419	Auxiliary Hardtop	236.75
426	Electric Power Windows	59.20
441	Direct Flow Exhaust System	nc
473	Power Operated Folding Top Mechanism	139.90
488	24 Gallon Fuel Tank	118.40
583	Optional 300 HP, 327 CI Engine	53.80
396	Optional 340 HP, 327 CI Engine	107.60
582	Optional 370 HP, 327 CI Engine (Fuel Inj)	484.20
675	Positraction Rear Axle	43.05
685	4-Speed Transmission	188.30
686	Metallic Brakes	37.70
687	Heavy Duty Brakes and Suspension	333.60
1832	Whitewall Tires, 6.70x15	31.55
1833	Nylon Tires, 6.70x15	15.70

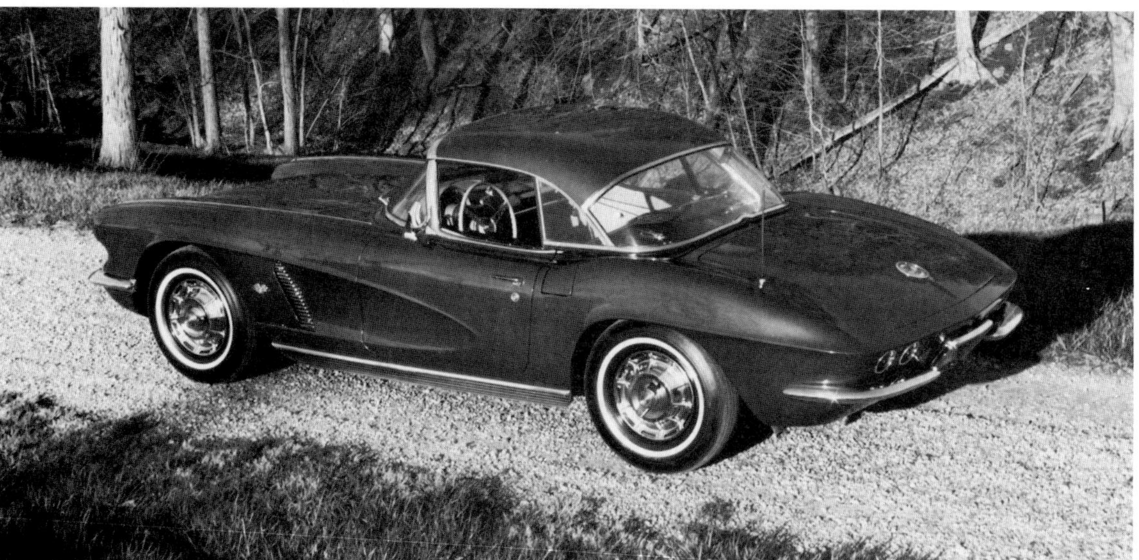

Though very similar to 1961, the 1962 Corvette had its differences. It was the first year for thin whitewall tires (between ⅞" and 1"), and the first with the higher displacement, 327-cubic-inch engines. The bright molding was removed from the side cove area and the cove could no longer be ordered in a contrasting color. Author photos.

A lot ended in 1962. This was the last Corvette with an externally opening trunk (excluding the rear window hatches of the new generation.) And it was the last Corvette with exposed headlights. Chevrolet and author photos.

This staged promotional photo illustrates the high seating characteristics of all Corvettes built before 1963. This, plus a wide upper door section, created a comfortable "arm out the window" driving style unmatched by any Corvette built since. Chevrolet photo.

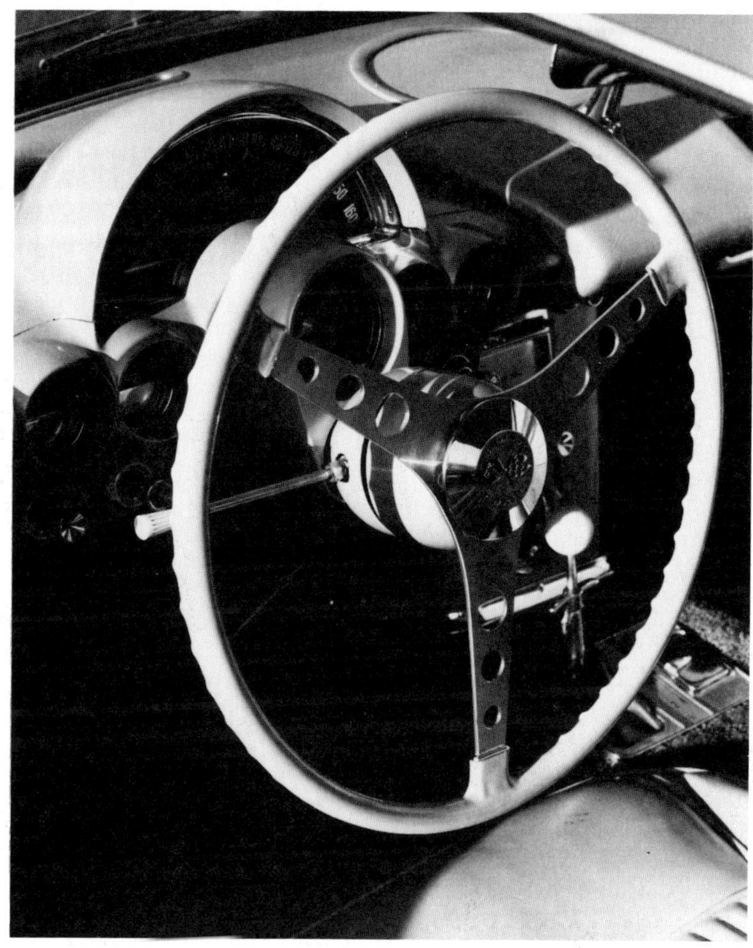

The 1961 and 1962 (1962 shown) instrument cluster changed little from that introduced in 1958. Author photo.

1961-1962 Corvette

BASE ENGINE

Type: .... Chevrolet ohv V-8
Bore x stroke, inches: 3.875 x 3.0 (1961), 4.0 x 3.25 (1962)
Displacement, inches: 283 (1961), 327 (1962)
Compression ratio: 9.5:1 (1961), 10.5:1 (1962)
Carburetion: .... Single four-barrel carburetor
Horsepower: 230 (1961), 250 (1962)
Distributor: .... Single point breaker
Other engines offered: ... Higher horsepower variations were available in both 1961 and 1962. See option charts.

CHASSIS AND DRIVETRAIN

Clutch: .... Single dry-plate
Transmission: .... Three-speed manual
Front suspension: ... Coil springs, tube-type shock absorbers, stabilizer bar
Rear suspension: ... Leaf springs, tube-type shock absorbers, rigid axle
Axle ratio: 3.36:1
Frame: .... Steel box sections, welded

GENERAL:

Wheelbase, inches: 102
Track, front, inches: 57.0
rear, inches: 58.8
Brakes: .... Drum
Tire size, front and rear: 6.70-15
Wheels: .... Steel
Body material: .... Fiberglass
Assembly plant: .... St. Louis, Missouri

CHAPTER 6

1963-1964 CORVETTE

(1963 Coupe)

Serial Nos. 1963: 30867S100001 - 30867S121513*
1964: 40867S100001 - 40867S122229*
(*for coupes, fourth digit is a 3)

Chevrolet uncorked a dandy in 1963. The engines and transmissions carried over from 1962, but otherwise the Corvette was brand new. It had a beautiful new body, available for the first time as either a closed coupe or open convertible. The chassis was new and included independent rear suspension and a novel, single transverse rear spring. What a car.

And what an introduction! Cloaked in secrecy right up to release, the Corvette exploded onto the market. There wasn't much dickering for a few dollars off sticker prices. These were instant hits and in tremendous demand from the first day.

This was one of those rare times when everything came together just right. The Corvette engine was already highly thought of. After all, the Chevy V-8 is one of the all-time favorites and the Corvette had the Chevy engine in its best form. A wrecked Corvette was worth its weight in gold for the engine alone.

Prior to 1963, Corvettes were criticized for having an outdated chassis and inconsistent styling that, the 1956-57 models excluded, were hard to rave about. Styling is a subjective thing, but the chassis complaints were certainly valid. The first Corvettes were designed around a chassis which some people felt was already obsolete.

All this ceased in 1963. The chassis which made its debut in 1963 was good enough to last almost untouched right through the 1982 model. And the body styling was on a par with anything anywhere. This new body/chassis combination left critics with very little to criticize. The 1963 could have done with a few less styling frills, and drum brakes were still being used to stop very potent machines. That was about it, and Chevrolet took care of these shortcomings in short order.

The styling of the 1963 Corvette was a shock, but not a total surprise to real auto buffs. The Corvette look was influenced strongly by a one-off race car called the Mitchell Sting Ray. The story of how this racer came about and the part it played in the development of the beautiful production Corvettes starting with the 1963, is a great part of Corvette folklore.

The story centers on two events and three men. The events were the Automobile Manufacturers Association ban on racing in 1957, with which General Motors went along, and the promotion of William L. Mitchell as successor to Harley Earl as head of all GM styling. The men were Mitchell, his chief Corvette stylist Larry Shinoda, and Zora Arkus-Duntov.

Duntov was the most pro-racing individual of some influence in the modern history of General Motors. He had personally raced in Europe with and against

1963 Corvette "Split Window" Coupe. Chevrolet photo.

The Corvettes starting with the 1963 model had a history before they were even introduced, thanks to the Mitchell racing Sting Ray. This gorgeous vehicle was campaigned on the race circuit under the sponsorship of Bill Mitchell, GM's vice president in charge of design, four years before the production vehicles based on it were released. Chevrolet photo.

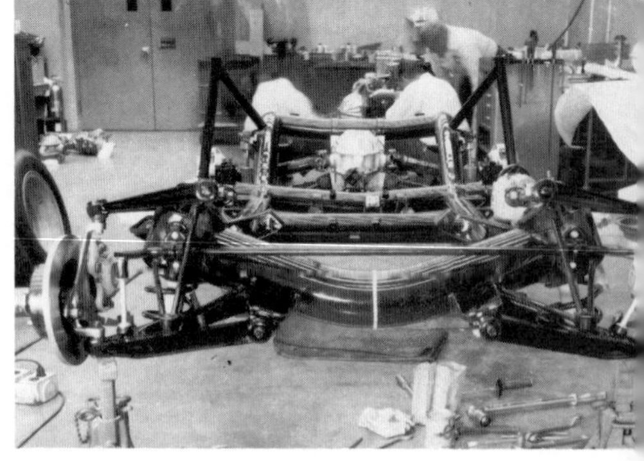

In 1963, Zora Arkus-Duntov decided to end the racetrack domination of the Ford-powered Cobra by building 125 lightweight (1908 lbs.) "Grand Sport" Corvettes. Chevrolet management approved but GM corporate did not and Duntov's program was stopped after only five cars were built. Three were immediately sold to private individuals and made their way to racetracks with some success despite not being equipped with the 550 horsepower, cast-aluminum hemi V-8 Duntov had planned. Duntov held back two cars in reserve in case the corporate winds shifted again. He changed these from coupes to convertibles but wasn't allowed to go racing, so these were also sold. All five Grand Sports survive today in private hands and occasionally one is for sale. It's difficult to figure out what one is worth, though asking prices have ranged as high as $175,000. That's a little out of reach for most of us, but we can all dream. And a Grand Sport tops the most wanted list of many Corvette enthusiasts. Chevrolet photos.

the best cars in the world and he was convinced the Corvette could and should dominate racing worldwide.

In order to accomplish this lofty task, Duntov figured a special Corvette racer would be needed for events like Sebring and Le Mans so he built something called the Corvette SS for the 1957 season.

The SS was approved by GM management, but Duntov's budget called for just one SS to be built. The brass wanted the SS to look nice for fan appeal, and Duntov realized that it could get hung up in Styling. So he secretly built an extra SS chassis and dumped an ugly fiberglass shell over it in order to have something for shakedown tests. The appearance of the shakedown car earned it the nickname "mule."

Duntov was right about the real SS getting bogged down in Styling. The SS arrived for its debut at Sebring in 1957 at the very last minute with stylists still working on it in the transport van. To the surprise of no one, it failed early in the race. The SS and the mule (which tested very well at Sebring and was actually faster) were shipped back to Detroit where Duntov planned to rework both of them for entry later in the year at Le Mans. But then the AMA ban came along and ended the SS forever.

But not the mule.

We now switch to the Mitchell-Shinoda side of the story. William L. Mitchell replaced Harley Earl as head of all GM styling in 1958. Earl was responsible for starting the Corvette in the first place and Mitchell loved it equally. Mitchell thought it essential for the Corvette to have a racing heritage, AMA ban or no AMA ban. He also wanted Chevrolet's image leader to bear his styling influence. He hatched an ingenious plan.

Mitchell knew that the mule was wasting away in a warehouse and that it was a wolf in sheep's clothing, a potential champion. Mitchell persuaded Ed Cole, Chevrolet's general manager and a race-lover himself, to allow a secret Chevrolet styling studio to rebody the mule and turn it loose on the track. To get around the AMA ban, Mitchell paid General Motors one dollar for the car and campaigned it as the Mitchell Sting Ray, with Dick Thompson driving. There was considerable personal time given by Mitchell and his "crew" but this was very definitely a corporate project. Everyone involved just snickers about it today.

Mitchell turned to his secret studio, managed by Larry Shinoda, to create the body for the Sting Ray and Shinoda and company created a masterpiece. Simply put, the original Sting Ray racer is one of the neatest cars ever. The reaction of everyone who saw it was just what Mitchell had hoped for and he turned Shinoda's studio loose on adapting the design to a new Corvette production model for 1963. The Sting Ray name appropriately captured the aggressive look of the racer's flowing fender lines and was used for the production cars.

Nineteen sixty-three was the year of the split-window coupe. From the first moment Mitchell saw the split rear window proposal in Shinoda's studio, he liked it and adamantly insisted it stay in. Others, including Duntov, said it was dumb and blocked rear vision severely. Duntov and those who agreed with him got their way in 1964 when the split was removed. Mitchell admits today the split wasn't very practical; he just liked the way it looked.

One thing is for sure. The 1963 coupe is now one of the greatest collector Corvettes of all. It's hard to believe that in the sixties people actually chopped the split out of 1963 coupes and put in glass from later models. A few years later they were reinstalling the split glass. And more than one 1964 Corvette has acquired the split and changed its identity.

1963 Corvette Colors/Options

Color Code	Body Color	Soft Top Color
900	Tuxedo Black	Black/White/Beige
936	Ermine White	Black/White/Beige
923	Riverside Red	Black/White/Beige
912	Silver Blue	Black/White/Beige
916	Daytona Blue	Black/White/Beige
932	Saddle Tan	Black/White/Beige
941	Sebring Silver	Black/White/Beige

INTERIOR COLORS: Black, Red, Saddle, Dark Blue

Order #	Item Description	Sticker Price
837	Base Corvette Sport Coupe	4257.00
867	Base Corvette Convertible	4037.00
898	Genuine Leather Seat Trim	80.00
941	Sebring Silver Exterior Paint	80.70
A01	Soft Ray Tinted Glass, All Windows	16.15
A02	Soft Ray Tinted Glass, Windshield	10.80
A31	Electric Power Windows	59.20
C07	Auxiliary Hardtop (for roadster)	236.75
C48	Heater and Defroster Deletion (credit)	−100.00
C60	Air Conditioning	421.80
G81	Positraction Rear Axle, All Ratios	43.05
G91	Special Highway 3.08:1 Axle	2.20
J50	Power Brakes	43.05
J65	Sintered Metallic Brakes (power)	37.70
L75	Optional 300 HP, 327 CI Engine	53.80
L76	Optional 340 HP, 327 CI Engine	107.60
L84	Optional 370 HP, 327 CI Engine (Fuel Inj)	430.40
M20	4-Speed Transmission	188.30
M35	Powerglide Automatic Transmission	199.10
N03	36 Gallon Fuel Tank (coupe only)	202.30
N11	Off Road Exhaust System	37.70
N34	Woodgrained Plastic Steering Wheel	16.15
N40	Power Steering	75.35
P48	Special Cast Aluminum Knock-Off Wheels	322.80
P91	Blackwall Nylon Tires, 6.70x15	15.70
P92	Whitewall Rayon Tires. 6.70x15	31.55
T86	Back-Up Lamps	10.80
U65	Signal Seeking AM Radio (early)	137.75
U69	AM-FM Radio	174.35
Z06	Special Performance Equipment for Coupe	1818.45

Everything about the 1963 Corvette was new, including interior vinyl trim. A leather interior option became available for the first time in a Corvette in 1963, but it included only the seats, and just the tan color could be ordered in leather. In 1964, all interior color choices could be ordered in either vinyl or extra-cost leather. Author photo.

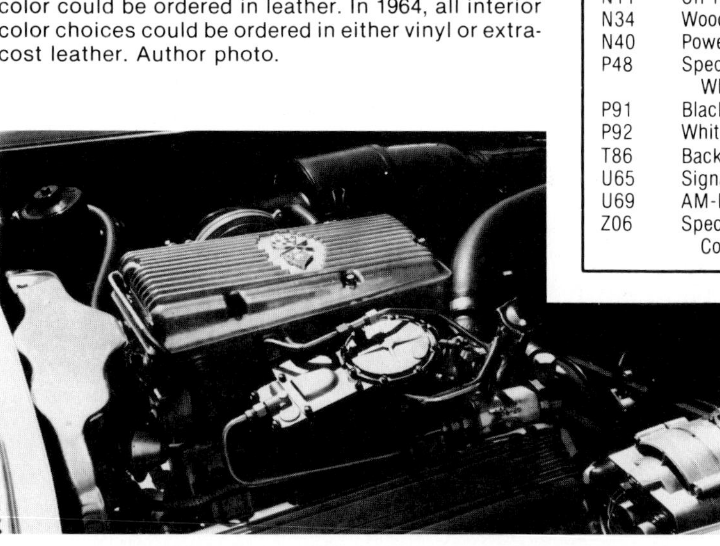

The Corvette fuel-injected engine continued to be available in both 1963 and 1964. The system was similar to previous years, but a new-style air cleaner and doghouse (plenum chamber) made their debut in 1963. The 1963 engines carried over from 1962, and all were 327 cid. The same was true of 1964 except that horsepower ratings of two engines were increased. Author photo.

The 1963 and 1964 Corvettes are very similar, but the 1963 started the show and it commands higher prices. The difference between convertibles is sometimes negligible, but there's no comparison between coupes. The 1964 is every bit as good a car, but that twenty-inch split down the 1963's rear glass makes it worth more, sometimes fifty percent more. It's nuts but it's true. And it probably won't change.

The 1963 Corvette started the hidden headlight trend for Corvettes. In the 1963, the revolving unit was fiberglass on all but very late production cars. The late ones and all later Sting Rays had metal shells.

Real "knock off" wheels made the option list in 1963, but it's doubtful that any were actually factory-installed until 1964 due to leak problems. The wheels have become so popular that reproductions of the wheels are now available. The repros cost less than $1,000 per set. Originals are more desirable and cost two or three times as much, depending on condition. The real knock-off style was used through the 1966 model, but only the 1963-64 wheel style was left unpainted between the fins.

Air conditioning became a Corvette option for the first time in 1963 but late introduction resulted in less than two-percent usage in 1963 models. A few more have been "built" by owners. Nineteen sixty-three also marked the first availability of power steering and power brakes in Corvettes.

Leather seat material was also introduced in 1963. It was only available in tan, but in 1964 all interior colors could be ordered in leather. Trim code tags under the gloveboxes of 1963 and newer Corvettes specify not only the interior color but material as well. Changing worn-out vinyl seats to leather doesn't lower a Corvette's value greatly because it's easy to change back to vinyl, but a Corvette with leather seats which is properly coded for leather is definitely more valuable.

Horsepower ratings for two engines increased in 1964. The solid lifter, non-injected engine increased from 340 to 365 horsepower. The fuel-injected engine went from 360 to 375 horsepower.

The 1963 had two hood depressions with fake vent plates in each. These plates were styled to look like the functional hood vents of the Mitchell Sting Ray racer. In 1964, the plates were eliminated, but the hood depressions remained. Both years had a thirty-six-gallon fuel tank available as an option in coupes. The tanks ate up most of the storage space behind the seats, but Corvettes with them are prized by collectors. Both 1963 and 1964 models had AM-FM radios as options, except for early 1963's, which were signal-seeking AM types.

Production for the two years was almost equal. The 21,513 made in 1963 were slightly surpassed by 1964's 22,229. The coupe-to-convertible mix in 1963 was nearly even, but 1964 coupe production was only thirty-seven percent.

Some 1963 and 1964 models are excellent investments; but be selective. The 1963 coupe is one of the fastest appreciating Corvettes. Combined with desirable options like fuel-injection or air conditioning, the split-window coupe makes a prized collector car.

In any measurable way, the 1964 is as good a car as the 1963, but it doesn't share the same mystique nor the same appreciation rate. Granted, some specially equipped 1964's are very valuable; but when comparing similar cars the 1963 will sell for more. The 1964 is caught in an unfortunate squeeze. It followed the lead car in what many consider to be the best Corvette series, but it preceded the model year that brought four-wheel disc brakes to the Corvette.

The price differential between 1963 and 1964 models is substantial, but less so when comparing convertibles. In investment terms, it would be most accurate to lump the 1963 convertibles in with both 1964 body styles, then consider the split-window coupe in a category by itself.

Is the 1963 coupe really worth the extra expense? Not from any objective standpoint. But it has a unique place in Corvette history and nothing else will ever quite equal it. It's worth it.

1963-1964 Corvette

BASE ENGINE

Type:	Chevrolet ohv V-8
Bore x stroke, inches:	4.00 x 3.25
Displacement, inches:	327
Compression ratio:	10.5:1
Carburetion:	Single four-barrel carburetor
Horsepower:	250
Distributor:	Single point breaker
Other engines offered:	Higher horsepower variations were available in both 1963 and 1964. See option charts.

CHASSIS AND DRIVETRAIN

Clutch:	Single dry-plate
Transmission:	Three-speed manual
Front suspension:	Coil springs, tube-type shock absorbers, stabilizer bar
Rear suspension:	Single transverse leaf spring, tube-type shock absorbers, independent with lateral struts
Axle ratio:	3.36:1
Frame:	Steel box sections, welded

GENERAL:

Wheelbase, inches:	98
Track, front, inches:	56.25
rear, inches:	57.0
Brakes:	Drum
Tire size, front and rear:	6.70 x 15
Wheels:	Steel
Body material:	Fiberglass
Assembly plant:	St. Louis, Missouri

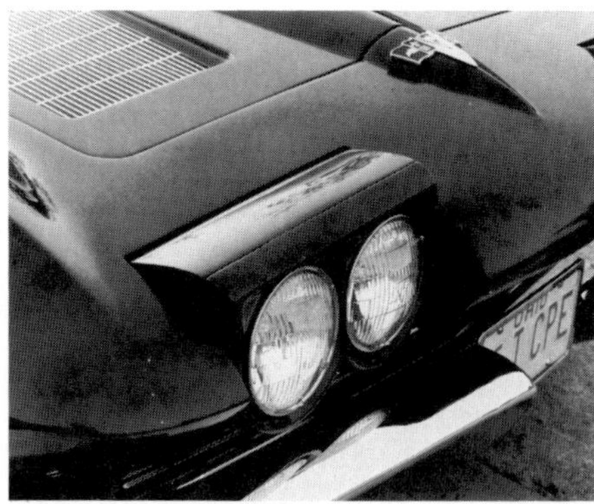

The 1963 Corvette wasn't the first in automotive history to feature hidden headlights, but it certainly started the modern trend to use them. The 1963-67 units were each operated by electric motors. The units were the same for 1963-67 except that the headlight housings were fiberglass in the 1963 (except for a few late cars) and metal in all others. Author photos.

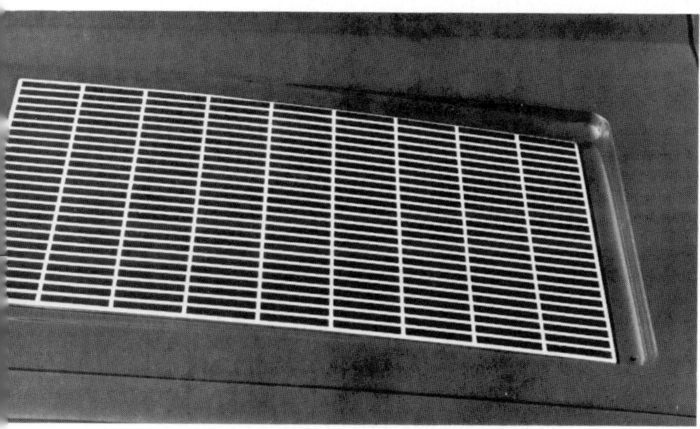

The 1963 Corvette instrument cluster was a little fancy, but drew raves for its functional layout. The silver center cones and silver outer bezels changed to black for the 1964 model. The hood grilles were styled to look like the functional heat exhausts of the racing Sting Ray. The side fender ducts were also nonfunctional in both 1963 and 1964 models. Author photos.

All 1963 through 1967 Corvettes had beautiful removable hardtops available for the convertible models (1964 shown). The 1964 had hood depressions but no fake vent trim like the 1963. Author photos.

1964 Corvette Colors/Options

Color Code	Body Color	Soft Top Color
900	Tuxedo Black	Black/White/Beige
936	Ermine White	Black/White/Beige
923	Riverside Red	Black/White/Beige
940	Satin Silver	Black/White/Beige
912	Silver Blue	Black/White/Beige
916	Daytona Blue	Black/White/Beige
932	Saddle Tan	Black/White/Beige

INTERIOR COLORS: Black, Red, Silver, White, Saddle, Dark Blue

Order #	Item Description	Sticker Price
837	Base Corvette Sport Coupe	4252.00
867	Base Corvette Convertible	4037.00
—	Genuine Leather Seat Trim	80.70
A01	Soft Ray Tinted Glass, All Windows	16.15
A02	Soft Ray Tinted Glass, Windshield	10.80
A31	Electric Power Windows	59.20
C07	Auxiliary Hardtop (for roadster)	236.75
C48	Heater and Defroster Deletion (credit)	—100.00
C60	Air Conditioning (not available with L84)	421.80
F40	Special Front and Rear Suspension	37.70
G81	Positraction Rear Axle, All Ratios	43.05
G91	Special Highway 3.08:1 Axle	2.20
J50	Power Brakes	43.05
J56	Special Sintered Metallic Brake Package	629.50
J65	Sintered Metallic Brakes (power)	53.80
K66	Transistor Ignition System	65.35
L75	Optional 300 HP, 327 CI Engine	53.80
L76	Optional 365 HP, 327 CI Engine	107.60
L84	Optional 375 HP, 327 CI Engine (Fuel Inj)	538.00
M20	4-Speed Transmission	188.30
M35	Powerglide Automatic	199.10
N03	36 Gallon Fuel Tank (coupe only)	202.30
N11	Off Road Exhaust System	37.70
N40	Power Steering	75.35
P48	Special Cast Aluminum Knock-Off Wheels	322.80
P91	Blackwall Nylon Tires, 6.70x15	15.70
P92	Whitewall Rayon Tires, 6.70x15	31.85
T86	Back Up Lamps	10.80
U69	AM-FM Radio	176.50

Cast aluminum wheels with real knock-off hubs were offered for 1963-64 Corvettes, though it's likely none were factory-installed on any 1963 models due to leak problems. The surface between the fins was unpainted on the 1963-64 style. The wheels' popularity has resulted in their remanufacture, but originals had thinner fins. Author photo.

CHAPTER 7

1965-1966 CORVETTE

(1965 Fuel Injection)

Serial Nos. 1965: 194675S100001 - 194675S123562*
1966: 194676S100001 - 194676S127720*
(*for coupes, fourth digit is a 3)

Chevrolet did the impossible in 1965. It made the Corvette better again.

The big news for the 1965 Corvette was a four-wheel disc brake system. Previous Corvettes had used a drum brake setup front and rear that was lifted from the Chevy passenger car line. That was fine for the first Blue Flame models, but Corvettes were getting faster every year and the brakes just stayed the same. Ten years into production, the 150-horsepower Blue Flame had given way to a 1963 model that could be purchased right out of the show room with 340 horsepower. A sintered metallic brake option had been offered but these were racing brakes that had to be "heated up" to work properly. They were not practical for street use.

Chevy engineers didn't fool around with an interim disc front/drum rear arrangement. They went right to discs at all four wheels. In so doing, they catapulted the Corvette right into the ranks of the world's best cars in fadeproof stopping power. The system remained virtually unchanged in every Corvette built through the end of 1982, and the 1982 model still stopped with the best.

The new disc brake system was standard equipment starting with the 1965 Corvette, but for a while Chevrolet offered a "delete cost" option of drum brakes to reduce inventory. For a measly savings of $64.50, it's difficult to understand the logic of specifying the drums, unless for their simplicity and anticipated lower maintenance costs.

As it turned out, the discs did develop reliability problems. The system was complex, using four pistons driving dual calipers at each wheel. As pads wore, piston seals encountered areas of their steel bores which were subject to corrosion. With sixteen pistons per car, leaks were all but inevitable. In one of the great mysteries of all time, Chevrolet did nothing about the problem until it completely redesigned the brakes with aluminum calipers for its all-new 1984 model.

The leak-prone calipers for 1965 Corvettes turned into a gigantic headache for Corvette owners. The corroded steel caliper bores could be honed, but it was a temporary fix. New calipers from GM were expensive and prone to the same problems after they were in service. In retrospect, that 1965 drum brake substitution option didn't look so dumb after all.

Had Corvettes of the era not developed such a cult following, the brake problem would never have been solved. But the cult did develop and if GM wouldn't solve it, enthusiasts would. And they did.

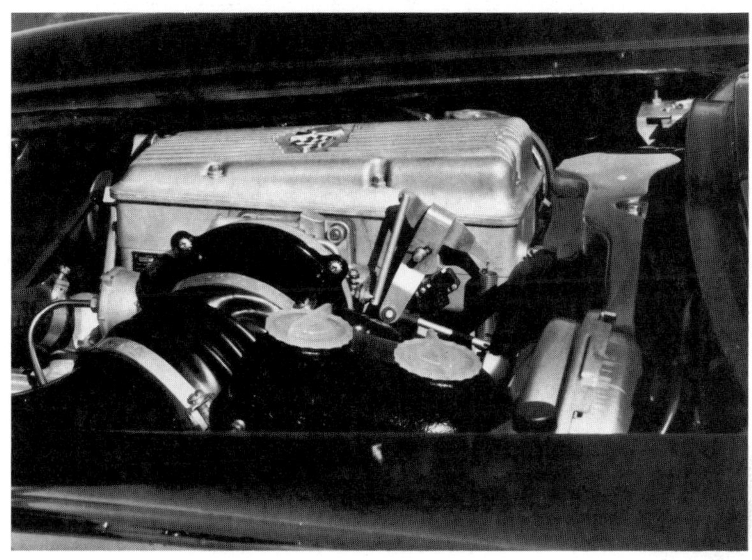

The 1965 Corvette was the last one available with the fuel-injection system developed by Zora Arkus-Duntov and John Dolza. It has been said many times that fuel injection was replaced during the 1965 model year by the 396 cid "big-block" motors, but records now show that fuel injection was available until near the end of the model run. Author photo.

The 1965 Corvette was the last with fuel injection available and the first with disc brakes. The combination of these two make a terrific and widely acknowledged collector car. Author photo.

The fix turned out to be stainless steel inserts for the caliper bores. There are several aftermarket companies doing this now, some good and some not, but the good ones produce a product that is a lifetime cure and is so guaranteed.

If a disc brake Corvette you're considering for purchase has leaky calipers or originals that haven't started leaking yet, plan to spend about $600 for a permanent fix. That will include sleeving your calipers, new pads and a switch to silicone fluid.

Sadly, fuel-injection was phased out by the end of 1965 production. Its high cost had prevented the degree of market penetration Chevrolet deemed necessary to justify its production. Its replacement, though both were available simultaneously for a time, was the 396-cubic-inch "big-block" with 425 horsepower. Brutal.

The 1965 Corvette enjoys several distinctions. It is the first with disc brakes and big-block motors. It's the last with fuel-injection available, creating just one year that both fuel-injection and disc brakes could be had on the same Corvette. This is a very desirable combination, one that Zora Arkus-Duntov once told an interviewer was the Corvette's zenith from an engineering standpoint.

The 1965 body was a carryover from the previous year, but there were differences. The indentations were removed from the 1965 hood, but models with 396-cubic-inch engines (427 in 1966) received special hoods with newly designed air scoops. The horizontal side fender indentions of the 1963-64 models were replaced by vertical functional slots in 1965 and 1966 models.

Instruments in 1963 and 1964 had long, bent needles; but in 1965 they were changed to a flat dial/straight needle design with strong aircraft design influence. Seats were redesigned in 1965 for better support and the interior door panels starting in 1965 became one-piece molded units, replacing the vinyl-on-fiberboard type of earlier years.

The 1966 was a near twin to the 1965. There were trim changes, an extra batch of pleats in the seats to cure splitting problems and a plated cast grille to replace the earlier extruded aluminum units.

Beautiful side-mounted exhaust systems could be ordered on both years as could telescopic steering columns. A Corvette first and last, a genuine teak steering wheel was optional on both years but on no others. Another Corvette first for both years was the availability of gold-stripe tires. Blackwall tires were still standard and whitewalls were available, too.

1965-1966 Corvette

BASE ENGINE

Type: . . . . Chevrolet ohv V-8
Bore x stroke, inches: 4.00x3.25
Displacement, inches: 327
Compression ratio: 10.5:1 (1965), 10.25:1 (1966)
Carburetion: . . . . Single four-barrel carburetor
Horsepower: 250
Distributor: . . . . Single point breaker
Other engines offered: ...Higher horsepower variations were available in both 1965 and 1966. See option charts.

CHASSIS AND DRIVETRAIN

Clutch: . . . . Single dry-plate
Transmission: . . . . Three-speed manual
Front suspension: ...Coil springs, tube-type shock absorbers, stabilizer bar
Rear suspension: ...Single transverse leaf spring, tube-type shock absorbers, independent with lateral struts
Axle ratio: 3.36:1
Frame: . . . . Steel box sections, welded

GENERAL:

Wheelbase, inches: 98
Track, front, inches: 56.8
rear, inches: 57.6
Brakes: . . . . Disc, four-wheel
Tire size, front and rear: 7.75-15
Wheels: . . . . Steel
Body material: . . . . Fiberglass
Assembly plant: . . . . St. Louis, Missouri

Production in 1966 reached the highest level of the 1963-67 series. There were 27,720 Corvettes made in 1966, of which 9,958 were coupes. Nineteen sixty-five production totaled 23,562 and just 8,186 were coupes. It was the lowest production year for coupes of the 1963-67 models.

Collectors view the 1965 as slightly more desirable than the 1966, but the difference is minimal, certainly nothing like the spread between 1963 and 1964 coupes. Value for both of these years is mainly determined by equipment and the option list for each year was immense.

Some are obvious winners. A 1965 with fuel-injection is a top-notch collector car and the awesome performance of the big-blocks make either year valuable if so equipped.

But no matter how equipped, all 1965 and 1966 Corvettes are potentially terrific cars. They are noticeably tighter than the previous Sting Rays, especially in convertible form. In fact, convertibles have enjoyed a new round of popularity since their demise in the mid-seventies, and Corvette enthusiasts consider the 1965-66 models (and 1967) great choices. Equipped with the removable hardtop and fold-down convertible top, they're three cars in one and drive like three different cars. Great fun.

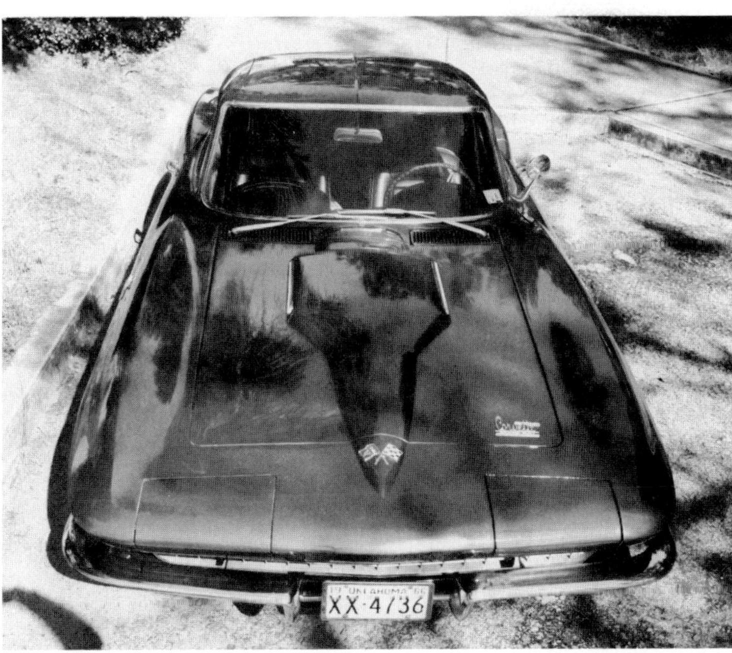

The 1965 and 1966 Corvettes with big-block motors were distinguished by special hoods. Although the big-blocks added more weight where the Corvette least needed it, they are so unbelievably powerful that they can't help but be prized investment cars. But many have been badly abused. Exercise caution in purchasing one of these beasts. Wellington Morton photo.

1965 Corvette Colors/Options

Color Code	Body Color	Soft Top Color
AA	Tuxedo Black	Black/White/Beige
CC	Ermine White	Black/White/Beige
FF	Nassau Blue	Black/White/Beige
GG	Glen Green	Black/White/Beige
MM	Milano Maroon	Black/White/Beige
QQ	Silver Pearl	Black/White/Beige
UU	Rally Red	Black/White/Beige
XX	Goldwood Yellow	Black/White/Beige

INTERIOR COLORS: Black, Red, Blue, Saddle, Silver, White, Green, Maroon

Order #	Item Description	Sticker Price
19437	Base Corvette Sports Coupe	4321.00
19467	Base Corvette Convertible	4106.00
—	Genuine Leather Seat Trim	80.70
A01	Soft Ray Tinted Glass, All Windows	16.15
A02	Soft Ray Tinted Glass, Windshield	10.80
A31	Electric Power Windows	59.20
C07	Auxiliary Hardtop (for roadsters)	236.75
C48	Heater and Defroster Deletion (credit)	—100.00
C60	Air Conditioning	421.80
F40	Special Front and Rear Suspension	37.70
G81	Positraction Rear Axle, All Ratios	43.05
G91	Special Highway 3.08:1 Axle	2.20
J50	Power Brakes	43.05
J61	Drum Brake Substitution (credit)	—64.50
K66	Transistor Ignition System	75.35
L75	Optional 300 HP, 327 CI Engine	53.80
L76	Optional 365 HP, 327 CI Engine	129.15
L78	Optional 425 HP, 396 CI Engine	292.70
L79	Optional 350 HP, 327 CI Engine	107.60
L84	Optional 375 HP, 327 CI Engine (Fuel Inj)	538.00
M20	4-Speed Transmission	188.30
M22	4-Speed Close Ratio Transmission	236.95
M35	Powerglide Automatic Transmission	199.10
N03	36 Gallon Fuel Tank (coupe only)	202.30
N11	Off Road Exhaust System	37.70
N14	Side Mount Exhaust System	134.50
N32	Teakwood Steering Wheel	48.45
N36	Telescopic Steering Column	43.05
N40	Power Steering	96.85
P48	Special Cast Aluminum Knock-Off Wheels	322.80
P92	Whitewall Tires, 7.75x15	31.85
T01	Goldwall Tires, 7.75x15	50.05
U69	AM-FM Radio	203.40
Z01	Backup Lamps and Inside Day/Night Mirror	16.15

1966 Corvette Colors/Options

Color Code	Body Color	Soft Top Color
900	Tuxedo Black	Black/White/Beige
972	Ermine White	Black/White/Beige
976	Nassau Blue	Black/White/Beige
982	Mosport Green	Black/White/Beige
988	Milano Maroon	Black/White/Beige
986	Silver Pearl	Black/White/Beige
974	Rally Red	Black/White/Beige
984	Sunfire Yellow	Black/White/Beige
978	Laguna Blue	Black/White/Beige
980	Trophy Blue	Black/White/Beige

INTERIOR COLORS: Black, Red, Bright Blue, White-Blue, Silver, Saddle, Green, Blue

Order #	Item Description	Sticker Price
19437	Base Corvette Sport Coupe	4295.00
19467	Base Corvette Convertible	4084.00
—	Genuine Leather Seats	79.00
A01	Soft Ray Tinted Glass, All Windows	15.80
A02	Soft Ray Tinted Glass, Windshield	10.55
A31	Electric Power Windows	59.20
A82	Headrests	42.15
A85	Shoulder Harness	26.35
C07	Auxiliary Hardtop (for roadster)	231.75
C48	Heater and Defroster Deletion (credit)	—97.85
C60	Air Conditioning	412.90
F41	Special Front and Rear Suspension	36.90
G81	Positraction Rear Axle, All Ratios	42.15
J50	Power Brakes	43.05
J56	Special Heavy Duty Brakes	342.30
K66	Transistor Ignition System	73.75
L36	Optional 390 HP, 427 Engine	181.20
L72	Optional 427 HP, 427 CI engine	312.85
L79	Optional 350 HP, 327 CI Engine	105.35
M20	4-Speed Transmission	184.30
M21	4-Speed Close Ratio Transmission	184.30
M22	4-Speed Close Ratio Transmission HD	237.00
M35	Powerglide Automatic Transmission	194.85
N03	36 Gallon Fuel Tank	198.05
N11	Off Road Exhaust System	36.90
N14	Side Mount Exhaust System	131.65
N32	Teakwood Steering Wheel	48.45
N36	Telescopic Steering Column	42.15
N40	Power Steering	94.80
P48	Special Cast Aluminum Knock-Off Wheels	326.00
P92	Whitewall Tires, 7.75x15	31.30
T01	Goldwall Tires, 7.75x15	46.55
U69	AM-FM Radio	199.10
V74	Traffic Hazard Lamp Switch	11.60

1966 Corvette 427 Coupe. Wellington Morton photo.

The side fender vents were made functional in 1965 and 1966. In both years a side exhaust system was available. There was no muffler, just a chambered pipe that wrapped from the engine down the sides of the body. The outer surface was an aluminum heat shield. These systems can be added to any 1963-67 model, but they were only factory available from 1965-67. If you're contemplating adding side exhausts, ride in a Corvette with them first. They are loud! And the acoustics of coupes make side exhausts particularly irritating. But in a convertible with the top down, there's nothing more exhilarating. Wellington Morton photo.

The knock-off aluminum wheel option continued in 1965 and 1966 but with small differences. Both were painted a flat gray-black between the fins. The 1965 had a bright center cone like the 1963 and 1964, but the cones of the 1966 had a brushed finish. Wellington Morton photo.

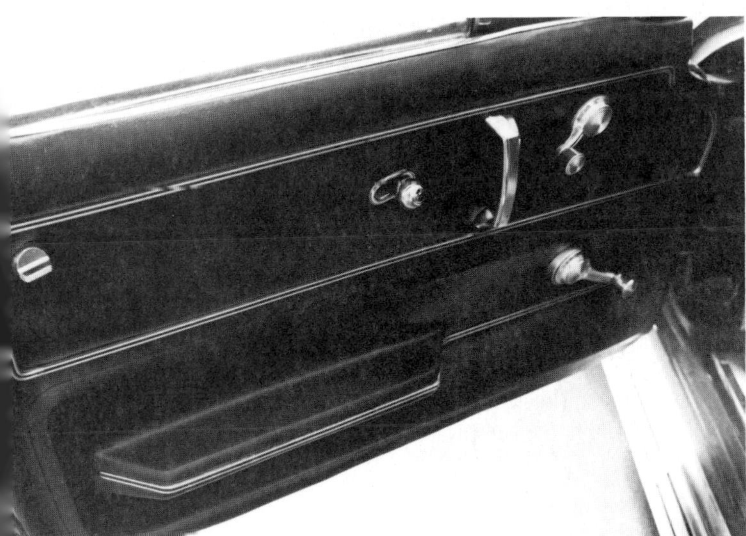

The door panels of the 1965 and 1966 models were a molded vinyl-on-foam design. They tended to crack along the sides of the armrest, but excellent reproductions are available today. The pull handle of the 1965 was plastic, colored to match the interior. Unfortunately, many pulled apart; the 1966 was metal as shown. The instrument layout of the 1965 and 1966 was the same as earlier Sting Rays, but the faces were flat, aircraft style. Beautiful. Wellington Morton photos.

CHAPTER 8

1967 CORVETTE

Serial Nos. 194677S100001 - 194677S122940*
(*for coupes, fourth digit is a 3)

The "mid-year" Corvettes are those built between 1963 and 1967, and often they're written about as a single group or series. Sometimes the mid-years are divided into two groups, 1963-64 and 1965-67. The logic most often cited is that the '65 and later cars should be segregated because disc brakes replaced drums in 1965.

But a lot of Corvette buffs group the 1967 model all by itself so I've done it here. To some of these folks, there are 1967's and there are the rest of 'em.

An analysis of mid-year selling prices will show the top prices are consistently paid for the 1963 and the 1967. The 1963 is understandable, but what's so special about the 1967?

First, understand that the 1967 is a Corvette that shouldn't even exist. Chevrolet had planned to put a new body on the Corvette chassis in 1967, but the new shape was delayed at the last minute by a year and finally arrived as the 1968 model. Chevrolet had to make do with the same old Sting Ray body for a fifth year. Stylists were told to change a few things, but time was short.

Normally, when this happens—change for the sake of change—the results are disastrous. But this time the opposite happened.

Rather than come up with new emblems and scripts, they just left most of them off. The 1967 is the cleanest, least adorned of any Sting Ray body.

Somebody in the government concluded that spinners on hubcaps and wheels posed a threat to society, so manufacturers were told to get them off their 1967 models. This meant the knock-off wheels optional on the 1963-66 Corvettes had to go. Chevrolet, possibly fearing the 1967 would turn out to be a slow seller since a new design was expected, decided to retool the aluminum wheel in a bolt-on style. This was particularly surprising because Chevrolet went to this expense for a wheel that would only be used for the 1967 Corvette. The 1968 was to use a wider rim to accommodate wider tires.

Again, a last minute redesign of a gorgeous wheel could be expected to yield dismal results, but it didn't. The 1967 bolt-on aluminum wheel was a masterpiece of exquisite detail and elegance. It was so nice, Corvette stylists dusted the design off and used a modified version on the 1982 Collector Edition.

Everything done to the 1967, the new side-fender louver treatment, the relocation of the handbrake from under the dash to between the seats, the new hood for 427-cubic-inch engines . . . everything came out right.

Demand did soften during 1967 and production dropped to 22,940, less than in either 1965 or 1966. Some feel the lighter schedule had a positive effect on quality. It's hard to say now, but the 1967 does get a lot of votes as the best-built Corvette ever.

1967 Corvette. Chevrolet photo.

It's rare to see a Corvette without a radio but this one didn't even have a heater. To discourage novice purchase of its L-88 engine option, a pure race machine sold to the public as a technicality to qualify it as a production vehicle, Chevrolet would not install radios or heaters. Bill Miller photo.

This was the L-88 engine, rated by Chevrolet at 430 horsepower, but actually having close to 600! Note the unusual air-cleaner-in-hood arrangement. Just 20 of the L-88 models were sold in 1967. Needless to say, these are very valuable today. Bill Miller photo.

Engines available in 1967, in addition to the standard 300-horsepower, 327-cubic-inch, included the 350-horsepower version of the 327, and three 427-cubic-inch variations rated at 390, 400 and 435 horsepower. Also, aluminum heads could be specified for the 435-horsepower mill for an extra $368.65. Oh, and there were a few other—twenty to be exact—427 engine models sold to retail customers called L-88's.

Ah yes, the L-88. Rated at 430 horsepower, it had five less horsepower than the 435-horsepower L-71 engine. But at $947.90, the L-88 was more than twice as expensive. See, Chevrolet wasn't being exactly honest about the horsepower. The L-88 put out over 500, but the engine was intended expressly for racing and Chevrolet tried to discourage unknowing customers from ordering it by giving it a lower horsepower rating than the L-71.

A total of 216 L-88 Corvettes were retailed to customers in 1967, 1968 and 1969 models. But the twenty built in the 1967 model year qualifies them as the most rare. While these are very valuable collector cars, their usefulness is limited to just that, collecting. They were not intended for street use and no one should buy one with that in mind.

The 1967 is as close to a "can't lose" Corvette investment as you can get. The 1963 has a slightly stronger appreciation history but the 1967 has the reputation of being one of the best-driving Corvettes ever. It's the latest of the mid-years and with its many Corvette firsts—things like foam- and fiber-cushioned headliner, four-way flashers, turn signals with the lane-change feature added, dual master cylinders, six-inch rim widths, larger interior vent ports and folding seat back latches—the 1967 Corvette is thought by many to be the most refined Sting Ray of all. If Chevrolet had followed it with an even greater 1968 model, the 1967 would be thought of now as just another nice older Corvette. But the 1968 didn't turn out that way. A lot of potential new Corvette buyers in 1967 waited for the new body style coming in 1968. It was an understandable decision, but it looks now as if it wasn't the best one.

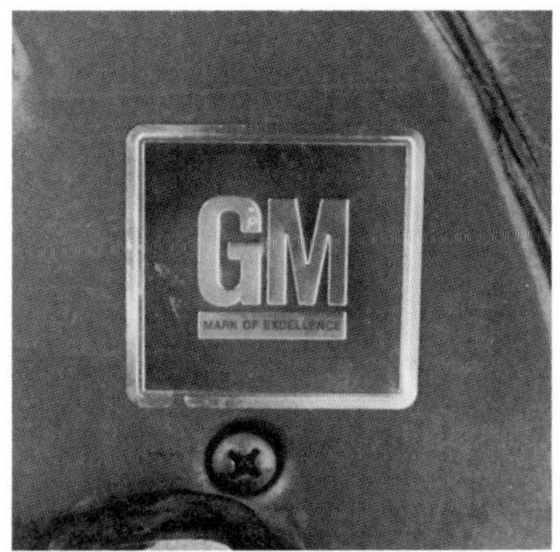

The GM Mark of Excellence sticker appeared in the door jamb of 1967 Corvettes. It was exclusive to the year. Author photo.

The handbrake moved to between the seats in 1967. Also, the inside door lock button moved forward several inches. Various reasons have been speculated for the move of the lock button, but the most likely is that it simply made it easier to reach. Author photos.

The side exhaust system introduced in 1965 continued to be available in 1967. But the backup light above the license plate was new and exclusive to the 1967 model. Author photos.

The 1967's instruments were similar to those of the previous two years, but 1967 did have the optional speed warning buzzer device pictured above. Author photo.

The 1967 Corvette was one of the first to show signs of federal input in the area of safety. One such result in 1967 was a flatter design for the control knobs. Author photo.

1967 Corvette Colors/Options

Color Code	Body Color	Soft Top Color
900	Tuxedo Black	Black/White/Teal Blue
972	Ermine White	Black/White/Teal Blue
980	Elkhart Blue	Black/White/Teal Blue
977	Lyndale Blue	Black/White/Teal Blue
976	Marina Blue	Black/White/Teal Blue
983	Goodwood Green	Black/White/Teal Blue
974	Rally Red	Black/White/Teal Blue
986	Silver Pearl	Black/White/Teal Blue
984	Sunfire Yellow	Black/White/Teal Blue
988	Marlboro Maroon	Black/White/Teal Blue

INTERIOR COLORS: Black, Red, Bright Blue, Saddle, White-Blue, White-Black, Teal Blue, Green

Order #	Item Description	Sticker Price
19437	Base Corvette Sport Coupe	$4388.75
19467	Base Corvette Convertible	4240.75
—	Genuine Leather Seats	79.00
A01	Soft Ray Tinted Glass, All Windows	15.80
A02	Soft Ray Tinted Glass, Windshield	10.55
A31	Electric Power Windows	57.95
A82	Headrests	42.15
A85	Shoulder Belts (coupe only)	26.35
C07	Auxiliary Hardtop (for roadster)	231.75
C08	Vinyl Covering for Auxiliary Hardtop	52.70
C48	Heater and Defroster Deletion (credit)	−97.85
C60	Air Conditioning	412.90
F41	Special Front and Rear Suspension	36.90
J50	Power Brakes	42.15
J56	Special Heavy Duty Brakes	342.30
K66	Transistor Ignition System	73.75
L36	Optional 390 HP, 427 CI Engine	200.15
L68	Optional 400 HP, 427 CI Engine	305.50
L71	Optional 435 HP, 427 CI Engine	437.10
L79	Optional 350 HP, 327 CI Engine	105.35
L88	Optional 430 HP, 427 CI Engine	947.90
L89	Aluminum Cylinder Heads for L71	368.65
M20	4-Speed Transmission	184.35
M21	4-Speed Close Ratio Transmission	184.35
M22	4-Speed Close Ratio Transmission HD	237.00
M35	Powerglide Automatic Transmission	194.35
N03	36 Gallon Fuel Tank (coupe only)	198.05
N11	Off Road Exhaust System	36.90
N14	Side Mount Exhaust System	131.65
N36	Telescopic Steering Column	42.15
N40	Power Steering	94.80
N89	Special Cast Aluminum Bolt-On Wheels	263.30
P92	Whitewall Tires, 7.75x15	31.35
QB1	Redline Tires, 7.75x15	46.65
U15	Speed Warning Indicator	10.55
U69	AM-FM Radio	172.75

As if 427 cubic inches weren't enough, in 1967 you could even get a 3x2 carburetor setup with either 400 or 435 horsepower. This arrangement was characterized by the unusual triangular air cleaner. The distinctive hood was unique to 1967 models with the 427 motors. Author photos.

The "rally" wheel was standard fare in 1967. Federal law mandated the removal of spinners from wheels in 1967 so the knock-off wheel of 1963-66 was replaced with the "bolt-on" in 1967. The center cone of this gorgeous wheel pried off to reveal lug nuts. Like the knock-offs, the popularity of this wheel has resulted in reproductions, but originals are detectible and more valuable. Bill Miller and author photos.

1967 Corvette

BASE ENGINE

Type: . . . . Chevrolet ohv V-8
Bore x stroke, inches: . . . . 4.00 x 3.25
Displacement, inches: 327
Compression ratio: 10.25:1
Carburetion: . . . . Single four-barrel carburetor
Horsepower: 300
Distributor: . . . . Single point breaker
Other engines offered: ... Higher horsepower variations were available in both 1965 and 1966. See option charts.

CHASSIS AND DRIVETRAIN

Clutch: . . . . Single dry-plate
Transmission: . . . . Three-speed manual
Front suspension: ... Coil springs, tube-type shock absorbers, stabilizer bar
Rear suspension: ... Single transverse leaf spring, tube-type shock absorbers, independent with lateral struts
Axle ratio: 3.36:1
Frame: . . . . Steel box sections, welded

GENERAL:

Wheelbase, inches: 98
Track, front, inches: 57.6
rear, inches: 58.3
Brakes: . . . . Disc, four-wheel
Tire size, front and rear: 7.75-15
Wheels: . . . . Steel
Body material: . . . . Fiberglass
Assembly plant: . . . . St. Louis, Missouri

CHAPTER 9

1968-1969 CORVETTE

Serial Nos. 1968: 194678S400001 - 194678S428566*
1969: 194679S700001 - 194679S738762*
(*for coupes, fourth digit is a 3)

The 1968 Corvette was restyled with a new body shape; a toned-down version of the Mako Shark-inspired design originally planned for introduction as the 1967 model. The new shape was lower, slightly wider and more aerodynamic. No one realized it at the time, but the Corvette wouldn't see another complete body change until 1983, a full fifteen years later.

Magazine journalists have always found it difficult to accept anything American built as a "real sports car," whatever that means. And Corvette fit and finish was always open to some complaints. But Corvettes built in the mid-sixties, especially the 1965-67 models, were very well designed and constructed cars and didn't offer anything really juicy for the critics. This changed in 1968. The critics had a field day.

Part of the negative press reaction to the 1968 Corvette was design related. Few could argue the car didn't look good, "dramatic" being a favorite adjective. But the new design required compromises. The body was a little wider at its widest point, but the "Coke-bottle" shape and a transmission tunnel made bigger to accommodate the three-speed automatics created a cabin that was noticeably cramped. Some called it cave-like.

To accommodate the lower roofline, seat backs were raked at thirty-three degrees compared to twenty-five degrees the year before. The seats had little support of any kind and a sliding-board effect caused occupants to have to constantly reposition themselves. Side vent windows were eliminated and the window-to-seat relationship was such that driving with an elbow out the window was uncomfortable at best. The doors didn't close with the reassuring "thunk" purists preferred, but rather with a crash of internal rattles.

Starting with the doors, the 1968 Corvette's real problem lay in a perceived lack of quality control. Magazine reviews, particularly one by *Car and Driver,* literally roasted Chevrolet for building a piece of junk. *Car and Driver* recited a litany of quality ailments and proclaimed its test Corvette too shabby to merit testing. The *Car and Driver* road test—actually, the lack of it—sent shock waves through General Motors.

Reviews of this sort can have enormous impact on a new car and its reputation. Some of the *Car and Driver* criticisms pointed out real problems that required design attention and correction. Most were of a nuisance nature, things a fairly competent owner could correct in a weekend. So someone looking at the car now as a restoration candidate isn't too concerned, but the new-car buyer in 1968

No one could deny the beauty of 1968 styling; the shape was good enough to last fifteen years. But the 1968 met a barrage of criticism for quality problems and design glitches. It has never recovered, but watch this one—it could be a sleeper. Note that the side exhaust system shown has been owner-added. This side exhaust style was a factory option, but only in 1969. Author photo.

The body sides of the 1968 and 1969 models wrapped under the tires, exposing painted surfaces to debris thrown by the extra-wide rubber. The side exhaust style shown was available only in 1969. Author photo.

certainly was turned off. The 1968 Corvette got saddled early with the reputation of being a quality disaster, and it has never shaken that reputation to this day.

The magazine criticism of the 1968 Corvette did wake Chevrolet up and serve it notice that the Corvette market couldn't be taken for granted. The Corvette had already attracted a tremendous following, a momentum a couple of bad reviews couldn't halt. But Chevrolet realized the Corvette couldn't rest on its laurels for long.

Quality problems were attacked and reduced, and components were redesigned to make the car more livable. One example was a quick redesign of the inner door panels to get more desperately needed shoulder room in the cramped cockpit.

Chevrolet stopped calling its Corvette the Sting Ray in 1968 but thought better of it and put the name back on in 1969. A subtle point, but the 1963-67 Corvettes were Sting Rays (two words), whereas the 1969 was a Stingray. The body styling of both the 1968 and 1969 was identical other than details like the Stingray script on the side fenders of the latter. Other details included a different type of exterior door opener. The 1968 had a thumb button and a finger depression plate above it. The button was removed in 1969 and the depression plate triggered the door mechanism. Also, the 1968 had separate backup lights placed under the bumpers whereas the 1969 had them incorporated into the regular taillights.

Nineteen sixty-eight Corvettes had the ignition switch on the dash, but it moved to the steering column in 1969. The cutaway dash design left no room for a glovebox in the normal location in the 1968, but at least the 1969 got some map pockets.

The 1968 and 1969 Corvettes retained hidden headlights but the units were vacuum-operated rather than electrically. The vacuum units moved the lights into driving position more quickly and have proven to be very trouble-free. The hidden headlights of Corvettes were vacuum-operated through 1982.

But the 1968 and 1969 Corvettes also had a vacuum-operated lid which covered the windshield wipers when not in use. The lid was a styling gimmick borrowed from the Mako Shark dream car. Its tendency to malfunction was one of the items that tarnished the quality image of these cars. I remember that the lid of my own 1969 would pop up whenever it felt like it, then crunch down on the wiper arms when the wiper switch was turned on. Also, some owners have complained about the lid icing over, but my own experience was that the lid mechanism was powerful enough to crack through anything an Ohio winter could produce.

Both coupe and convertible body styles continued in 1968, but the coupe was a different breed than before. It was a "T" top with two removable roof panels and a rear window which could also be removed. Both years and body styles had a fiber-optics light-monitoring system with a display panel on the center console.

Wheel width in 1968 increased from six inches to seven, an increase made possible by the body's redesign to accommodate wider tires. Rim width increased again, to eight inches, in 1969. But the steering-wheel diameter was reduced from sixteen inches in the 1968 to fifteen in the 1969.

Stereo radios could be ordered on both years, but the side-mount exhaust systems were available only in 1969.

The quality problems associated with the 1968 and, to a lesser degree, the 1969 have obviously tarnished these models. Collectors don't hold them in great esteem but this very fact has kept prices reasonable. There has always been a small band of Corvette enthusiasts who draw an analogy between the 1963 and 1968 models and assume that 1968's will eventually explode in value.

Anything's possible, but the analogy falls apart under scrutiny. The 1963 Corvette was widely praised from its first introductory day and led a procession of wildly popular cars. The 1968 was tainted from day one. It did lead off a fifteen-year Corvette series, but those were years of much higher volume than the four that followed 1963.

Both big- and small-blocks continued in 1968 and 1969. The big engines for both years were still 427 cubic inches, but the small-blocks went from 327 cubic inches in 1968 to 350 in 1969. Government-mandated emission devices were starting to creep in, but blistering performance packages could be ordered in both years. In 1968 and 1969, the L-88 version of the 427 was available. This was a pure racing engine capable of over 500 horsepower. It was sold quietly to the public to qualify it as a "production" vehicle.

In 1969, Chevrolet offered another engine that had no business in a street car, the ZL-1. This one also pumped out over 500 horsepower, but was aluminum for weight savings. The ZL-1 option was a racing package consisting of the engine and suspension components. The option cost was $3,000, which seemed outrageous but really wasn't. Though ZL-1 parts found their way out of Chevrolet Engineering to the racetracks, official records show that only two ZL-1-optioned 1969 Corvettes were delivered to retail customers.

These thundering engines available from the factory prompted John Greenwood, the famous Corvette road racer, to comment in a recent interview that the 1968-69 Corvettes were his personal favorites because they were so nearly race-ready right off the show room floor.

While these racing engines make for great conversation—imagine driving away from your local Chevy dealer in a bone-stock automobile capable of speeds in excess of 170 mph—they're for serious drivers and collectors only. Corvettes equipped with these engines are practically useless for street driving. To discourage anything but race customers, Chevrolet wouldn't even install heaters in L-88 or ZL-1 Corvettes. These cars were offered to the public only as a technicality necessary to qualify them as "production" race vehicles.

The body of the 1968-69 was wrapped under the wheels so that rocks thrown by the tires chipped the lower body sides. Without a doubt, the big tires hanging out from the body gave these models a very hairy business-only look. But the body was altered the following year to solve the chip problem.

Despite a slow start, production of the 1968 Corvette jumped to 28,566, a new Corvette record. Strikes stalled the start of 1969 production, so when things finally got rolling Chevrolet decided to just let them roll. Nineteen sixty-nine production went four months into the 1970 production schedule and resulted in a whopping 38,762 1969's built.

Corvette buffs rate the 1968 and 1969 models about equally in desirability, with the 1968 having perhaps a small edge. It has the advantage of lower production, it was the first of the series, and it has several unique features collectors look for. The 1969 is less unique and more plentiful but has a better quality image. As a restoration candidate, the 1968 is preferred by some for the reasons listed and because the quality problems associated with fit and finish can be corrected during refurbishing.

Unique features of the 1968 included a push-button door release and a dash-mounted ignition switch. In the 1969, the depression plate in the door activated the door mechanism and the ignition switch moved to the steering column. Author photos.

The 1968 introduced a new interior with seats raked at 33 degrees, the most severe in Corvette's history. Author photo.

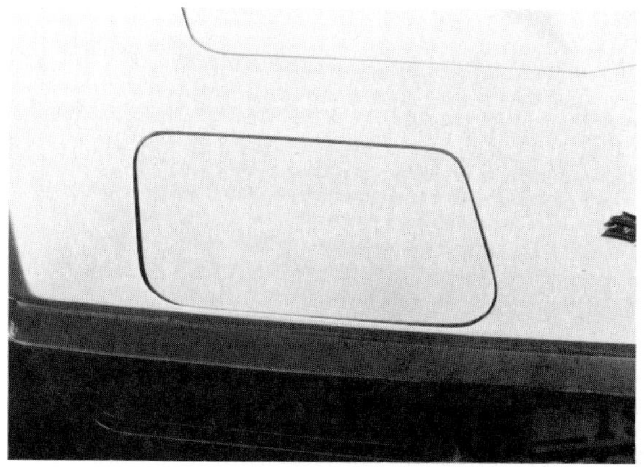

Hidden headlights continued with the 1968 model, but these popped up instead of revolving into position. Also, these and all subsequent Corvette headlight units through 1982 were vacuum-operated rather than electrically. Author photos.

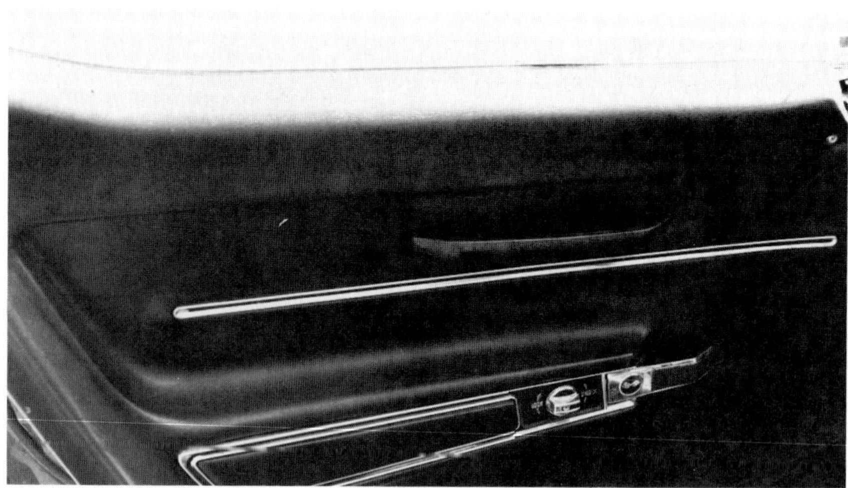

The 1968 inner door panel (late style shown above) was unique to the year with a horizontal pull handle and a thick upper section that limited shoulder room. The 1969 panel (right) used a vertical pull and a thinner section in the shoulder area. Author photos.

The 1968 model introduced a number of styling touches, some of which didn't work out well in service. One was this vacuum-operated lid, which covered the windshield wipers when not in use. The lid's vacuum action tended to be a little unpredictable and icing could cause difficulty. Author photo.

The Stingray name was not used on the 1968 Corvette, but returned in 1969. The trim liners for the side fender slots were optional only in 1969. Author photo.

1968 Corvette Colors/Options

Color Code	Body Color	Soft Top Color
900	Tuxedo Black	Black/White/Beige
972	Polar White	Black/White/Beige
992	Corvette Bronze	Black/White/Beige
976	LeMans Blue	Black/White/Beige
978	International Blue	Black/White/Beige
988	Cordovan Maroon	Black/White/Beige
974	Rally Red	Black/White/Beige
986	Silverstone Silver	Black/White/Beige
983	British Green	Black/White/Beige
984	Safari Yellow	Black/White/Beige

INTERIOR COLORS: Black, Red, Medium Blue, Dark Blue, Dark Orange, Tobacco, Gunmetal

Order #	Item Description	Sticker Price
19437	Base Corvette Sport Coupe	4663.00
19467	Base Corvette Convertible	4320.00
—	Genuine Leather Seat Trim	79.00
A01	Soft Ray Tinted Glass, All Windows	15.80
A31	Electric Power Windows	57.95
A82	Head Restraints	42.15
A85	Custom Shoulder Belts	26.35
C07	Auxiliary Hardtop (for roadster)	231.75
C08	Vinyl Covering For Auxiliary Hardtop	52.70
C50	Rear Window Defroster	31.60
C60	Air Conditioning	412.90
F41	Special Front and Rear Suspension	36.90
G81	Positraction Rear Axle, All Ratios	46.35
J50	Power Brakes	42.15
J56	Heavy Duty Breaks	384.45
K66	Transistor Ignition System	73.75
L36	Optional 390 HP, 427 CI Engine	200.15
L68	Optional 400 HP, 427 CI Engine	305.50
L71	Optional 435 HP, 427 CI Engine	437.10
L79	Optional 350 HP, 327 CI Engine	105.35
L88	Optional 435 HP, 427 CI Engine	947.90
L71/81	Optional 435 HP, 427 CI Engine	805.75
M20	4-Speed Transmission	184.35
M21	4-Speed Close Ratio Transmission	184.35
M22	4-Speed Close Ratio Transmission HD	263.30
M40	Turbo-Hydramatic Transmission	226.45
N11	Off Road Exhaust System	36.90
N36	Telescopic Steering Column	42.15
N40	Power Steering	94.80
P01	Bright Metal Wheel Cover	57.95
PT6	Red Stripe Nylon Tires, F70x15	31.30
PT7	White Stripe Nylon Tires, F70x15	31.30
UA6	Alarm System	26.35
U15	Speed Warning Indicator	10.55
U69	AM-FM Radio	172.75
U79	AM-FM Stereo Radio	278.10

1969 Corvette Colors/Options

Color Code	Body Color	Soft Top Color
900	Tuxedo Black	Black/White/Beige
972	Can-Am White	Black/White/Beige
974	Monza Red	Black/White/Beige
976	LeMans Blue	Black/White/Beige
990	Monaco Orange	Black/White/Beige
983	Fathom Green	Black/White/Beige
984	Daytona Yellow	Black/White/Beige
986	Cortez Silver	Black/White/Beige
988	Burgundy	Black/White/Beige
980	Riverside Gold	Black/White/Beige

INTERIOR COLORS: Black, Bright Blue, Green, Red, Gunmetal, Saddle

Order #	Item Description	Sticker Price
19437	Base Corvette Sport Coupe	$4780.95
19467	Base Corvette Convertible	4437.95
—	Genuine Leather Seat Trim	79.00
A01	Soft Ray Tinted Glass, All Windows	16.90
A31	Electric Power Windows	63.20
A85	Custom Shoulder Belts	42.15
C07	Auxiliary Hardtop (for roadster)	252.80
C08	Vinyl Covering for Auxiliary Hardtop	57.95
C50	Rear Window Defroster	32.65
C60	Air Conditioning	428.70
F41	Special Front and Rear Suspension	36.90
—	Positraction Rear Axle, All Ratios	46.35
J50	Power Brakes	42.15
K05	Engine Block Heater	10.55
K66	Transistor Ignition System	81.10
L36	Optional 390 HP, 427 CI Engine	221.20
L46	Optional 350 HP, 350 CI Engine	131.65
L68	Optional 400 HP, 427 CI Engine	326.55
L71	Optional 435 HP, 427 CI Engine	437.10
L88	Optional 435 HP, 427 CI Engine	1032.15
L89	Optional 435 HP, 427 CI Engine	832.05
ZL1	Optional Special 427 CI Engine	3000.00
M20	4-Speed Transmission	184.80
M21	4-Speed Close Ratio Transmission	184.80
M22	4-Speed Close Ratio Transmission Heavy Duty	290.40
M40	Turbo Hydramatic Transmission	221.80
N14	Side Mount Exhaust System	147.45
N37	Tilt-Telescopic Steering Column	84.30
N40	Power Steering	105.35
P02	Wheel Covers	57.95
PT6/PT7	Red Stripe/White Stripe Nylon Tires	31.30
TJ2	Front Fender Louver Trim	21.10
UA6	Alarm System	26.35
U15	Speed Warning Indicator	11.60
U69	AM-FM Radio	172.45
U79	AM-FM Stereo Radio	278.10

1969 Corvette convertible. Author photo.

1968-1969 Corvette

BASE ENGINE

Type: Chevrolet ohv V-8
Bore x stroke, inches: 4.00 x 3.25 (1968), 4.00 x 3.48 (1969)
Displacement, inches: 327 (1968), 350 (1969)
Compression ratio: 10.25:1
Carburetion: Single four-barrel carburetor
Horsepower: 300
Distributor: Single point breaker
Other engines offered:...Higher horsepower variations were available in both 1968 and 1969. See option charts.

CHASSIS AND DRIVETRAIN

Clutch: Single dry-plate
Transmission: Three-speed manual
Front suspension:...Coil springs, tube-type shock absorbers, stabilizer bar
Rear suspension:...Single transverse leaf spring, tube-type shock absorbers, independent with lateral struts
Axle ratio: 3.36:1
Frame: Steel box sections, welded

GENERAL

Wheelbase, inches: 98
Track, front, inches: 58.3 (1968), 58.7 (1969)
rear, inches: 59.0 (1968), 59.4 (1969)
Brakes: Disc, four-wheel
Tire size, front and rear: F70-15
Wheels: Steel
Body material: Fiberglass
Assembly plant: St. Louis, Missouri

CHAPTER 10

1970-1972 CORVETTE

Serial Nos. 1970: 194670S400001 - 194670S417316*
1971: 194671S100001 - 194671S121801*
1972: 1Z67K2S500001 - 1Z67K2S527004**
(*for coupes, fourth digit is a 3)
(**for coupes, third digit is a 3. Fifth digit varies with engine installed)

The seventies saw a tremendous evolution occur in the Corvette. When introduced in 1953, it was aimed at the country club crowd. Zora Arkus-Duntov guided it into a performance image where all else was secondary. As government mandates forced their way into the industry, the Corvette changed again. This time it turned into a more sedate but luxurious personal touring machine. It went from street scorcher to gran turisimo. The evolution went quite smoothly even though the Beach Boys did stop singing about it.

The engine option list was shortened in 1970 but strong versions of the small-block 350-cubic-inch engines and a new 454-cubic-inch engine were available. One factor making 1970 Corvettes so desirable to many is that it was the last year of high-compression engines. Compression went down the following year to permit burning lower octane fuels so the oil companies could start phasing in low- and no-lead fuels at their stations before the advent of catalytic converters.

In 1970, Chevrolet introduced a new engine for the Corvette called the LT-1, and it turned out to be a honey! It was a solid-lifter version of the 350-cubic-inch engine and developed 370 horsepower. The Corvette hadn't had anything like it since 1965.

The 1970 got a very late production start due to an extra long 1969 model run. There were 17,316 Corvettes built in 1970 compared to 21,801 in 1971. Other than a few color changes and a switch to amber turn-signal lenses early in 1971 production, the two models were virtual duplicates. Something did end in 1971. It was the last year for the fiber-optics light-monitoring system.

A lot ended in 1972. Fewer engine varieties were available and power ratings went down. The drop in horsepower was due to terminology, a change from gross ratings to net ratings, as-installed figures which included the losses from the fan, air cleaners, mufflers and the like.

The 1972 was the last Corvette to have a removable rear window. This deletion went pretty much unnoticed at the time, but it's interesting to note that the original concept for the '68 body style was for a single "targa" type of roof panel combined with the removable panel. As originally planned, this would have yielded a coupe with a much airier feel than the center support design, which was

The 1970 Corvette had the reputation of being a vastly improved model. Additions included square exhaust ports and flared wheel wells to solve the tire debris problems of the 1968-69 models. The 1970 was also the last Corvette with high-compression engines. Chevrolet photo.

Front turn lamps were redesigned in 1970 and the grille texture was new. Chevrolet photo.

dictated by the lack of a storage area large enough to accommodate the single removable panel. But in their first production form, the "T" top coupes did at least keep the removable rear window concept. In 1973, even it was gone.

The 1972 was the last Corvette with conventional chrome bumpers at both ends. It was the last with the hidden windshield wiper feature and the last with a metal egg-crate grille. It was the last year for the LT-1 engine and the only year the popular engine could be combined with air conditioning.

Today, the 1970 Corvette is a popular year. Problems with the preceding two years were mostly sorted out, yet the 1970 still had the high-compression engines including the new LT-1. And production of the 1970 was the lowest since 1962.

Nineteen seventy-one is viewed less favorably, mainly because of the switch to lower compression. In truth, the performance differential is negligible in everyday driving and the compression change permits using the lower octane fuels that are common today.

The 1972 has emerged as another Corvette "keeper." This takes some explaining since it was nearly the same as the 1971 model. What apparently happens in enthusiasts' minds is that the 1970 and 1971 get lumped together and the 1970 wins because of its stronger engines. The 1972 gets separate consideration. Since so much ended with the 1972 model, it seems to get the nostalgia vote.

A real favorite is the 1972 equipped with LT-1 engine and air conditioning. This is a combination Chevrolet didn't particularly like to offer. The problem is that the LT-1 has solid lifters, which permit higher rpm; and higher revolutions spin air-conditioning belts off their pulleys. Some of the mid-year Corvettes got the solid lifter/air conditioning combination, but not many. According to *Corvette News,* a mere 240 of the 1972 models were so equipped, though some sources place the number slightly higher.

1970-1971-1972 Corvette

BASE ENGINE

Type: .... Chevrolet ohv V-8
Bore x stroke, inches: .... 4.00 x 3.48
Displacement, inches: 350
Compression ratio: 10.25:1 (1970), 8.5:1 (1971, 1972)
Carburetion: .... Single four-barrel carburetor
Horsepower: 300 (1970), 270 (1971), 200 (1972)
Distributor: .... Single point breaker
Other engines offered:...Higher horsepower variations were available in 1970, 1971 and 1972. See option charts.

CHASSIS AND DRIVETRAIN

Clutch: .... Single dry-plate (manual)
Transmission: . . Four-speed manual or three-speed automatic
Front suspension:...Coil springs, tube-type shock absorbers, stabilizer bar
Rear suspension:...Single transverse leaf spring, tube-type shock absorbers, independent with lateral struts
Axle ratio: .... 3.36:1 (manual), 3.08:1 (automatic)
Frame: .... Steel box sections, welded

GENERAL:

Wheelbase, inches: 98
Track, front, inches: 58.7
rear, inches: 59.4
Brakes: .... Disc, four-wheel
Tire size, front and rear: F70-15
Wheels: .... Steel
Body material: .... Fiberglass
Assembly plant: .... St. Louis, Missouri

The 1970-72 Corvettes were the last to feature chrome bumpers front and rear. In 1973, the front bumper changed to body-colored flexible plastic. In 1974, the rear followed suit. Author photos.

1970 Corvette Colors/Options

Color Code	Body Color	Soft Top Color
976	Mulsanne Blue	Black/White
979	Birdgehampton Blue	Black/White
982	Donnybrooke Green	Black/White
992	Laguna Gray	Black/White
975	Marlboro Maroon	Black/White
993	Corvette Bronze	Black/White
974	Monza Red	Black/White
986	Cortez Silver	Black/White
972	Classic White	Black/White
984	Daytona Yellow	Black/White

INTERIOR COLORS: Black, Blue, Brown, Red, Green, Saddle

Order #	Item Description	Sticker Price
19437	Base Corvette Sport Coupe	5192.00
19467	Base Corvette Convertible	4849.00
—	Custom Interior Trim	158.00
A31	Electric Power Windows	63.20
A85	Custom Shoulder Belts	42.15
C07	Auxiliary Hardtop (for roadster)	273.85
C08	Vinyl Covering for Auxiliary Hardtop	63.20
C50	Rear Window Defroster	36.90
C60	Air Conditioning	447.65
—	Positraction Axle, Optional Ratio	12.65
J50	Power Brakes	47.40
L46	Optional 350 HP, 350 CI Engine	158.00
LS5	Optional 390 HP, 454 CI Engine	289.65
LT1	Optional 370 HP, 350 CI Engine	447.60
M21	4-Speed Close Ratio Transmission	nc
M22	4-Speed Close Ratio Transmission Heavy Duty	95.00
M40	Turbo Hydramatic Transmission	nc
N37	Tilt-Telescopic Steering Column	84.30
N40	Power Steering	105.35
P01	Custom Wheel Covers	57.95
PT7	White Stripe Nylon Tires, F70x15	31.30
PU9	White Letter Nylon Tires, F70x15	33.15
T60	Heavy Duty Battery	15.80
UA6	Alarm System	31.60
U69	AM-FM Radio	172.75
U79	AM-FM Stereo Radio	278.10

1971 Corvette Colors/Options

Color Code	Body Color	Soft Top Color
976	Mulsanne Blue	Black/White
979	Birdgehampton Blue	Black/White
983	Brands Hatch Green	Black/White
988	Steel Cities Gray	Black/White
987	Ontario Orange	Black/White
973	Mille Miglia Red	Black/White
905	Nevada Silver	Black/White
972	Classic White	Black/White
912	Sunflower Yellow	Black/White
989	War Bonnet Yellow	Black/White

INTERIOR COLORS: Black, Dark Blue, Dark Green, Red, Saddle

Order #	Item Description	Sticker Price
19437	Base Corvette Sport Coupe	5496.00
19467	Base Corvette Convertible	5259.00
—	Custom Interior Trim	158.00
A31	Electric Power Windows	79.00
A85	Custom Shoulder Belts	42.00
C07	Auxiliary Hardtop (for roadster)	274.00
C08	Vinyl Covering for Auxiliary Hardtop	63.00
C50	Rear Window Defroster	42.00
C60	Air Conditioning	459.00
—	Positraction Axle, Optional Ratio	13.00
J50	Power Brakes	47.00
LS5	Optional 365 HP, 454 CI Engine	295.00
LS6	Optional 425 HP, 454 CI Engine	1221.00
LT1	Optional 330 HP, 350 CI Engine	483.00
ZR1	Optional 330 HP, 350 CI Engine	1010.00
ZR2	Optional 425 HP, 454 CI Engine	1747.00
M21	4-Speed Close Ratio Transmission	nc
M22	4-Speed Close Ratio Transmission Heavy Duty	100.00
M40	Turbo Hydramatic Transmission	nc
N37	Tilt-Telescopic Steering Column	84.30
N40	Power Steering	115.90
P02	Wheel Covers	63.00
PT7	White Stripe Nylon Tires, F70x15	28.00
PU9	White Lettered Nylon Tires, F70x15	42.00
T60	Heavy Duty Battery	15.80
U69	AM-FM Radio	178.00
U79	AM-FM Stereo Radio	283.00

A lot ended for the Corvette in 1972. This was the last Corvette to have a removable rear window (coupes), and the last to have a solid-lifter engine available. The car shown had the particularly nice combination of an LT-1 engine and air conditioning. Author photos.

This beautiful side fender grille treatment was exclusive to the 1970, 1971 and 1972 models. Author photo.

The hidden wiper treatment was used on the 1970-72 Corvettes, but 1972 was the last year. In the down position, the door nicely hides the wipers, but the mechanism proved somewhat troublesome for everyday use. Author photos.

At left is the release button for the removable rear window, a feature that ceased with the 1972 model. The buttons and knob under the steering column were manual overrides for the vacuum-operated headlight units and windshield wiper lid. Author photos.

Chevrolet dropped solid-lifter engines from the Corvette lineup in 1966, but enthusiasts weren't happy about it. In 1970, a new solid-lifter engine called the LT-1 became available and was a real favorite. This engine was available only during the 1970-72 period and was characterized by a distinctive hood (1972 shown). Author photo.

Cast aluminum wheels were not available in the 1968-72 period, but this finely detailed wheel disc was optional. Author photo.

1972 Corvette Colors/Options

Color Code	Body Color	Soft Top Color
945	Bryar Blue	Black/White
979	Targa Blue	Black/White
988	Steel Cities Gray	Black/White
946	Elkhart Green	Black/White
987	Ontario Orange	Black/White
973	Mille Miglia Red	Black/White
924	Pewter Silver	Black/White
972	Classic White	Black/White
912	Sunflower Yellow	Black/White
989	War Bonnet Yellow	Black/White

INTERIOR COLORS: Black, Blue, Red, Saddle

Order #	Item Description	Sticker Price
19437	Base Corvette Sport Coupe	5533.00
19467	Base Corvette Convertible	5296.00
—	Custom Interior Trim	158.00
A31	Electric Power Windows	85.35
A85	Custom Shoulder Belts	26.35
C07	Auxiliary Hardtop (for roadster)	273.85
C08	Vinyl Roof Covering For Auxiliary Hardtop	158.00
C50	Rear Window Defroster	42.15
C60	Air Conditioning	464.50
—	Positraction Axle, Optional Ratio	12.65
J50	Power Brakes	47.40
LS5	Optional 270 HP, 454 CI Engine	294.90
LT1	Optional 255 HP, 350 CI Engine	483.45
ZR1	Optional 255 HP, 350 CI Engine	1010.05
M21	4-Speed Close Ratio Transmission	nc
M40	Turbo Hydramatic Transmission	nc
N37	Tilt-Telescopic Steering Column	84.30
N40	Power Steering	115.90
P02	Custom Wheel Covers	63.20
PT7	White Stripe Nylon Tires, F70x15	30.35
PU9	White Lettered Nylon Tires, F70x15	43.65
T60	Heavy Duty Battery	15.80
U69	AM-FM Radio	178.00
U79	AM-FM Stereo Radio	283.35

CHAPTER 11

1973-1977 CORVETTE

 (1975 Convertible)

Serial Nos. 1973: 1Z67J3S400001 - 1Z67J3S434464*
1974: 1Z67J4S400001 - 1Z67J4S437502*
1975: 1Z67J5S400001 - 1Z67J5S438465*
1976: 1Z37L6S400001 - 1Z37L6S446558
1977: 1Z37L7S400001 - 1Z37L7S449213
(*for coupes, third digit is a 3)
(fifth digit in all serial numbers varies with engine installed)

Corvettes got heavier and slower during the years from 1973 to 1977. The option list shrank and by 1977 optional engine choices were down to one. The body didn't change much and after 1975 wasn't even available in convertible configuration.

Yet during this period Chevrolet built and sold 202,202 Corvettes, more than any previous five-year period, almost more than all previous Corvette models combined.

The reason is that every other company wishing to sell its products in the United States faced the same federal mandates that Chevrolet did. The Corvettes of the period may have been overshadowed by earlier Corvettes, but Corvette's competitors were in the same pollution control soup and the Corvette more than held its own. There were always better cars to be had. But "for the money," always the great equalizer in the Corvette's favor, kept Chevy's two-seater in its premier position. You can't attribute the Corvette's success during 1973-77 merely to its rich heritage. Chevrolet's engineers coped with and met the challenges of the day as well as any competition, what little there was.

This isn't to say that nothing significant happened during the period. The 1973 got a new hood, designed around the elimination of the troublesome hidden wiper setup. Its front bumper was body-colored, designed to meet federal 5-mph crash standards, but the rear remained the same as the previous year. Engineers were determined to make the 1973 quieter and changed the chassis mounts to isolate road noise more effectively. Also, sound-deadening material was sprayed on selected inner panels and a pad was added to the inner hood.

The 1974 was the first to have body-colored bumper treatment both front and rear. It was the last with a real dual exhaust, non-catalytic converter system. It was the last with the 454-cubic-inch engine on the option list. Even though the engines were all weaker, the 454 still propelled the 1974 Corvette in a most exciting manner.

Nineteen seventy-five was the year of the catalytic converter, not a wonderful distinction. It was the first for standard electronic (point-less distributor) ignitions and bladder-style fuel cell. But the 1975's real claim to fame is that it was

The 1973 Corvette was the only one with the soft body-colored nose and abrupt rear with chrome bumpers. Larry Shinoda, the famous Corvette designer, once commented in an interview that the 1973 was his favorite of the post-1967 era because the front and rear styling were closest to what the stylists originally had in mind when this series was first designed. The aluminum wheels shown in this photo were offered briefly in 1973, then canceled due to strength problems. They kept reappearing on the option sheets, but weren't actually available again until 1976. Author photo.

the year the convertible was phased out. Everyone concluded right away that the 1975 convertible was sure to be a collector piece. It is, but the lofty prices some had predicted haven't materialized.

The 1976 set a new production record of 46,558. This had more to do with a strong market in general than any new innovations. Aluminum wheels became optional, a maintenance-free battery was added, and a new "sport steering wheel" borrowed from the Vega was added. Hardly the things enthusiasts dream about.

Things started perking up in 1977. Major changes were in the works for 1978, the Corvette's silver anniversary, and stylists allowed a few of the new things to trickle into the 1977. The center console was a new design that included a deeper radio slot to accept standard Delco radios. This was good, since it allowed the full line of Delco products to be made available in the Corvette. Previously, the need for a unique Corvette radio and the Corvette's relatively low volume meant a limited radio choice. Nobody seemed to notice that the style of the new console didn't match the rest of the interior too well. The rest was coming the following year.

In 1977, cruise control became optional for the first time, but only with automatic transmissions. The headlight dimmer, windshield wiper and washer controls all moved to the directional-signal stalk.

With the possible exception of models like the 1975 convertible and 1974 with 454-cubic-inch motor, Corvettes built in the 1973-77 period can never be seriously considered as collector cars. That doesn't mean some won't hold their value well or make attractive purchases. Considering the number built and the lack of strong identity between years, these will be the affordable Corvettes. New models are getting ever more expensive, and the lower-production older favorites will continue to skyrocket. The 1973-77 series will likely emerge as the "drivers," the Corvettes easiest to buy and sell at modest prices.

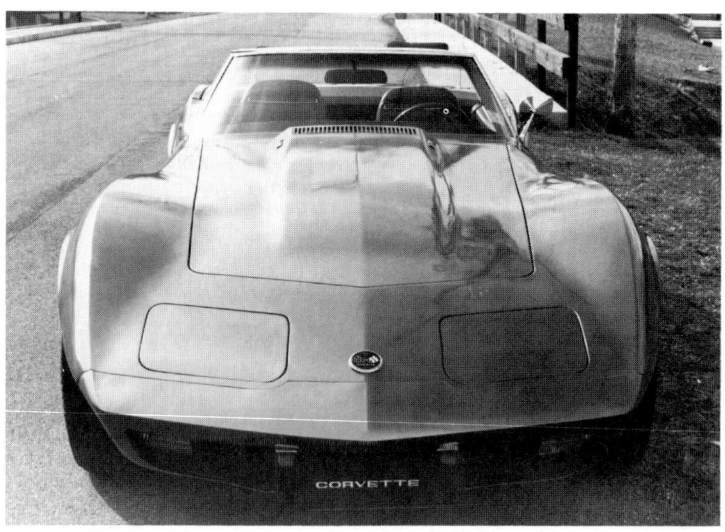

1975 Corvette convertible. Author photo.

1973 Corvette Colors/Options

Color Code	Body Color	Soft Top Color
922	Medium Blue	Black/White
927	Dark Blue	Black/White
945	Blue-Green	Black/White
947	Elkhart Green	Black/White
980	Orange	Black/White
976	Mille Miglia Red	Black/White
914	Silver	Black/White
910	Classic White	Black/White
952	Yellow	Black/White
953	Yellow (Metallic)	Black/White

INTERIOR COLORS: Black, Midnight Blue, Dark Red, Dark Saddle, Medium Saddle

Order #	Item Description	Sticker Price
1YZ37	Base Corvette Sport Coupe	5561.50
1YZ67	Base Corvette Convertible	5398.50
—	Custom Interior Trim	154.00
A31	Electric Power Windows	83.00
A85	Custom Shoulder Belts	41.00
C07	Auxiliary Hardtop (for roadster)	267.00
C08	Vinyl Roof Covering for Auxiliary Hardtop	62.00
C50	Rear Window Defroster	41.00
C60	Air Conditioning	452.00
—	Positraction Axle, Optional Ratio	12.00
J50	Power Brakes	46.00
L82	Optional 250 HP, 350 CI Engine	299.00
LS4	Optional 275 HP, 454 CI Engine	250.00
M21	4-Speed Close Ratio Transmission	nc
M40	Turbo Hydramatic Transmission	nc
N37	Tilt-Telescopic Steering Column	82.00
N40	Power Steering	113.00
P02	Custom Wheel Covers	62.00
QRM	White Stripe SBR Tires, GR70x15	32.00
QRZ	White Letter SBR Tires, GR70x15	45.00
T60	Heavy Duty Battery	15.00
U58	AM-FM Stereo Radio	276.00
U69	AM-FM Radio	173.00
UF1	Map Light	5.00
YJ8	Cast Aluminum Wheels	175.00
Z07	Off Road Suspension and Brake Package	369.00

1974 Corvette Colors/Options

Color Code	Body Color	Soft Top Color
922	Corvette Med Blue	Black/White
968	Dark Brown	Black/White
917	Corvette Gray	Black/White
910	Classic White	Black/White
980	Corvette Orange	Black/White
976	Mille Miglia Red	Black/White
974	Medium Red	Black/White
914	Silver Mist	Black/White
948	Dark Green	Black/White
946	Bright Yellow	Black/White

INTERIOR COLORS: Black, Dark Blue, Neutral, Dark Red, Saddle, Silver

Order #	Item Description	Sticker Price
1YZ37	Base Corvette Sport Coupe	6001.50
1YZ67	Base Corvette Convertible	5765.50
—	Custom Interior Trim	154.00
A31	Electric Power Windows	86.00
A85	Custom Shoulder Belts	41.00
C07	Auxiliary Hardtop (for roadster)	267.00
C08	Vinyl Covered Auxiliary Hardtop	329.00
C50	Rear Window Defroster	43.00
C60	Air Conditioning	467.00
FE7	Gymkhana Suspension	7.00
—	Positraction Axle, Optional Ratio	12.00
J50	Power Brakes	49.00
L82	Optional 250 HP, 350 CI Engine	299.00
LS4	Optional 270 HP, 454 CI Engine	250.00
M21	4-Speed Close Ratio Transmission	nc
M40	Turbo Hydramatic Transmission	nc
N37	Tilt-Telescopic Steering Column	82.00
N41	Power Steering	117.00
QRM	White Stripe SBR Tires, GR70x15	32.00
QRZ	White Letter SBR Tires, GR70x15	45.00
U05	Dual Horns	4.00
U58	AM-FM Stereo Radio	276.00
U69	AM-FM Radio	173.00
UA1	Heavy Duty Battery	15.00
UF1	Map Light	5.00
Z07	Off Road Suspension and Brake Package	400.00

1973-1974-1975-1976-1977 Corvette

BASE ENGINE

Type: . . . . Chevrolet ohv V-8
Bore x stroke, inches: . . . . 4.00 x 3.48
Displacement, inches: 350
Compression ratio: 8.5:1
Carburetion: . . . . Single four-barrel carburetor
Horsepower:...190 (1973), 195 (1974), 165 (1975), 180 (1976-7)
Distributor:...Single point breaker (1973, 1974), high energy ignition (1975, 1976, 1977)
Other engines offered:...Higher horsepower variations were available in 1973, 1974, 1975, 1976 and 1977. See option charts.

CHASSIS AND DRIVETRAIN

Clutch: . . . . Single dry-plate (manual)
Transmission:...Four-speed manual or three-speed automatic
Front suspension:...Coil springs, tube-type shock absorbers, stabilizer bar
Rear suspension:...Single transverse leaf spring, tube-type shock absorbers, independent with lateral struts
Axle ratio: . . . . 3.36:1 (manual), 3.08:1 (automatic)
Frame: . . . . Steel box sections, welded

GENERAL:

Wheelbase, inches: 98
Track, front, inches: 58.7
rear, inches: 59.5
Brakes: . . . . Disc, four-wheel
Tire size, front and rear: GR70-15
Wheels: . . . . Steel
Body material: . . . . Fiberglass
Assembly plant: . . . . St. Louis, Missouri

1974 L-82 engine. Author photo.

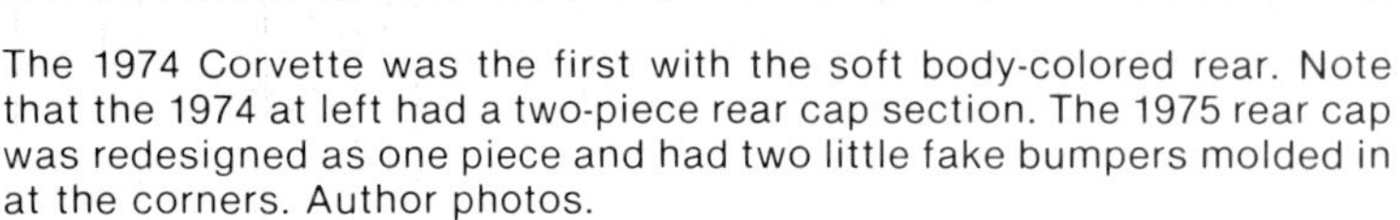

The 1974 Corvette was the first with the soft body-colored rear. Note that the 1974 at left had a two-piece rear cap section. The 1975 rear cap was redesigned as one piece and had two little fake bumpers molded in at the corners. Author photos.

1975 interior with leather trim. Ed Olson photo.

As was the case in the rear, designers added little bumper pads to the body-colored front end cap of the 1975. They were styled to look like black rubber pads, but were actually molded as part of the cap and painted black. They did have the effect of giving both ends of the 1975 a slimmer, less blunt appearance. Author photos.

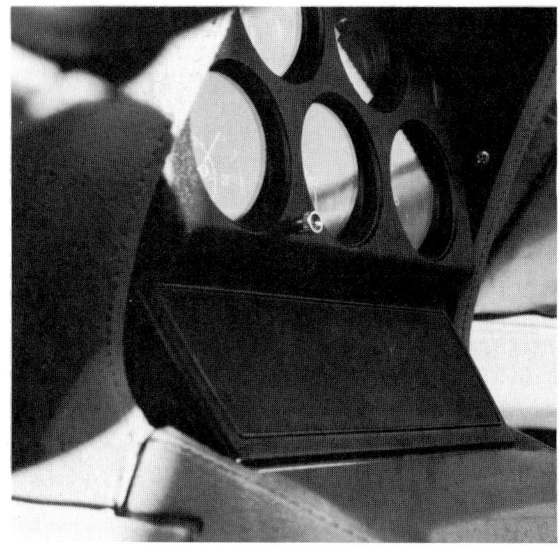

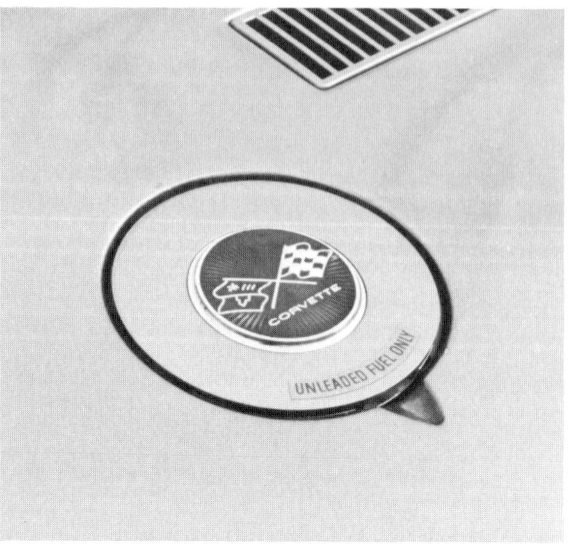

Radios were not standard equipment in Corvettes until 1979 but very few Corvettes left the factory without one. This 1975 is one that did. Some collectors attach special value to no-radio Corvettes because of their scarcity, something most owners who use their cars for pleasure would disagree with. At right, the 1975 was the first Corvette to require unleaded fuel. Ed Olson and author photos.

1976 base engine. Author photo.

1975 Corvette Colors/Options

Color Code	Body Color	Soft Top Color
22	Bright Blue	Black/White
27	Steel Blue	Black/White
42	Bright Green	Black/White
70	Orange Flame	Black/White
74	Dark Red	Black/White
76	Mille Miglia Red	Black/White
67	Medium Saddle	Black/White
13	Silver	Black/White
10	Classic White	Black/White
56	Bright Yellow	Black/White

INTERIOR COLORS: Black, Dark Blue, Neutral, Dark Red, Medium Saddle, Silver

Order #	Item Description	Sticker Price
1YZ37	Base Corvette Sport Coupe	6810.10
1YZ07	Base Corvette Convertible	6550.10
—	Custom Interior Trim	154.00
A31	Electric Power Windows	93.00
A85	Custom Shoulder Belts	41.00
C07	Auxiliary Hardtop (for roadsters)	267.00
C08	Vinyl Covered Auxiliary Hardtop	350.00
C50	Rear Window Defroster	46.00
C60	Air Conditioning	490.00
FE7	Gymkhana Suspension	7.00
—	Positraction Axle, Optional Ratio	12.00
J50	Power Brakes	50.00
L82	Optional 205 HP, 350 CI Engine	336.00
M21	4-Speed Close Ratio Transmission	nc
M40	Turbo Hydramatic Transmission	nc
N37	Tilt-Telescopic Steering Column	82.00
N41	Power Steering	129.00
QRM	White Stripe SBR Tires, GR70x15	35.00
QRZ	White Letter SBR Tires, GR70x15	48.00
U05	Dual Horns	4.00
U58	AM-FM Stereo Radio	284.00
U69	AM-FM Radio	178.00
UA1	Heavy Duty Battery	15.00
UF1	Map Light	5.00
Z07	Off Road Suspension and Brake Package	400.00

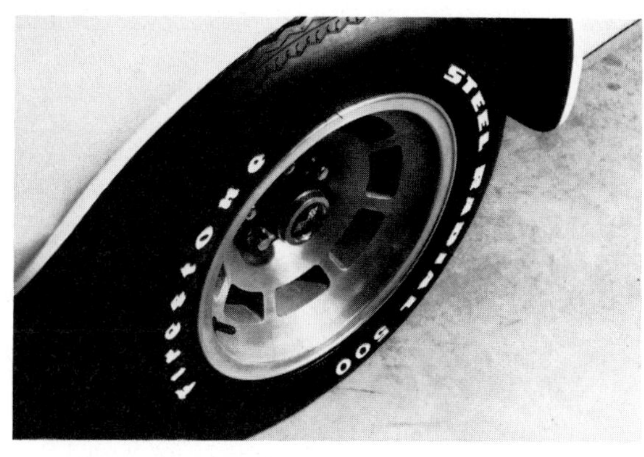

This style of aluminum wheel was first available on the 1973 Corvette, but Chevrolet rejected the wheels supplied by a California vendor and attempted to recall those that had been released. The wheel appeared again in 1976 in the same style but produced by Kelsey-Hayes in its Mexican facility (and so identified on the wheel's interior surface). Author photo.

1976 Corvette Colors/Options

Color Code	Body Color
22	Bright Blue
69	Dark Brown
64	Buckskin
33	Dark Green
37	Mahogany
70	Orange Flame
72	Red
13	Silver
10	Classic White
56	Bright Yellow

INTERIOR COLORS: Black, Firethorn, Buckskin, Smoked Grey, Dark Brown, Blue-Green, White

Order #	Item Description	Sticker Price
1YZ37	Base Corvette Sport Coupe	7604.85
—	Custom Interior Trim	164.00
A31	Power Windows	107.00
C49	Rear Window Defogger	78.00
C60	Air Conditioning	523.00
FE7	Gymkhana Suspension	35.00
—	Positraction Axle, Optional Radio	13.00
J50	Power Brakes	59.00
L82	Optional 210 HP, 350 CI Engine	481.00
M21	4-Speed Close Ratio Transmission	nc
M40	Turbo Hydramatic Transmission	nc
N37	Tilt-Telescopic Steering Column	95.00
N40	Power Steering	151.00
QRM	White Stripe SBR Tires, GR70x15	37.00
QRZ	White Letter SBR Tires, GR70x15	51.00
U58	AM-FM Stereo Radio	281.00
U69	AM-FM Radio	187.00
UA1	Heavy Duty Battery	16.00
UF1	Map Light	10.00
YJ8	Aluminum Wheels	299.00

Enthusiasts didn't care for the addition of the Vega steering wheel to the 1976 interior and it lasted just one year. The 1976 was the last Corvette with the center console style shown, which required a unique radio because of space limitations. Author photo.

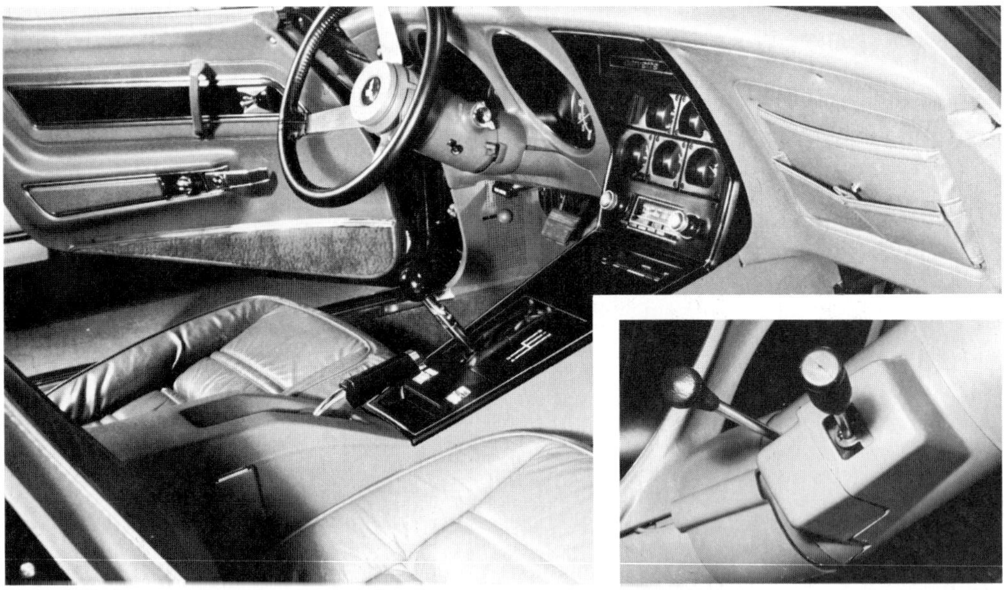

The 1977 center console was new and had additional radio room so that the entire range of Delco products would fit. The steering wheel and column were new for 1977 and the headlight dimmer switch, windshield wiper and windshield washer controls all moved to the steering column. Author photos.

1977 Corvette. Chevrolet photo.

1977 Corvette Colors/Options

Color Code	Body Color
19	Black
28	Corvette Dark Blue
26	Corvette Light Blue
66	Corvette Orange
83	Corvette Dark Red
72	Medium Red
13	Silver
80	Corvette Tan
10	Classic White
52	Corvette Yellow

INTERIOR COLORS: Black, Blue, Brown, Buckskin, Red, Smoked Grey, White

Order #	Item Description	Sticker Price
1YZ37	Base Corvette Sport Coupe	8647.65
A31	Power Windows	116.00
B32	Color Keyed Floor Mats	22.00
C49	Rear Window Defogger	84.00
C60	Air Conditioning	553.00
D35	Sport Mirrors	36.00
FE7	Gymkhana Suspension	38.00
G95	Positraction Axle, Optional Ratio	14.00
K30	Cruise Control	88.00
L82	Optional 210 HP, 350 CI Engine	495.00
M21	4-Speed Close Ratio Transmission	nc
M40	Turbo Hydramatic Transmission	nc
N37	Tilt-Telescopic Steering Column	165.00
QRZ	White Letter SBR Tires, GR70x15	57.00
UA1	Heavy Duty Battery	17.00
U58	AM-FM Stereo Radio	281.00
U69	AM-FM Radio	187.00
UM2	AM-FM Stereo Radio W/Tape System	414.00
V54	Luggage And Roof Panel Rack	73.00
YJ8	Aluminum Wheels	321.00
ZN1	Trailer Package	83.00
ZX2	Convenience Group	22.00

Corvettes built in the 1973-77 period weren't known for blistering speed, as engineers struggled to meet ever more stringent federal emission standards. The 1977 L-82 engine shown was rated at 210 hp, a far cry from the 435 hp available a decade earlier. Author photo.

CHAPTER 12

1978 CORVETTE

Serial Nos. 1Z87L8S400001 - 1Z87L8S440274*
1Z87L8S900001 - 1Z87L8S906502* (Pace Car)
(*fifth digit varies with engine installed)

It wasn't all-new, but the 1978 was the most changed Corvette since 1968. It was the Corvette's silver anniversary, twenty-five years since the introduction of the Blue Flame six-cylinder. Chevrolet celebrated by adding some nice improvements to the 1978.

For starters, the Corvette became a full fastback again. The restyling of the Corvette's rear doubled the usable area behind the seats, a real shortcoming of the post-1968 cars.

On the inside, Chevrolet finished what was started in 1977. The 1977 got a new console, but in the 1978 the rest of the dash was new. It even got a real glovebox. Inner door panels were redone. The windshield wiper and washer controls moved back to the dash after a one-year stint on the turn-signal lever.

Chevrolet further commemorated the Corvette's twenty-fifth with a two-tone silver paint scheme. These are not special models, just optional paint choices. But some options, like aluminum wheels, had to be purchased when the special paint was ordered. There is no way to differentiate a silver anniversary paint Corvette by its serial numbers.

Not so for the 1978 Corvette Pace Car replica. This is the car that had the world talking about Corvettes again; and it's a great story.

It began when Chevrolet accepted an invitation from the Indianapolis Motor Speedway to provide a pace vehicle for the 1978 race. Early on, it was decided by Chevrolet management that the Corvette would pace the race and that a special model would be created to do it. And replicas would be sold to the public.

What wasn't immediately clear was just what the car would be and how many would be sold. Initially, it was to be two shades of silver with a red dividing stripe, but this changed to silver and black to set it off more from the silver anniversary paint option. There was talk of special Goodyear tires with Corvette spelled out in the sidewalls in white letters. Novel idea, but it was scrubbed due to cost and anticipated replacement headaches.

The first rumored quantity was 300, obviously picked to honor those first 300 Corvettes made in Flint. Next it was 1,000, then 5,000. But long before the Pace Cars were actually built, things were heating up and Chevrolet feared the wrath of its dealers and possible legal action resulting from not providing at least one Pace Car to each. So that's what it did. The final quantity built, 6,502, was based on one for every dealer plus a handful of extras for promotional purposes.

After a few years of hibernation, new Corvettes were being talked about again in 1978. It was the Corvette's twenty-fifth anniversary and Chevrolet celebrated by introducing the most-improved Corvette in a decade, including two specials: the silver anniversary model and the limited edition Pace Car replica. Author photos.

This was no longer a small quantity by any collector's standards, but Pace Car hysteria was already in full bloom and it didn't matter. The cars came into dealerships with a sticker of $13,653.21 which included most options. But the cars soon changed hands for $25,000 and more. Some dealers who had committed themselves to selling their Pace Car at or below sticker price tried to back out. Many got sued as a result.

To put it mildly, the Pace Car Corvette caused a commotion. *The Wall Street Journal* even got into the picture with a front-page article on the mania, quoting some "experts" who predicted prices of $50,000 and more.

Of course it was not to be. Six thousand cars with special paint schemes and a few other geegaws do not a true collector car make. Six thousand is still twenty times the number of 1953's built and few of those would bring $50,000 in 1978. No one is sure what the most paid for a Pace Car was—probably somewhere in the mid-thirties for an L-82 with four-speed transmission, the combination deemed best. The Pace Car basked in the hype until the Indy race, then the bottom fell out. Ads appeared for a long time with exorbitant prices, and still do, but it wasn't too long before Pace Cars were selling for close to their original sticker prices.

All this aside, the 1978 models are among the few in the whole 1968-82 range of Corvettes that come close to being real collector cars. It was a year people recognized and talked about. It was a well-built car and most people viewed the new rear window treatment, interior redesign and a larger fuel tank as definite improvements.

What isn't so clear is which 1978 models will prove to be the best investments in the long run. While the Pace Car is thought to be too gaudy for many tastes, the silver anniversary paint scheme is widely popular. All Pace Car replica Corvettes had silver cloth or leather interiors. Even more silver anniversary paint 1978's were built, but these could be ordered with any interior color. Perhaps a rare silver anniversary paint trim combination, such as dark blue leather, will emerge from the herd.

Maybe it'll still be the Pace Car. It was one of the most publicized Corvettes ever. Publicity alone doesn't create classic cars and there are still too many new Pace Cars tucked away in garages for any great price explosion to occur. But over the years, as other Corvettes of the era fade away, the Pace Car may yet emerge as the high-dollar Corvette of the period. It does have unique credentials.

1978 Corvette

BASE ENGINE

Type: .... Chevrolet ohv V-8
Bore x stroke, inches: .... 4.00 x 3.48
Displacement, inches: 350
Compression ratio: 8.2:1
Carburetion: .... Single four-barrel carburetor
Horsepower: 185
Distributor: .... High energy ignition
Other engines offered: ... A 220-hp engine was optional in 1978

CHASSIS AND DRIVETRAIN

Clutch: .... Single dry-plate (manual)
Transmission: .. Four-speed manual or three-speed automatic
Front suspension: ... Coil springs, tube-type shock absorbers, stabilizer bar
Rear suspension: ... Single transverse leaf spring, tube-type shock absorbers, independent with lateral struts
Axle ratio: .... 3.36:1 (manual), 3.08:1 (automatic)
Frame: .... Steel box sections, welded

GENERAL:

Wheelbase, inches: 98
Track, front, inches: 58.7
rear, inches: 59.5
Brakes: .... Disc, four-wheel
Tire size, front and rear: P255/70 R-15
Wheels: .... Steel
Body material: .... Fiberglass
Assembly plant: .... St. Louis, Missouri

The limited edition Pace Car Corvette came with a silver interior in either leather or cloth trimmed in leather. The seats were a completely new design unique to the Pace Car in 1978, but standard in all Corvettes starting in 1979. The main instrument cluster was new for 1978 in all Corvettes and was beautifully executed. Ed Olson Photos.

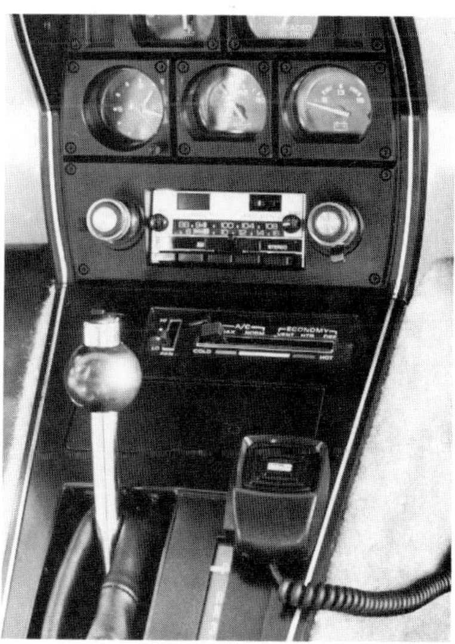

The center console designed for the new 1978 interior actually appeared in 1977. But the 1978 was the first to have an AM-FM radio with CB available . . . at a whopping $638. Ed Olson and author photos.

The limited edition Pace Car replica Corvette is perhaps the most famous Corvette in recent memory. These were being sold for double their sticker price even before their release. Many dealers renigged on purchase agreements in attempts to squeeze more profits; and the subsequent law suits, bad publicity and ill will left a cloud over what was one of the finer Corvettes in modern history. The inflated price bubble burst shortly after the Indy 500 race in 1978 and Pace Car replicas can now be purchased for very reasonable prices. Author photo.

The lesser-known special Corvette in 1978 was the silver anniversary edition. This was just a paint option, but the two-tone silver Corvette offered an excellent alternative to those who felt the Pace Car Corvette was too gaudy. Defying logic, the silver anniversary 1978 Corvettes have held their value nearly as well as the Pace Cars. Author photo.

"CORVETTE PACES INDY 500—A special 'Limited Edition' Corvette will lead the 33-car field at the 62nd annual Indianapolis 500 race May 28, 1978. The pace car features two-tone black and silver paint treatment along with front air dam, rear deck lid spoiler, polished aluminum spoked wheels with red stripe, glass roof panels, white-lettered tires, sport mirrors, special 'smoke' color interior and 'Indy Pace Car' decals on the front fenders. The L-82 high performance 350-cubic inch (5.7 liter) V-8 with Turbo Hydramatic transmission will power the vehicle. This year also marks Corvette's 25th anniversary in the Chevrolet lineup as America's one-of-a-kind sports car." Chevrolet press release from 1978. Chevrolet photos.

1978 Corvette Colors/Options

Color Code	Body Color
59	Corvette Light Beige
19	Black
83	Corvette Dark Blue
26	Corvette Light Blue
89	Corvette Dark Brown
82	Corvette Mahogany
72	Corvette Red
13	Silver
13	Silver Anniversary
10	Classic White
52	Corvette Yellow

INTERIOR COLORS: Black, Dark Blue, Light Beige, Red, Mahogany, Oyster

Order #	Item Description	Sticker Price
1YZ87	Corvette Sport Coupe	9351.89
1YZ87/78	Limited Edition Corvette (Pace Car)	13,653.21
A31	Power Windows	130.00
AU3	Power Door Locks	120.00
B2Z	Silver Anniversary Paint	399.00
CC1	Removable Glass Roof Panels	349.00
C49	Rear Window Defogger	95.00
C60	Air Conditioning	605.00
D35	Sport Mirrors	40.00
FE7	Gymkhana Suspension	41.00
G95	Positraction Axle, Optional Highway Ratio	15.00
K30	Cruise Control	99.00
L82	Optional 220 HP, 350 CI Engine	525.00
M21	4-Speed Close Ratio Transmission	nc
MX1	Turbo Hydramatic Transmission	nc
N37	Tilt-Telescopic Steering Column	175.00
QBS	White Letter SBR Tires, P255/60R-15	216.32
QGR	White Letter SBR Tires, P255/70 R-15	51.00
UA1	Heavy Duty Battery	18.00
UM2	AM-FM Stereo Radio W/Tape System	419.00
UP6	AM-FM Stereo Radio W/CB System	638.00
U58	AM-FM Stereo Radio	286.00
U69	AM-FM Radio	199.00
U75	Power Antenna	49.00
U81	Dual Rear Speakers	49.00
YJ8	Aluminum Wheels	340.00
ZN1	Trailer Package	89.00
ZX2	Convenience Group	84.00

Chevrolet used the aluminum wheels available since 1976 for the Pace Car Corvette but polished them to a bright finish and added a red tape stripe. Limited edition stickers appeared on the Pace Car but the big Indy 500 decals for the doors and rear fenders were packed loose with the car for installation by the owner. Most chose not to use them. Author photos.

CHAPTER 13

1979-1982 CORVETTE

 (1982 Collector's)

Serial Nos. 1979: 1Z8789S400001 - 1Z8789S453807
1980: 1Z878AS400001 - 1Z878AS440614
1981: 1G1AY8764BS400001 - 1G1AY8764BS431611 (St. Louis)
1981: 1G1AY8764B5400001 - 1G1AY8764B5108995 (Bowling Green)
1982: 1G1AY8786C5100001 -1G1AY8786C5125407 (sixth digit for 1982 Collector Edition is a 0) (ninth digit for 1981-82 is a check digit and varies)

Rumors of a "brand-new Corvette next year" have been part of the Corvette scene since its earliest days. Finally, the rumors heard around 1979 were based on fact. A new Corvette really was on the way for 1983.

The Corvette chassis introduced in 1963 models had a twenty-year life and the 1968 body style lasted fifteen. Considering the upheaval the industry went through during these years, the longevity of the Corvette body and chassis designs is a tribute to the soundness of both. All in all, this is one of auto history's more successful series of cars.

But it came to an end. The 1979-82 models were the end of the series. They were thought of as those built after the anniversary/Pace Car year and before the new generation. With a new car coming, major changes weren't in the cards for the 1979-82 models, but notable things did happen.

The 1979 Corvette carried the same body as the 1978 except for detail changes like emblems. The new-style seat introduced in the Pace Car became standard equipment in 1979. These seats employed extensive plastic to cut weight. Also, the front and rear bolt-on spoilers, which made their debut on the Pace Car, became optional on the 1979. Chevrolet reported these capable of reducing aerodynamic drag by fifteen percent. Nineteen seventy-nine production reached 53,807.

In 1980, new bumper caps for both the front and rear were introduced. These had integral spoilers which eliminated the add-on appearance of the previous type. They offered aerodynamic gains and a fifty-percent increase of airflow into the radiator.

Engineers went after weight reductions in the 1980 model. An aluminum differential housing and cross-member replaced steel units. Fiberglass body panels, door and windshield glass, and the frame were all made thinner. A 350-cubic-inch engine was standard in all states except California which got a 305-cubic-incher. To the horror of Corvette enthusiasts, a federal mandate resulted in a speedometer with a maximum reading of 85 mph. Production for the year totaled 40,614.

1980 Corvette. Chevrolet photo.

Some of the 1978 Pace Car Corvette features rubbed off onto the 1979 production Corvettes. The bolt-on front air dam and rear spoiler became options for the 1979. But the silver anniversary emblems that adorned the 1978 were removed and the 1979 emblems were the same as those used in 1977. Author photos.

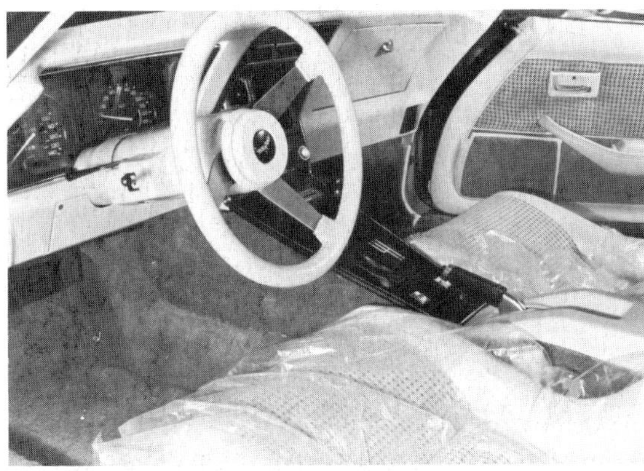

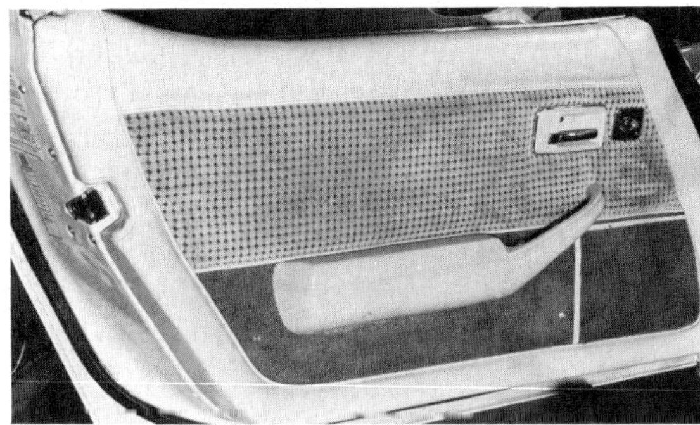

The Pace Car influence was also evident in the interior of the 1979. The new seat design used first in the Pace Car became the standard seat for 1979. This unusual checkered fabric was also tried in 1979. Author photos.

1979 Corvette Colors/Options

Color Code	Body Color
59	Corvette Light Beige
19	Black
83	Corvette Dark Blue
28	Corvette Light Blue
82	Corvette Dark Brown
58	Corvette Dark Green
72	Corvette Red
13	Silver
52	Corvette Yellow
10	Classic White

INTERIOR COLORS: Black, Dark Blue, Dark Brown, Light Beige, Red, Dark Green, Oyster

Order #	Item Description	Sticker Price
1YZ87	Corvette Sport Coupe	10,220.23
A31	Power Windows	141.00
CC1	Removable Glass Roof Panels	365.00
C49	Rear Window Defogger	102.00
C60	Air Conditioning	635.00
D35	Sport Mirrors	45.00
FE7	Gymkhana Suspension	49.00
F51	Heavy Duty Shock Absorbers	33.00
G95	Highway Ratio Rear Axle	19.00
K30	Cruise Control	113.00
L82	Optional 225 HP, 350 CI Engine	565.00
MM4	4-Speed Transmission	nc
M21	4-Speed Transmission, Close Ratio	nc
MX1	Turbo-Hydramatic Transmission	nc
N37	Tilt-telescopic Steering Column	190.00
N90	Aluminum Wheels	380.00
QGR	White Letter SBR Tires, P225/70 R-15	54.00
QBS	White Letter Aramid BR Tires, P225/60 R-15	226.20
U58	AM/FM Stereo Radio	90.00
UM2	AM/FM Stereo Radio w/tape	228.00
UN3	AM/FM Stereo Radio w/cassette	234.00
UP6	AM/FM Stereo Radio w/CB and power antenna	439.00
U75	Power Antenna	52.00
U81	Dual Rear Speakers	52.00
UA1	Heavy Duty Battery	21.00
ZN1	Trailer Package	98.00
ZQ2	Power Windows and Door Locks	272.00
ZX2	Convenience Group	94.00

1980 Corvette Colors/Options

Color Code	Body Color
19	Black
13	Silver
58	Dark Green
83	Red
52	Yellow
28	Dark Blue
59	Frost Beige
76	Dark Claret
47	Dark Brown
10	White

INTERIOR COLORS: Black, Oyster, Red, Dark Blue, Claret, Doeskin

Order #	Item Description	Sticker Price
1YZ87	Corvette Sport Coupe	13,140.24
AU3	Power Door Locks	140.00
CC1	Removable Glass Roof Panels	391.00
C49	Rear Window Defogger	109.00
FE7	Gymkhana Suspension	55.00
F51	Heavy Duty Shock Absorbers	35.00
K30	Cruise Control	123.00
LG4	180 HP, 305 CI Engine (Req'd California)	—50.00
L48	190 HP, 350 CI Engine (Base except Calif)	nc
L82	230 HP, 350 CI Engine	595.00
MM4	4-Speed Transmission	nc
MX1	4-Speed Transmission, Close Ratio	nc
MX1	Trubo-Hydramatic Transmission	nc
N90	Aluminum Wheels	407.00
QGB	White Letter SBR Tires, P225/70 R-15	62.00
QXH	White Letter SBR Tires, P225/60 R-15	426.16
UA1	Heavy Duty Battery	22.00
U58	AM/FM Stereo Radio	46.00
UM2	AM/FM Stereo Radio w/8 track	155.00
UN3	AM/FM Stereo Radio w/cassette	168.00
UP6	AM/FM Stereo Radio w/CB and power antenna	391.00
U75	Power Antenna	56.00
UL5	Radio Delete	—126.00
U81	Dual Rear Speakers	52.00
V54	Roof Panel Carrier	125.00
YF5	California Emissions	250.00
ZN1	Trailer Package	105.00

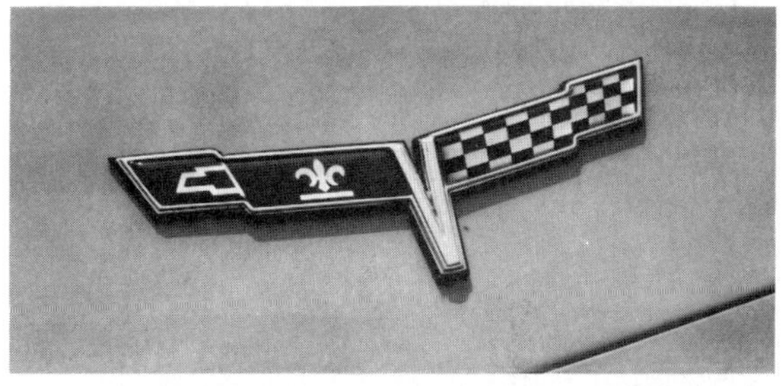

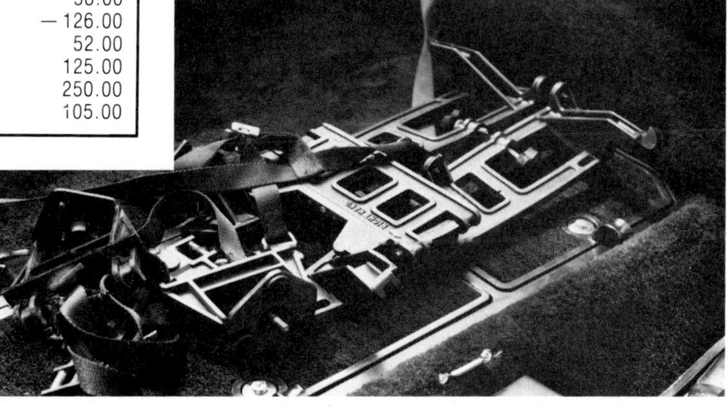

Detail changes for 1980 included a new side fender treatment, new emblems and a new apparatus to attach the roof panels to the rear deck area of the exterior. Author photos.

Aerodynamics became the key word in auto design for the eighties, and Corvette designers improved airflow over the Corvette by incorporating a front air dam and rear spoiler into the bumper caps. The storage bins behind the seats were reduced from three to two in 1980 and the hand of the government struck again in the form of a speedometer in America's premier sports car that could read to only 85 mph. Author photos.

The Corvette changed little in 1981. Chevrolet photo.

1981 Corvette Colors/Options

Color Code	Body Color
75	Red
52	Yellow
19	Black
10	White
59	Beige
13	Silver Metallic
28	Dark Blue Metallic
24	Bright Blue Metallic
79	Maroon Metallic
84	Charcoal Metallic
33/38M	Silver/Dark Blue
50/74M	Beige/Dark Bronze
33/39M	Silver/Charcoal
80/98M	Claret/Dark Claret

INTERIOR COLORS: Camel, Blue, Black, Rust, Red, Silver

Order #	Item Description	Sticker Price
1YY87	Corvette Coupe	16,258.52
L81	5.7 Liter V-8 engine	nc
G92	Performance Rear Axle	20.00
V54	Roof Panel Carrier	135.00
ZN1	Trailering Equipment	110.00
C49	Rear Window Defogger	119.00
AU3	Power Door Locks	145.00
DG7	Electric Sport Mirrors	117.00
U58	AM/FM Stereo Radio	95.00
UM4	Electronically Tuned Stereo/8-track	386.00
UM5	Electronically Tuned Stereo/CB/ 8-track	712.00
UN5	Electronically Tuned Stereo/CB/ Cassette	750.00
UM6	Electronically Tuned Stereo/Cassette	423.00
U75	Power Antenna	55.00
UL5	Radio Delete	−118.00
CC1	Removable Glass Roof Panels	414.00
A42	Power Driver's Seat	183.00
F51	Heavy Duty Shock Absorbers	37.00
K35	Cruise Control w/Resume	155.00
FE7	Gymkhana Suspension	57.00
QGR	White Letter SBR Tires, P225/60R-15	72.00
QXH	White Letter SBR Tires, P255/60R-15	491.92
MM4	4-Speed Transmission	nc
MX1	Turbo-Hydramatic Transmission	nc
N90	Aluminum Wheels	428.00
D84	Two-Tone Exterior Paint	399.00

1982 Corvette Colors/Options

Color Code	Body Color
19	Black
31	Bright Blue
26	Dark Blue
24	Silver Blue
39	Charcoal
99	Dark Claret
56	Gold
40	Silver Green
70	Red
13	Silver
10	White
59	Silver Beige (Collector)
24/26M	Silver Blue/Dark Blue
13/99M	Silver/Dark Claret
13/39M	Silver/Charcoal
10/13M	White/Silver

INTERIOR COLORS: Dark Blue, Camel, Charcoal, Dark Red, Silver Grey, Silver Green, Silver Beige

Order #	Item Description	Sticker Price
1YY87	Corvette Coupe	18,290.07
1YY07	Collector Edition Hatchback	22,537.59
D84	Two-Tone Exterior Paint	428.00
L83	5.7 Liter V-8 Engine	nc
V54	Roof Panel Carrier	144.00
V08	Heavy Duty Cooling	57.00
C49	Rear Window Defogger	129.00
AU3	Power Door Locks	155.00
DG7	Electric Sport Mirrors	125.00
U58	AM/FM Stereo Radio	101.00
UM4	Electronically Tuned Stereo/8-track	386.00
UN5	Electronically Tuned Stereo/ CB/Cassette	755.00
	w/ 1YY07	695.00
UM6	Electronically Tuned Stereo w/Cassette	423.00
U75	Power Antenna	60.00
UL5	Radio Delete	−124.00
CC1	Removable Glass Roof Panels	443.00
AG9	Power Driver's Seat	197.00
K35	Cruise Control w/Resume	165.00
FE7	Gymkhana Suspension	61.00
QGR	White Letter SBR Tires, P225/70R-15	80.00
QXH	White Letter SBR Tires, P255/60R-15	542.52
N90	Aluminum Wheels	458.00

cross-fire injection

The 1982 collector edition had a tasteful gold and silver paint scheme and very nice detailing. In addition to trim changes, the collector edition differed from other 1982 models by the lifting rear hatch window. But it didn't come cheap. The 1982 collector edition's base price cracked the twenty-thousand-dollar figure for the first time in the Corvette's history at an attention-getting $22,537.59. John Amgwert photos.

1979-1980-1981-1982 Corvette

BASE ENGINE

Type: . . . . Chevrolet ohv V-8
Bore x stroke, inches: . . . . 4.00 x 3.48*
Displacement, inches: 350*
Compression ratio: . . . 8.2:1 (1979, 1980, 1981), 9:1 (1982)
Carburetion:...Single four-barrel carburetor (1979, 1980, 1981), throttle body injection (1982)
Horsepower: 195 (1979), 190 (1980, 1981), 200 (1982)
Distributor: . . . . High energy ignition
Other engines offered:...*The 350 engine was not certified for sale in California during the 1980 model year. California Corvettes were equipped with 305 engines. See option tables for additional engines available in 1979 and 1980.

CHASSIS AND DRIVETRAIN

Clutch: . . . . Single dry-plate (manual)
Transmission:...Four-speed manual (1979, 1980, 1981) or three-speed automatic
Front suspension:...Coil springs, tube-type shock absorbers, stabilizer bar
Rear suspension:...Single transverse leaf spring, tube-type shock absorbers, independent with lateral struts
Axle Ratio:...3.36:1 (1979 manual), 3.55:1 (1979 automatic), 3.07:1 (1980), 2.72:1 (1981 manual, 1982), 2.87:1 (1981 automatic, 1982 collectors)
Frame: . . . . Steel box sections, welded

GENERAL:

Wheelbase, inches: 98
Track, front, inches: 58.7
rear, inches: 59.5
Brakes: . . . . Disc, four-wheel
Tire size, front and rear: P255/70 R-15
Wheels: . . . . Steel
Body material: . . . . Fiberglass
Assembly plant:...St. Louis, Missouri (1979, 1980, 1981 partial), Bowling Green, Kentucky (1981 partial, 1982)

The weight-reduction campaign continued in the 1981 models equipped with automatic transmissions and standard suspensions by the replacement of the steel rear leaf spring by a unit made of fiberglass. The steel spring weighed thirty-three pounds, compared to just seven for the plastic spring. Emblems changed slightly, seat design was modified, Californians got the 350-cubic-inch engine again and Delco offered a snazzy new radio.

But the big news for 1981 was the end of Corvette production in St. Louis and the start of production in Bowling Green, Kentucky. St. Louis built its last Corvette on July 31, 1981. Bowling Green built its first on June 1, 1981, so there was a two-month overlap. Production of 1981 models by the St. Louis plant totaled 31,611 compared to 8,995 at Bowling Green.

Even before 1982 production began, enthusiasts drew an analogy between the 1982 and the 1967 and 1962 models, as each ended Corvette eras. Chevrolet thought about this too and created a "Collector Edition" for 1982. Production was not limited and the Collector Edition comprised about thirty percent of 1982 production. It was a beautiful package, featuring silver-gold metallic paint with a clear lacquer overcoat for gloss. It was highly optioned and even had special wheels with a design lifted right from the "bolt-on" cast aluminum wheel of 1967, a particularly interesting touch which confirmed the 1967 analogy.

Other than the Collector Edition, the 1982 body was no different from 1981 models except for small details. But there was news in the engine department. Chevrolet introduced "cross fire injection," also called "throttle body injection." This new fuel-injection system eliminated conventional carburetors and had its function controlled constantly by a small computer. Just as it had done in the 1962-63 transformation years, Chevrolet had chosen to introduce the drive train package ahead of the new body/chassis by one year.

The 1979-82 Corvettes are fine automobiles but will never be collector cars because of the sheer quantity built, their general sameness, and the lack of genuine performance packages. In 1982, for instance, a manual transmission wasn't even available. But even though their body design dates to 1968 and their chassis to 1963, these are refined and very popular automobiles. Tremendous gains in the design combined with the proven chassis to make these Corvettes handle very well. The space gains of the new rear end design make them much more practical to own. The Collector Edition was the only one with an opening rear window and the stylists' good taste exemplified in the car's trim make it a particularly good choice.

1982 Corvette. Chevrolet photo.

CHAPTER 14

1984-1987 CORVETTE

(Convertible)

(Callaway Turbo)

Serial Nos. 1984: 1G1AY0781E5100001 - 1G1AY0781E5151547
1985: 1G1YY0787F5100001 - 1G1YY0787F5139727
1986: 1G1YY0789G5100001 - 1G1YY0789G5127794 (Coupe)
1986: 1G1YY6789G9100001 - 1G1YY6789G9107315 (Convertible)
1987: 1G1YY2182H5100001 - 1G1YY2182H51-----
(Sixth digit for 1987 convertibles is a 3)
(Ninth digit for all years is a check digit and varies)

"Is this the new Corvette?"

Not a year passed between 1968 and 1982 without at least one of the major auto magazines having that question on its cover, along with a spy photo or artist's sketch. Corvette features do sell magazines, but the editors weren't necessarily being deceptive. Chevrolet *did* start and stop several development programs for the elusive, all-new Corvette.

Each abort is a story in itself, but it can generally be said the Corvette suffered a priority penalty. Building and selling automobiles was a different ball game in the seventies, and General Motors had more important matters to concern itself with than creating a successor for its relatively low-volume sports car.

Zora Arkus-Duntov, the famous Corvette engineering guru, retired in 1975. If one of the Corvette programs started prior to 1975 had seen completion, the new Corvettes today would be mid-engine designs. Duntov, first and foremost an engine genius, saw the logical evolution of the Corvette leading it to mid-engine placement, because the rearward weight bias would put more of the engine's tractive power at the driving wheels.

Duntov's successor was David McLellan, brilliant engineer, veteran of fifteen chassis development years at GM's Milford proving grounds, and a graduate of GM's Sloan Fellowship Management Program. McLellan brought an open mind to the question of a new Corvette's configuration. After thorough analysis, he concluded mid-engine placement created more problems than it solved. While acknowledging the Corvette had grown obsolete, he felt its big front-mounted V-8 driving the rear wheels was still the best configuration to meet the Corvette's mission.

McLellan's vision for an all-new Corvette was at the same time conservative and radical. The engine and its placement would be traditional Corvette, but virtually everything else would be scrapped and replaced with the latest in state-of-the-art thinking. In 1978, McLellan's group began engineering work on the project that resulted in the 1984 Corvette.

Oddly, there was no 1983 Corvette model. What should have been a 1983 Corvette introduction in September 1982 was delayed until March 1983, a simple case of schedule slippage. In the interim, Chevrolet realized its "1983" model

1985 Corvette. Author photos.

could meet 1984 federal regulations and substantial savings achieved by just calling it a 1984 and forgetting about a model changeover six months later. This was much to the dismay of Corvette enthusiasts, especially those proud owners of the Corvette's first year, 1953, who'd written Chevrolet in hopes of getting a 1983 with a corresponding serial number.

The 1984 Corvette catapulted America's sports car into the ranks of the world's best contemporary performance automobiles. In fact, the cornering capability of the new Corvette was nearly beyond belief. You can almost imagine Chevy engineers, after reading endless magazine road tests during the seventies when g-meters and skidpad tests became the rage, saying, "Okay, you want a car that stays glued to the skidpad, we'll give you one." Did they ever! But the cornering asset turned into a liability when the public perceived the car's suspension as bone crushing, and resale values plummeted. Understanding this issue is one key to making a smart purchase of a 1984-87 Corvette. Here's the story:

One indication of cornering ability is how much force it takes to break the tires' adhesion. Magazine testers measure this with a g-meter (a "g" equals the force of gravity) on a skidpad. Where the family sedan might register a 0.70g or less, performance-oriented cars would be in the 0.75g to 0.85g range. Different skidpads yield slightly different results, but readings over 0.85g are always considered exceptional.

Corvette engineers worked with Goodyear to develop a tire-and-suspension combination that would yield very high skidpad adhesion results. Since high cornering adhesion requires minimal body lean, Corvette engineers specified very stiff springs, then combined these springs with other performance items in an option labeled RPO Z51.

Using non-stock camber settings and the RPO Z51, a prototype 1984 Corvette reached 1.01g in GM skidpad tests. Even in showroom trim, GM's tests yielded 0.95g for the Z51 and 0.90g for the base suspension. (*Road & Track*'s September 1986 issue road test summary put the Z51 Corvette at 0.91g, best of seventy five cars tested.) Even before the 1984 Corvette was officially introduced, news of its extraordinary cornering ability was out. The Z51 option had a magic ring; customers demanded it, dealers ordered it, and almost half of the 1984 Corvettes sold were Z51-equipped.

This was ridiculous. The Z51 spring rates were much too hard for everyday driving. After the hoopla surrounding the introduction died down, owners started complaining about the Corvette's harsh ride. The car magazines, universally euphoric at first exposure to the new Corvette (at a smooth Riverside racetrack in California, by the way), changed their tune after extensive road testing. They became critical of the Corvette's ride quality, *Car & Driver* calling it an "F16" kind of car, unsuitable for "civilians." Rough ride wasn't the only problem brought on by the hard suspension; the 1984 was notorious for squeaks and rattles.

Chevrolet reacted quickly. The springs for both Z51 and base suspension 1985 models were softened, so that the Z51 in 1985 rode much like the base suspension of 1984. In 1986, the base suspension was softened again. In 1987, RPO Z52 combined softer base suspension springs with performance items previously part of the Z51 package; things like wider wheels, heavy-duty cooling, and quicker steering. To keep hard suspension models out of unsuspecting hands, Chevrolet started making four-speed manual transmissions mandatory with the Z51 option starting in late 1986. Even as spring rates were reduced, the Corvette's handling

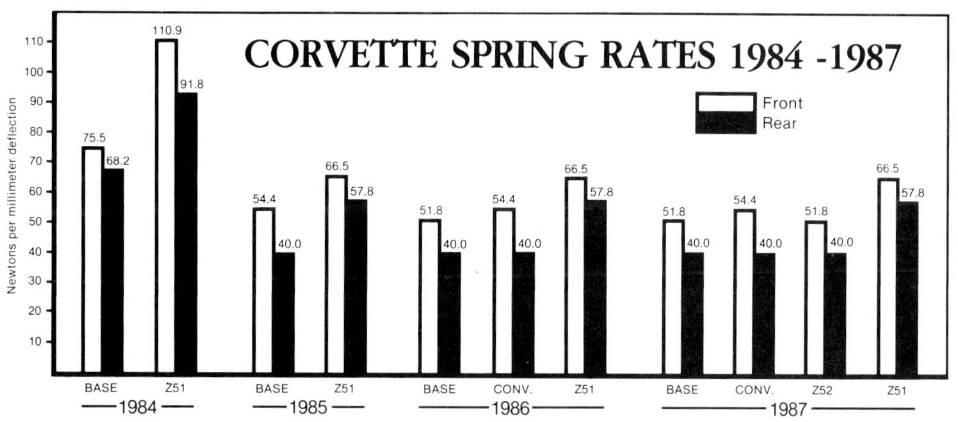

1984 Corvette Colors/Options

Color Code	Body Color
10	White
16	Bright Silver
18	Medium Gray
19	Black
20	Light Blue
23	Medium Blue
53	Gold
63	Light Bronze
66	Dark Bronze
72	Bright Red
16/18M	Silver/Gray
20/23M	Light Blue/Medium Blue
63/66M	Light Bronze/Dark Bronze

INTERIOR COLORS: Graphite, Medium Gray, Medium Blue, Light Saddle, Carmine, Dark Bronze

Order #	Item Description	Sticker Price
1YY07	Corvette Sport Coupe	21,800.00
—	Leather Seats	400.00
AG9	Power Driver Seat	210.00
AQ9	Sport Seats (Cloth)	625.00
AU3	Power Door Locks	165.00
CC3	Removable Transparent Roof Panel	595.00
D84	Two-Tone Paint	428.00
FG3	Delco/Bilstein Shock Absorbers	189.00
G92	Performance Axle Ratio	22.00
KC4	Engine Oil Cooler	158.00
K34	Cruise Control	185.00
MM4	4-Speed Transmission	n/c
MX0	Automatic Transmission	n/c
UL5	Radio Delete	-256.00
UM6	Electronically Tuned Stereo/Cassette	153.00
UN8	Electronically Tuned Stereo/CB	215.00
UU8	Delco-Bose Stereo System	895.00
V01	Heavy Duty Radiator	57.00
YF5	California Emissions	75.00
Z51	Performance Handling Package	600.20
Z6A	Defogger System	160.00

1985 Corvette Colors/Options

Color Code	Body Color
13	Silver
18	Medium Gray
20	Light Blue
23	Medium Blue
40	White
41	Black
53	Gold
63	Light Bronze
66	Dark Bronze
81	Bright Red
13/18M	Silver/Gray
20/23M	Light Blue/Medium Blue
63/66M	Light Bronze/Dark Bronze

INTERIOR COLORS: Graphite, Medium Gray, Medium Blue, Light Saddle, Carmine, Dark Bronzo

Order #	Item Description	Sticker Price
1YY07	Corvette Sport Coupe	24,878.00
A—2	Leather Seats	400.00
A—8	Sport Seats, Leather	1,025.00
B—8	Sport Seats, Cloth	625.00
AG9	Power Driver Seat	215.00
AU3	Power Door Locks	170.00
CC3	Removable Transparent Roof Panel	595.00
D84	Two-Tone Paint	428.00
FG3	Delco/Bilstein Shock Absorbers	189.00
G92	Performance Axle Ratio	22.00
K34	Cruise Control	185.00
MM4	Four-Speed Transmission	n/c
MM0	Automatic Transmission	n/c
NN5	California Emissions	99.00
UL5	Radio Delete	-256.00
UM6	Electronically Tuned Stereo/Cassette	122.00
UN8	Electronically Tuned Stereo/CB	215.00
UU8	Delco-Bose Stereo System	895.00
V08	Heavy Duty Cooling	225.00
Z51	Performance Handling Package	470.00
Z6A	Defogger System	160.00

improved as engineers were able to fine tune other chassis components, like the anti-sway bars.

Chevrolet specialists scrutinized every assembly process to eliminate potential squeaks or rattles. Overall construction, including paint quality, improved steadily through 1984 and 1985 and stayed there. By the end of 1986, the Corvette was consistently vying with the Nova (the product of Chevy's joint venture with Toyota) for top spot in Chevrolet's internal quality audits. Engineers were concerned enough about the negative perception of the 1984 Corvette that they made sure magazine writers got 1985 test vehicles well in advance of normal previews. The motoring press reacted favorably, admitting the improvements left little to fault in the Corvette.

Meanwhile, enthusiasts reacted positively to the new Corvette with only a few exceptions. There was criticism of its appearance similarity to the Camaro. There's little argument that the Corvette's exterior was a magnificent design (as was the Camaro's), but the looks comparison was valid, no doubt because both vehicles were designed in the same studio, Chevrolet #3, managed by Jerry Palmer.

The interior's instrumentation also got a mixed reception. The latest in electronics was certainly dazzling, but the graphic speedometer and tach displays were difficult to read quickly. Cost was yet another common complaint, enthusiasts feeling Chevrolet had priced the Corvette beyond reach of too many of its traditional customers.

Here's the bright side. The public's perception of 1984 Corvettes and the number built (51,547) combined to drive resale prices down, and subsequent models got caught in the downslide, though less drastically. Considering the performance capabilities of these automobiles, some used 1984-87 Corvettes are outstanding values. But not all.

To select one of these Corvettes, first ignore the investment angle. Some will eventually appreciate, but selection should be based on personal driving enjoy-

1984-1985-1986-1987 Corvette

BASE ENGINE

Type: .... Chevrolet ohv V-8
Bore x stroke, inches: .... 4.00 x 3.48
Displacement, inches: 350
Compression ratio: .9.0:1 (1984), 9.5:1 (1985, 1986, 1987)
Carburetion: ...... throttle body injection (1984), tuned-port injection 1985, 1986, 1987)
Horsepower: 205 (1984), 230 (1985, 1986), 240 (1987)
Distributor: .... High energy ignition
Other engines offered: ..... Base engines were the only ones available in 1984, 1985 and 1986. In 1987, a Callaway Twin Turbo engine was available through Chevrolet dealers. The engine was built and installed by Callaway Engineering, but had standard emissions and the full Corvette warranty.

CHASSIS AND DRIVETRAIN

Clutch: .... Single dry-plate (manual)
Transmissions: .. 4-speed automatic with overdrive and high stall torque converter; 4-speed manual with computer-controlled overdrive (manual override) in 2nd, 3rd, and 4th gears.
Front suspension: ...... Single transverse leaf spring, tube-type shock absorbers, upper and lower A-arms, stabilizer bar.
Rear suspension: ... Single transverse leaf spring, tube-type shock absorbers, upper and lower control arms, stabilizer bar.
Frame: .... All-welded body-frame integral construction. Bolt-in front crossmember to allow bottom-loaded engine.

General:

Wheelbase, inches: 96.2
Track, front, inches: 59.6
rear, inches: 60.4
Brakes: .... Disc, four-wheel
Tire size, front and rear: P255/70R-15
Wheel material: .... Aluminum alloy
Wheel sizes, inches: .... 16 x 8.5, 16 x 9.5
Body material: .... Fiberglass
Assembly plant: .... Bowling Green, Kentucky

No one could deny the 1984 Corvette was one beautiful automobile. Its engine, shown at left, had a magnesium cover over its cross-fire injection fuel delivery system. For 1985-87 models, tuned-port injection (right) replaced the cross-fire, yielding both power and economy gains. Author photos.

For 1986-87 Corvette coupes, the mandatory central-mount stoplamp was located on top of the hatch hinge; for convertibles, it was in the rear facia above the Corvette name script. Author photos.

In 1986, for the first time in more than a decade, Corvette enthusiasts had a choice of either coupe or convertible models. The new convertible was built by Chevrolet in its Corvette facility in Bowling Green, Kentucky, but still cost $5,005 more than the coupe. Both models featured anti-lock brakes. The convertibles and later-production coupes also had aluminum cylinder heads. Chevrolet photo.

Leather sport seats (above left), had controls in the bolsters and were available in 1985-87 models. The standard seat was cloth (above right); the 1986-87 base cloth is shown. Chevrolet made small improvements to the instruments, including tilting the displays as shown in these 1986 model photos, but stayed with the electronic displays through the 1984-87 period. Author photos.

ment criteria. As others learn to do the same, yours will be that much more valuable.

Unlike earlier Corvettes which are sold primarily between individuals and specialty dealers, used 1984-87 Corvettes are mixed in with everything else in the used-car market. This means that a good percentage of the selling dealers aren't any more knowledgeable about Corvettes than the scores of other models they deal with. With Corvettes, they know reds and blacks are strong sellers, blues aren't, and other colors are somewhere between. They think automatics are easier to sell than four-speeds, and leather interiors are easier than cloth. Beyond that, they figure the more options, the better. These aren't bad criteria, just incomplete.

Color might be a resale consideration for a buyer who doesn't plan to keep a new Corvette long. Beyond that, it's not so clear. The popular colors are the safest choices, but the scarcity of some of the low runners can be an advantage in the long run. After all, some of the less common colors, like 1984-85's Dark Bronze and 1986-87's Silver Beige, are quite beautiful. Then again, a lousy color is a lousy color, scarce or not.

Like the popular colors, automatic-transmission Corvettes are the safer choices. Chevrolet sold about four automatic Corvettes to each four-speed in the 1984-87 period. But if hardcore enthusiasts are drawn to used 1984-87 Corvettes for their performance value, and if hardcores prefer manual shifting, four-speeds could be in short supply.

Leather seating has been preferred to cloth in the 1984-87 Corvettes by about the same eighty-percent margin as automatics to four-speeds. There were three seat choices with 1984 models, a base seat in a muted cloth, a base seat in optional leather, and an optional "sport" seat in a not-so-muted checkerboard cloth. Midway in 1985 production, leather became available in the sport seat, so for half of that model year there were four choices. For 1986 and 1987, the sport seat was available only in leather, and the base seat in cloth or optional leather as before, except that the cloth was the style previously used for the sport seats. Got that?

The earlier cloth was the better looking of the two. The most comfortable combination was the cloth sport seat of 1984 and 1985. Leather seats had a certain mystique and sold best because they looked better when new than the cloth choices, but they didn't wear as well as either cloth.

Chevrolet was selected for the Indy 500 pace car privilege in 1986 and used the occasion to showcase the return of a Corvette convertible, the first since 1975. Designed by Chevrolet with assistance from the American Sunroof Company, also factory-built by Chevrolet, the ragtop arrived as an interim 1986 model and all 1986 convertibles sold to the public were designated as pace car replicas. The actual Indy pace car was yellow, a new Corvette color for 1986, but the replicas could be any solid Corvette exterior color.

Anti-lock braking also arrived with the 1986 Corvette model. An adaptation of Bosch's system, the Corvette's ABS employed rotational speed sensors at each wheel to feed data to a computerized Electronic Control Unit. Brake line pressure was then automatically distributed under panic stop situations for optimum braking without wheel lockup and loss of steering control.

There were no engine choices during the 1984-86 period, but there were engine refinements each year. The 1984 engine was a carryover of the 1982's 350-cubic-inch V-8 with cross-fire injection. Despite the name, the fuel delivery

1987 Corvette Convertible. Chevrolet photo.

1986 Corvette Colors/Options

Color Code	Body Color	Soft Top Color
13	Silver	Black/White
18	Medium Gray	Black/White
20	Medium Blue	Black/White
35	Yellow	Black/White
40	White	Black/White/Saddle
41	Black	Black/White/Saddle
53	Gold	Black/Saddle
59	Silver Beige	Black
69	Medium Brown	Saddle
74	Dark Red	Black/White/Saddle
81	Bright Red	Black/White/Saddle
13/18	Silver/Gray	n/a
18/41	Gray/Black	n/a
40/13	White/Silver	n/a
59/69	Silver Beige/Brown	n/a

INTERIOR COLORS: Graphite, Medium Gray, Blue, Saddle, Bronze, Red

Order #	Item Description	Sticker Price
1YY07	Corvette Sport Coupe	27,502.00
1YY67	Corvette Convertible	32,507.00
A—2	Leather Seats	400.00
A—8	Sport Seats, Leather	1,025.00
AG9	Power Driver Seat	225.00
B4P	Radiator Boost Fan	75.00
C2L	Dual Removable Roof Panels	895.00
24S	Removable Roof Panel—Blue Tint	595.00
64S	Removable Roof Panel—Bronze Tint	595.00
C68	Electronic Air Conditioning Control	150.00
D84	Two-Tone Paint	428.00
FG3	Delco-Bilstein Shock Absorbers	189.00
G92	Performance Axle Ratio	22.00
KC4	Engine Oil Cooler	110.00
K34	Cruise Control	185.00
MM4	4-Speed Transmission	n/c
MX0	Automatic Transmission	n/c
NN5	California Emissions	99.00
UL5	Radio Delete	256.00
UM6	Electronically Tuned Stereo/Cassette	122.00
UU8	Delco-Bose Stereo System	895.00
V01	Heavy-Duty Radiator	40.00
Z51	Performance Handling Package	470.00
Z6A	Defogger System	165.00

1987 Corvette Colors/Options

Color Code	Body Color	Soft Top Color
13	Silver	Black/White
18	Medium Gray	Black/White
20	Medium Blue	Black/White
35	Yellow	Black/White
40	White	Black/White/Saddle
41	Black	Black/White/Saddle
53	Gold	Black/Saddle
59	Silver Beige	Black
66	Copper	Black/Saddle
69	Medium Brown	Saddle
74	Dark Red	Black/White/Saddle
81	Bright Red	Black/White/Saddle
13/18	Silver/Gray	n/a
18/41	Gray/Black	n/a
40/13	White/Silver	n/a
59/69	Silver Beige/Brown	n/a

INTERIOR COLORS: Graphite, Medium Gray, Blue, Saddle, Bronze, Red

Order #	Item Description	Sticker Price
1YY07	Corvette Sport Coupe	28,474.00
1YY67	Corvette Convertible	33,647.00
A—2	Leather Seats	400.00
A—8	Sport Seats, Leather	1,025.00
AC1	Power Passenger Seat	240.00
AC3	Power Driver Seat	240.00
B2K	Callaway Twin Turbo Engine	19,995.00
B4P	Radiator Boost Fan	75.00
C2L	Dual Removable Roof Panels	915.00
24S	Removable Roof Panel—Blue Tint	615.00
64S	Removable Roof Panel—Bronze Tint	615.00
C68	Electronic Air Conditioning Control	150.00
DL8	Twin Remote Heated Mirrors	38.00
D74	Illuminated Driver Vanity Mirror	58.00
D84	Two-Tone Paint	428.00
FG3	Delco-Bilstein Shock Absorbers	189.00
G92	Performance Axle Ratio	22.00
KC4	Engine Oil Cooler	110.00
K34	Cruise Control	185.00
MM4	4-Speed Transmission	n/c
MX0	Automatic Transmission	n/c
NN5	California Emissions	99.00
UJ6	Low Tire Pressure Indicator	325.00
UL5	Radio Delete	256.00
UM6	Electronically Tuned Stereo/Cassette	132.00
UU8	Delco-Bose Stereo System	905.00
V01	Heavy-Duty Radiator	40.00
Z51	Performance Handling Package	795.00
Z52	Sport Handling Package	470.00
Z6A	Defogger System	165.00

system was more carburetion than fuel injection. Real fuel injection came in 1985 with the debut of Corvette's tuned-port injection, a nifty change of hardware that yielded an increase from 205 horsepower to 230 horsepower, and ten percent better fuel economy. Aluminum heads were included with the 1986 models, but not during the first months of production (all convertibles *did* get aluminum heads). In addition to weight savings, the aluminum heads had a more efficient design that added another five horsepower.

For 1987, roller valve lifters were added to reduce internal engine friction in the standard Corvette engine, yielding five more horsepower than the 1986 aluminum-head motor. For the high rollers, Corvette engineers worked with Callaway Engineering to develop a 345-horsepower twin-turbo Corvette capable of 0-60 mph in 4.6 seconds and a top speed of 175 mph. Chevrolet shipped completed Corvettes to Callaway's shop in Old Lyme, Connecticut, where the engines were swapped for new units built from scratch by Callaway. Chevy dealers could order these ferocious machines by specifying RPO B2K. Additionally, the Callaway turbo Corvettes had street-legal emissions equipment and the regular Corvette warranty. The option cost for the twin turbo package was $19,995.00!

Speaking of warranty, Corvettes built during the 1984-87 period carried GM's twelve-month, 12,000-mile coverage, plus a General Motors Protection Plan warranty for three years or 36,000 miles. At extra cost, the original owner could buy additional coverage, the most expensive plan extending the Protection Plan to five years with unlimited mileage. These warranties are transferable to subsequent owners for a nominal fee. Repairs under the extended plans aren't completely free, and not all components are covered, but they're excellent insurance against most high-dollar failures.

So while the Corvettes built between 1984 and 1987 may look similar, there's a lot to consider when contemplating a purchase. Suspension, transmission, warranty, seat materials—all have to be weighed. There weren't engine choices during any of these model years, except for the ultra-expensive Callaway twin turbo in 1987, but improvements to the standard engine year to year were significant.

The used-car market seems to have put the big value break between 1985 and 1986, considering 1984 and 1985 to be the less desirable models. It's due to the addition of ABS braking to 1986 models, but the biggest refinements came between 1984 and 1985, so look at 1985 as the underpriced value leader of the four years. There are also great values in 1984 models, especially late production cars with base suspensions. Steer clear of the 1984 Z51, unless you have racetrack duty in mind.

The 1986 and 1987 models are the most refined of all. Remember, all 1986-87 convertibles had aluminum heads, but early 1986 coupes didn't. The 240-horsepower, roller-lifter engine of the 1987 made it the most powerful Corvette since 1974 (again, excluding the Callaway), and 1987's RPO Z52 suspension option was the best of the 1984-87 period for spirited street use.

The performance sports car of the eighties wore the Chevy bowtie, and the price of admission to the Corvette ownership group that takes a back seat to nothing, via a used 1984-87 Corvette, is within reach.

Appreciation? Be prepared to wait. But in pure performance value for the dollar, no wait required.

CORVETTE CLUB LISTING

No other automobile marque in the world can claim even close to as many clubs or club members as the Corvette. This unique phenomenon started in the late-fifties and was encouraged by *Corvette News*, the quarterly magazine published by Chevrolet for Corvette enthusiasts since 1957.

The first directory of Corvette clubs appeared in *Corvette News* during 1957 and for many years each issue contained a listing of all clubs. But the list became so long that *Corvette News* now publishes it annually.

Clubs offer a new enthusiast an excellent opportunity to meet Corvette owners and to become acquainted with the best local sources for various services. Most metropolitan areas have several clubs and it's wise to seek out one that emphasizes the desired phase of the hobby, be it concours, restoration, racing or just social.

This list of Corvette clubs is printed with permission from Chevrolet Motor Division General Motors Corporation.

ALABAMA

CORVETTE BIRMINGHAM
Keith Edge
Box 322
Birmingham, AL 35201
*Jim McGill Chevrolet
Birmingham, AL
(205) 956-6700

MAJESTIC GLASS 'VETTE CLUB
James Britton, President
5237 Huntsville Avenue
Brighton, AL 35020

MID-ALABAMA CORVETTE CLUB
Steve Thomas, President
P.O. Box 862
Alabaster, AL 35007
*Ivan Leonard Chevrolet
Birmingham, AL
(205) 823-5120

SMOKE CITY 'VETTES, INC.
P. O. Box 1053
Birmingham, AL 35201

UNTOUCHABLES CORVETTE CLUB
5030 Parkwood Dr. NW
Huntsville, AL 35810

ARIZONA

CORVETTE CLUB OF ARIZONA
Ed Newton
P. O. Box 27346
Tempe, AZ 85282
*Thorobred Chevrolet
Chandler, AZ
(602) 899-0131

DESERT CORVETTE ASSOCIATION
Hal Webb, President
P. O. Box 28301
Tempe, AZ 85282
*Ray Korte Chevrolet
Scottsdale, AZ
(602) 947-3535

NATIONAL CORVETTE RESTORERS SOCIETY
Southwest Chapter
Dick Daleiden
11420 N. 64th Street
Scottsdale, AZ 85254

PHOENIX CORVETTE CLUB
Shawn Lawson
324 W. Palm Lane
Phoenix, AZ 85003
*Lou Grubb Chevrolet
Phoenix, AZ
(602) 246-2300

SUN COUNTRY CORVETTES
Jerry Smith
P. O. Box 25321
Tempe, AZ 85282
*Chapman Chevrolet
Tempe, AZ
(602) 897-1900

VALLEY CORVETTE CLUB
Mike Muhs
7256 W. Indianola
Phoenix, AZ 85033
*Courtesy Chevrolet
Phoenix, AZ
(602) 279-3232

ARKANSAS

CORVETTES OF ARKANSAS, LTD.
Steve B. Tye
P. O. Box 652
Searcy, AR 72143
*Truman Baker Chevrolet
Company, Inc.
Searcy, AR
(501) 268-2423

TRI-LAKES CORVETTE CLUB
Tom Williams
48 Tomino Way
Hot Springs, AR 71909

CALIFORNIA

ALL STAR CORVETTES
John Noel
441 Bauchet Street
Los Angeles, CA 90022
*Jack Wall Chevrolet
Pasadena, CA
(818) 449-3333

BALLHOOTER CORVETTE CLUB
John Pawoll
345 Playa Blanca
Encinitas, CA 92024

BUTTE VALLEY CORVETTES
Tony Bevacqua
P. O. Box 1185
Yuba City, CA 95992
*Daoust Chevrolet
Marysville, CA
(916) 743-9233

BUTTERFIELD COUNTRY CORVETTE CLUB
Bob Eichel
38675 Esplanade Avenue
San Jacinto, CA 92383
*Mike Reade Chevrolet
Hemet, CA
(714) 658-4401

CENTRAL COAST CORVETTES
Keith Bing
P. O. Box 832
Lompoc, CA 93438
*Reilly Chevrolet
Lompoc, CA
(805) 736-7577

CHAPARRALS
Don Majestic, President
36356 Panorama Drive
Yucaipa, CA 92399

CORVETTE OWNERS CLUB OF SAN DIEGO
Rick Perry, President
476 Tyrone St.
El Cajon, CA 92020
*Courtesy Chevrolet
San Diego, CA
(619) 297-4321

C.O.R. VETTE SET
Ted Chase
P. O. Box 592
Summit City, CA 96089

CORVETTES OF DISTINCTION
Stephen Lemmon
P. O. Box 7
Joshua Tree, CA 92252
*Marshall Motor Cars, Inc.
Yucca Valley, CA
(619) 365-2211

CORVETTES OF FRESNO
Jack McLean, President
2777 W. Browning
Fresno, CA 93711
*Hallowell Chevrolet
Fresno, CA
(209) 291-7711

CORVETTES OF LODI
Cathy Newhall
P. O. Box 811
Lodi, CA 95240
*Sanborn Chevrolet
Lodi, CA
(209) 951-7071

CORVETTES OF NAPPA VALLEY
Jack Barlow
1701 Meek Avenue
Napa, CA 94559

CORVETTES OF SOUTHERN CALIFORNIA
Nancy Leonhardt, Secretary
P. O. Box 3603
Anaheim, CA 92803

CORVETTES ON THE MALL
Jeff Branson
2537 Central
Riverside, CA 92506

CORVETTES UNLIMITED
Rick Lieberman, President
P. O. Box 322
Van Nuys, CA 91408
*Baher Chevrolet
Northridge, CA
(818) 360-1011

CORVETTES WEST
Clyde Hamill
P. O. Box 945
Colton, CA 92324
*Mark Christopher Chevrolet
Ontario, CA

DELTA CORVETTES
Norman Ruddick
P. O. Box 737
Brentwood, CA 94513
*Winter Chevrolet
Antioch, CA

DIABLO VALLEY CORVETTES
Jim Neyland
P. O. Box 5824
Concord, CA 94524
*Fitzpatrick Chevrolet, Inc.
Concord, CA
(415) 689-6500

GOLDEN COAST CORVETTE CLUB
Jeff Buhler
P. O. Box 5155
San Luis Obispo, CA 93403
*Pete Johnston Chevrolet
Paso Robles, CA
(805) 238-7800

GULDSTRAND RACING ASSOCIATION
Grant Byers
11924 W. Jefferson Blvd.
Culver City, CA 90230

ITALIAN RACING TEAM
Dave Tozer
37394 Fremont Blvd.
Fremont, CA 94536

KINETIC KORVETTES LTD.
Roger Morgan
250 E. Beach St.
Watsonville, CA 95076

MONTEREY PENINSULA CORVETTE CLUB
Larry Miles
18882 Eisenhower St.
Salinas, CA 93901
*Richardson Motor Co.
Salinas, CA
(408) 758-6464

MOTHER LODE CORVETTES
Dave Christensen
P. O. Box 4550
Sonora, CA 95370

MOUNTAIN CORVETTES
Beverley Orr
400 Hiram Page Road 60
Yreka, CA 96097

NATIONAL CORVETTE RESTORERS SOCIETY
Northern California Chapter
Gregory Cosgrove
23355 Tanager Drive
Twain Harte, California 95383

NATIONAL CORVETTE RESTORERS SOCIETY
Southern California Chapter
R. J. Martinez
P. O. Box 141
Northridge, CA 91328

NEWPORT HARBOR CORVETTES
Allen Morris
24662 Vesta
Mission Viejo, CA 92691

NORTH BAY CORVETTE ASSOCIATION
John Brosnan
P. O. Box 2012
San Rafael, CA 94903
*Redwood Chevrolet
Novato, CA
(415) 897-2191

NORTH COAST 'VETTES
Gloria Graison
P. O. Box 1744
Oceanside, CA 92054

NORTHERN CALIFORNIA CORVETTE ASS'N.
Reno Luccesi
P. O. Box 6232
Hayward, CA 94544

NORTHERN CALIFORNIA CORVETTE CLUB
Gary Hacker
P. O. Box 330150
San Francisco, CA 94133
*Parker Robb Chevrolet
Walnut Creek, CA

ORANGE COUNTY 'VETTES
Alice Willard, Secretary
Box 414
Orange, CA 92666
*R & R Chevrolet
Yorba Linda, CA
(714) 579-5100

OWENS VALLEY CORVETTES
Carol Schaefer, Sec./Treas.
P. O. Box 367
Bishop, CA 93514
*Green Motors
Bishop, CA
(619) 873-3515

POMONA VALLEY CORVETTE ASSOC.
Jerry Coble, President
1952 Vinewood Street
La Verne, CA 91750

REDDING CORVETTES
Phil Craig
P. O. Box 875
Mt. Shasta, Ca 96067

RIALTO CORVETTES LTD.
Ray Farmer
P. O. Box 385
Rialto, CA 92376

RIVER CITY CORVETTE CLUB
Bob Schneider
1003 Oriole Ct.
Roseville, CA 95678
*Campus Chevrolet
Davis, CA
(916) 753-3352

RIVER CITY CORVETTES OF SACRAMENTO
Brenda Mounce, Treasurer
8813 On Court
Elk Grove, CA 95624

SANTA CLARA CORVETTES
Donna Bailey
P. O. Box 2634
Santa Clara, CA 95055
*Anderson Chevrolet
Menlo Park, CA
(415) 321-4280

SANTA CLARITA VALLEY CORVETTE CLUB
Mike McCloskey
P. O. Box 1175
Canyon Country, CA 91351

SIMI VALLEY CORVETTES
Jim Collins
1619 Sitka Avenue
Simi Valley, CA 93063

UNITED CORVETTES OF SO. CALIFORNIA
Joe Carpenter
P. O. Box 7284
Laverne, CA 91750
*Clippinger Chevrolet
Covina, CA
(818) 339-6261

VALLEY 'VETTES OF TURLOCK
Alice Gensalves
P. O. Box 3
Turlock, CA 95381

'VETTE SET
Barbara Heacox, President
P. O. Box 218
Manhattan Beach, CA 90266
*Champion Chevrolet
Manhattan Beach, CA
(213) 316-1234

VIEJO 'VETTES
Allen Morris
24662 Vesta
Mission Viejo, CA 92691

VINTAGE CORVETTES OF SOUTHTERN CA.
Charlie Ryia, President
P. O. Box 4873
Thousand Oaks, CA 91359

V.I.P. CORVETTE CLUB OF PALM SPRINGS
Bob Ferrell
P. O. Box 431
Palm Springs, CA 92263
*Mac Magruder Chevrolet
Palm Springs, CA
(619) 325-2901

COLORADO

ADEN CORVETTE CLUB
Douglas Gordon
Aden 218
Boulder, CO 80310

BOULDER CORVETTE ASSOCIATION, INC.
Howard Loomis
1282A Milo Cr.
Lafayette, CO 80026
*Fisher Chevrolet
Boulder, CO
(303) 443-0530

COLORADO SPRINGS CORVETTE CLUB
Bob Clayton
1707 Bates Dr.
Colorado Springs, CO 80909

CORVETTES WEST
Guy B. Limpitlaw
820 13 Street
Greeley, CO 80631
*Classic Chevrolet
Greeley, CO
(303) 352-7140

DENVER CORVETTE ASSOCIATION
Theresa Elmhorst
6095 S. Valleyview St.
Littleton, CO 80120
*Burt Chevy Center
Littleton, CA
(303) 761-0333

HIGH PLAINS CORVETTE ASSOCIATION
Mike Voycheske
P. O. Box 31
Atwood, CO 80722

LOOKING GLASS CORVETTE ASSOCIATION
Richard Purdy
5102 S. Laredo Ct.
Aurora, CO 80015
*Century Chevrolet
Broomfield, CO
(303) 469-3355
*Jerry Roth Chevrolet
Lakewood, CO
(303) 237-1311

NATIONAL CORVETTE RESTORERS SOCIETY
Rocky Mountain Chapter
David Egender
1022 South Memphis
Aurora, CO 80017

ROCKY MOUNTAIN CORVETTE ASSOCIATION
Larry Morrison
492 Meadowlark Way
Clifton, CO 81521
*Gary Dana Chevrolet
Delta, CO
*Steve Westphal Chevrolet
Grand Junction, CO

SOUTHERN COLORADO CORVETTE CLUB
Duilio A. Stricca
753 W. Abriendo Avenue
Pueblo, CO 81004

TOP OF THE ROCKIES CORVETTE ASSOC., INC.
Carol Boschee
2914 Mountain View
Longmont, CO 80501
*Hajek Chevrolet-Olds, Inc.
(303) 776-5530

CONNECTICUT

CANDLEWOOD VALLEY CORVETTES, INC.
P. O. Box 163
Newton, CT 06470
*Hayes Chevrolet-Buick, Inc.
New Milford, CT
(203) 354-5585

CLASSIC GLASS CORVETTE CLUB, INC.
Drew Papsun
4 Redcoat Road
Norwalk, CT 06850

CONNECTICUT CLASSIC CORVETTE CLUB
Armand Polverari
10 Apple Street
Wallingford, CT 06492

CORVETTES LTD. OF CONN.
Bert Higgins
218 Hope Valley Road
Amston, CT 06231

FOR CORVETTES ONLY
Mike Davidson
P. O. Box 1082
Norwich, CT 06360
*Mallon Chevrolet
Norwich, CT
(203) 889-3333

NATIONAL CORVETTE RESTORERS SOCIETY
Northeast Chapter
Carl Askenback
P. O. Box 390
Green Farms, CT 06436

PREDOMINATORS CORVETTE CLUB
Robert Ritchie, President
24 Agawam-Suite B
Stratford, CT 06497

DELAWARE

CORVETTE CLUB OF NORTHERN DELAWARE
Bob O'Hara
P. O. Box 1886
Wilmington, DE 19807
*Greytak Chevrolet
New Castle, DE
(302) 322-2438

FIRST STATE CORVETTE CLUB
Rick Berry
P. O. Box 275
Camden, DE 19934
*Townsend Bros. Chevrolet
Dover, DE
(302) 674-0100

DISTRICT OF COLUMBIA

METRO-VETTES CORVETTE CLUB
P. O. Box 56500
Washington, D.C. 20011

STING OF THE RAYS
P. O. Box 1356
Washington, D.C. 20001

FLORIDA

AMERICA'S CORVETTE CLUB
Judi Pawloski
1677s SW 5th Way
Ft. Lauderdale, FL 33326

BAY AREA CORVETTE CLUB
Alice Christensen
995 Corvette Drive
Largo, FL 33541

CAPE KENNEDY CORVETTE CLUB
Ted Taylor
P. O. Box 399
Cocoa Beach, FL 32931

CENTRAL FLORIDA CORVETTE ASSOC.
Gary A. Daugherty
5800 Hansel Avenue
Orlando, FL 32809

CORVETTE ASSOCIATION OF GAINESVILLE, INC.
Elaine Harden
2000 S.W. 19C
Archer, FL 32618
*Gary Massey Chevrolet
Gainesville, FL
(904) 376-7581

CORVETTE CLUB OF MARION COUNTY
Glen Sims, President
P. O. Box 1619
Silver Springs, FL 32688
*Turnipseed Chevrolet
Ocala, FL
(904) 629-8011

CORVETTE CLUB OF OSCEOLA COUNTY
Jackie Cosgrove
2403 Broadway
Riviera Beach, FL 33404
*Starling Chevrolet
Kissimmee, FL
(305) 396-4141

CORVETTE HOLLYWOOD
Billy G. Spivey, President
P. O. Box 3988
Hollywood, FL 33023
*Maroone Chevrolet
West Hollywood, FL
(305) 962-5310

CORVETTES OF NAPLES
Bob Shaffer
4718 Spring Creek Dr. S.W.
Bonita Springs, FL 33923
*Bob Taylor Chevrolet
Naples, FL
(813) 774-5621

CORVETTES OF SARASOTA
Rob Kerwin
3789 Mundy Ridge Road
Sarasota, FL 33583

CYPRESS GARDENS CORVETTE CLUB
Tom Bunn
60 Greenfield Ct.
Winter Haven, FL 33880
*Steve Sorensen Chevrolet
Lake Wales, FL
(813) 676-7671

FLORIDA CORVETTE ASSOCIATION
Louise Sudduth, President
744 Lighthouse Drive
N. Palm Beach, FL 33408
*Roger Dean Chevrolet
West Palm Beach, FL
(305) 683-8100

GOLD COAST VETTES, INC.
Don Ganzel, Governor
157 Howell Ln.
Lake Park, FL 33410
*Steve Moore Chevrolet
Lake Worth, FL
(305) 588-2000

GULF COAST CORVETTE CLUB
Joyce Alspaugh
6432 47th Avenue E.
Bradenton, FL 34203

JACKSONVILLE CORVETTE CLUB
Tom Martin
2314 Oakdale Dr. E.
Orange Park, FL 32073

MID-FLORIDA CORVETTE CLUB
Nancy J. Reed
205 Holiday Lane
Winter Springs, FL 32708

MIRACLE STRIP CORVETTE CLUB
Dale Faessel
P. O. Box 654
Pensacola, FL 32593
*Bob Salter Chevrolet
Pensacola, FL
(904) 476-2480

NATIONAL CORVETTE RESTORERS SOCIETY
Florida Chapter
Karl Volk
709 Tradewind Drive
North Palm Beach, FL 33408

NORTH FLORIDA CORVETTE ASSOCIATION
Cliff Payne
51 Beach Avenue
Atlantic Beach, FL 32233

PLAYGROUND CORVETTE CLUB
Wade Whitley
2445 Duncan Drive
Niceville, FL 32578

SOUTH FLORIDA CORVETTE ASSOC.
James Nace, President
3033 N.E. 15 Terrace
Ft. Lauderdale, FL 33334
*Gary Fronrath Chevrolet

SOUTHWEST FLORIDA CORVETTE CLUB
Judy Majercin
P. O. Box 6951
Ft. Myers, FL 33911
*Bill Branch Chevrolet
Ft. Myers, FL
(813) 936-8561

SUNCOAST CORVETTE ASSOCIATION
Ed Shuman
P. O. Box 425
Clearwater, FL 33517
*Quinlan Chevrolet
Clearwater, FL
(813) 531-5831

SUNSHINE CORVETTE CLUB
James Ferrare
27302 S.W. 164 Avenue
Homestead, FL 33031
*Leiphart Chevrolet
Homestead, FL
(305) 247-2121

SUNSHINE STATE CORVETTE CLUB
Ray Nolan
785 N. Ridgewood
Ormond Beach, FL 32074
*Tom Gibbs Chevrolet
Bunnell, FL
(904) 437-3314

TALLAHASSEE CORVETTE ASSOC.
Ray Tipson, President
1101 Waverly Road
Tallahassee, FL 32312
*Bill Thomas Chevrolet
Tallahassee, FL
(904) 385-2181

TITUSVILLE CORVETTE CLUB
Joe Munch
5415 Wendy Lee Drive
Titusville, FL 32780

VAGABOND CORVETTE CLUB
C. Anthony Marlow
19380 Collins Ave., 1016
Miami Beach, FL 33160

WEST FLORIDA CORVETTE ASSOCIATION
Larry Beebe
2011 Mission Valley Blvd.
Nokomis, FL 33555

GEORGIA

CLASSIC GLASS CORVETTE CLUB
George Chapman
2674 Eagle Ridge Road
Marietta, GA 30062

COASTAL CORVETTE CLUB
Arthur Richardson
120 Yorktown Drive
Brunswick, GA 31520

CORVETTE ATLANTA
Dave Flannery
3186 Westfield Walk
Roswell, GA 30075
*Leiphart Chevrolet
Decatur, GA
(404) 377-9161

CORVETTES OF AUGUSTA, INC.
Robert Cook
3524 Lost Tree Court
Augusta, GA 30907
*Milton Ruben Chevrolet
Augusta, GA
(404) 724-8224

CORVETTES LIMITED OF CENTRAL GA.
Al Hemstreet
300 Chestnut Road
Warner Robins, GA 31088
*Charlie Pike Chevrolet-Buick
Warner Robins, GA
(912) 922-9341

LIFE BEGINS AT 150
Rich Johnson
P. O. Box 2814
Smyrna, GA 30081

METRO VETTES UNLIMITED
P. O. Box 29
Red Oak, Georgia 30272

NATIONAL CORVETTE RESTORERS SOCIETY
Southeast Chapter
P. O. Box 3208
Augusta, GA 30904

PEACH STATE CORVETTE ASSOC.
Ed Tillirson
110 Wills Way
Fayetteville, GA7 30214
*Martin Burks Chevrolet
Forrest Park, GA
(404) 366-9245

RED 'VETTES OF GEORGIA
Ed Day
315 Kathie Court
Roswell, GA 30076

SOUTHERN CLASSIC COR-VETTES
Gary Grimes
P. O. Box 1244
Tifton, GA 31793

WEST GEORGIA CORVETTE ASSOCIATION
Darrell Smith
170 Henson Cr.
Carrollton, GA 30117

HAWAII

CORVETTE CLUB OF HAWAII
J. R. "Charlie" Brown
7536 Puumahoe Place
Honolulu, HI 96825

IDAHO

EASY VALLEY CORVETTE CLUB, INC.
Jerry Wilmot, President
6831 Butte Court
Boise, ID 83704
*Edmark Chevrolet
Nampa, ID
(208) 888-0031

ILLINOIS

BILL BOLGER CHEVROLET CORVETTE CLUB
Bill Bolger
300 Roosevelt Road
Glen Ellyn, IL 60137
*Bill Bolger Chevrolet
Chicago, IL
(312) 469-8100

BLACKHAWK VALLEY 'VETTES
Jan Hood, Secretary
502 S.W. 7th Street
Aledo, IL 61231

CENTRAL ILLINOIS CORVETTES, INC.
Dale E. Lael
1524 Jerome Avenue
Springfield, IL 62704
*Friendly Chevrolet

Springfield, IL
(217) 529-7100

CHICAGO CORVETTE CLUB
B. L. Gronberg, Secretary
209 S. Chase
Wheaton, IL 60187
*Tom Todd
Wheeling, IL
(312) 537-7000

CORVETTE CLUB OF ILLINOIS
Charles Mornout
805 Grant
Danville, IL 61832

CORVETTES UNLIMITED, INC.
Frank Garrone Jr.
719 West Shore Drive
Shorewood, IL 60436
*Bill Jacobs Chevrolet
(815) 725-7110

CROSSED FLAGS CORVETTE CLUB
Al Wologo
P. O. Box 925
South Holland, IL 60473
*Christenson Chevrolet, Inc.
Highland, IN
(219) 924-3344

FOX VALLEY CORVETTE CLUB
Bill Kane, President
P. O. Box 183
Montgomery, IL 60538
*Don McCue Chevrolet
St. Charles, IL
(312) 584-9700

GLASS FAVORITES
Jan Poloney
20 E. Tamarack
Canton, IL 61520
*Weaver-Yemm Chevrolet
Galesburg, IL

GOLDEN GLASS 'VETTE CLUB
Helen Zasadny, President
P. O. Box 94
Orland Park, IL 60462

GREAT RIVER CORVETTE CLUB
Herb Duffy
RR 1 Box 180A
Loraine, IL 62349

JARGON CORVETTE CLUB
Paul J. Ravenna
8131 Skokie Blvd.
Skokie, IL 60077

JIM DRISCOLL CORVETTE CLUB
Jim Driscoll
3623 N. St. Louis
Chicago, IL 60618

KANKAKEE VALLEY CORVETTE CLUB
Duane Phillips
Route 6, Box 370
Kankakee, IL 60901

LAKE COUNTY 'VETTE SET
Mary Courshon, President
P. O. Box 314
Lake Bluff, IL 60044
*Bernard Chevrolet
Libertyville, IL
(312) 362-1400

LAND OF LINCOLN
Deane Bohne
111th & Bell Road
Lemont, IL 60439

LOOKING GLASS CORVETTES
Susie Wildhaber
P. O. Box 82
Highland, IL 62249
*Jack Schmitt Chevrolet
Belleville, MI
(618) 234-0087

MID-WEST CORVETTES, INC.
Steven Bragg, President
P. O. Box 782
Rock Island, IL 61201
*Bob Eriksen Chevy Center
Milan, IL
(309) 787-1765

MISSISSIPPI VALLEY CORVETTE ASSOC.
Merle Hazelwonder, President
5212 Airport Road
Godfrey, IL 62035
*Albrecht-Hamlin Chevrolet Inc.
Woodriver, IL
(618) 259-4900

NATIONAL CORVETTE RESTORERS SOCIETY
Illinois Chapter
Paul C. Nicholson
4232 Harvey Avenue
Western Springs, IL 60558

NORTHERN ILLINOIS CORVETTE CLUB
Dale Samuelson
10530 Bluebonnet Drive
Rockford, IL 61111

NORTHERN RAYS LTD. CORVETTE CLUB
Vern Fagerberg
P. O. Box 1113
Itasca, IL 60143

NORTH SHORE CORVETTE CLUB
Val Jacques
P. O. Box 1167
Wheeling, IL 60090
*C-Frank Chevrolet
Highland Park, IL
(312) 432-4000

STAR CORVETTE CLUB, INC.
James Stathis
327 S. Lasalle Suite 920
Chicago, IL 60604
*Haggerty Chevrolet Inc.
Chicago, IL
(312) 737-4000

SUNBURST CORVETTE CLUB
Jerry Barron
131 Carlisle Ct.
Cary, IL 60013

VETTE SET
Aaron Patient, President
107 Fenway Drive
Decatur, IL 62521
*Miles Chevrolet
Decatur, IL
(217) 877-4440

INDIANA

ANDERSON CORVETTE ASSOCIATION, INC.
Timothy G. Harless
Rt. 1 Box 355
Markleville, IN 46056
*Weidner Chevrolet
Anderson, IN
(317) 642-8041

CHEVROLET ROLLS OUT THE THUNDER
Tom Torrolly
4613 Craftsbury Circle
Fort Wayne, IN 46818

CIRCLE CITY CORVETTE CLUB
Tom Trojan
11 Southway Ct.
Greenwood, IN 46142
*Blossom Chevrolet
Indianapolis, IN
(317) 357-1121

CIRCUS CITY CORVETTE CLUB
Bob Skinner, President
P. O. Box 1
Twelve Mile, IN 46988
*Paul Richards Chevrolet
Peru, IN
(317) 473-5551

CORVETTE CLUB OF COLUMBUS
Chuck Hanner
4730 Mission Ct.
Columbus, IN 47203
*Bill Dunfee Chevrolet
Columbus, IN
(812) 376-3327

CORVETTE CLUB OF INDIANA
Dennis McCarthy
2302 S. Indiana
Kokomo, IN 46902

DELCO ELECTRONICS CORVETTE CLUB
Mike Hickman
310 E. Baywood Ct.
Nobelsville, IN 46060
*Eriks' Chevrolet
Kokomo, IN
(317) 457-8333

DUNELAND CORVETTE CLUB, INC.
Joyce Dee, Secretary
1122 Cedar Street
Michigan City, IN 46360
*Vine Chevrolet
Michigan City, IN
(219) 879-5411

ELKHART 'VETTE SET
Mike Personette
58849 Cr. 1
Elkhart, IN 46517
*Kirk Chevrolet
Goshen, IN
(219) 534-2521

FORT WAYNE CORVETTE CLUB, INC.
Thomas West
21727 Woodburn Rd. 8B
Woodburn, IN 46797
*Kelley Chevrolet
Fort Wayne, IN
(219) 484-5566

GLASS GEMS CORVETTE CLUB
Steve Winters
51 S. New Jersey
Indianapolis, IN 46204

GLASS MENAGERIE CORVETTE CLUB
Larry Prickett
57 Warren Lane
Brownsburg, IN 46112
*Bud Wolf Chevrolet
Indianapolis, IN
(317) 257-4461

INDIANAPOLIS CORVETTE CLUB
Richard Satkamp
11933 Old Orchard Dr.
Indianapolis, IN 46236
*Dan Young
Indianapolis, IN
(317) 846-6666

INDY CLASSICAL GLASS CORVETTE CLUB
Willie E. Wardlow, President
4433 N. Ritter
Indianapolis, IN 46226

LAFAYETTE CORVETTE CLUB, INC.
Larry Mock, President
1611 Tanglewood
Lafayette, IN 47905
*DeFouw Chevrolet
Lafayette, IN
(317) 447-5010

MAGIC GLASS CORVETTE CLUB
Chuck Blank
7500 W. 84TH PLACE
Crown Point, IN 46307
*Carroll Chevrolet
Crown Point, IN
(219) 663-3000

MASS OF GLASS
Joe Biga
4681 Samuel Drive
Centerville, IN 47330

MICHIANA CORVETTE CLUB
Mike Eby
401 S. Lafayette Blvd.
South Bend, IN 46634
*Gates Chevrolet
South Bend, IN
(219) 237-4000

MID-WEST CORVETTE OWNERS
Jerry Myers
P. O. Box 8431
Evansville, IN 47715
*Cooke Chevrolet
Evansville, IN
(812) 477-6111

NATIONAL CORVETTE RESTORERS SOCIETY
Indiana Chapter
James Carr
1903 Pennsylvania Street
Columbus, IN 47201

ROAD AMERICA CORVETTE CLUB
Michael Miller
P. O. Box 273
Aurora, IN 47001

SIRMAL CORVETTE CLUB
Danny O'Brien
Rt. 4, Box 241
Tipton, IN 46072

STAR CITY CORVETTE CLUB
Larry R. Williams
1716 Scott Street
Lafayette, IN 47904

TERRE HAUTE CORVETTES
Russ Perry
P. O. Box 684
Terre Haute, IN 47808
*Sycamore Chevrolet
Terre Haute, IN
(812) 234-6661

VALPO 'VETTES
Mitch Mullins
609 Yellowstone Road
Valparaiso, IN 46383
*Hal Heuring Chevrolet-Cadillac
Valparaiso, IN
(219) 462-1175

IOWA

CEDAR RAPIDS CORVETTE CLUB
Donald J. Sedlacek
4029 Old Ferry Road
Palo, IA 52324
*Rapids Chevrolet Co.
Cedar Rapids, IA
(319) 366-2753

CENTRAL IOWA CORVETTE CLUB
Darol Carter
4204 E. Madison
Des Moines, IA 50317

CORVETTE CLUB OF IOWA
Larry Croskey
892 S.E. 72nd Avenue
Des Moines, IA 50237

CYCLONE CORVETTES, INC.
Jim Mertins, Secretary
2808 Greensboro Dr.
Ames, IA 50010
*George White Chevrolet
Ames, IA
(515) 233-2211

GLASS REFLECTION CORVETTE CLUB
Cindy Borgeson
3301 Mt. Vernon Drive
Waterloo, IA 50701

MUSCATINE CORVETTE CLUB
F. Eugene Logel, Governor
604 Sunrise Circle
Muscatine, Iowa 52761

RIVER CITY CORVETTE ASSOCIATION
Larry McCarty
R. R. 1 Box 211
Mediapolis, IA 52637

KANSAS

AIR CAPITAL CORVETTE CLUB
Ricke Rubin, President
P. O. Box 813
Wichita, KS 67201
*Don Hattan Chevrolet
Wichita, KS
(316) 744-1275

CENTRAL KANSAS CORVETTE ASSOCIATION
Fred Johnson
2007 Ridgelea Drive
Salina, KS 67401

CORVETTE CLUB OF KANSAS CITY
S. Davis
8835 Hemlock Drive
Overland Park, KS 66212
*Dammer Chevrolet
Independence, MO
(816) 836-8420

FLATLANDERS UNITED CORVETTE CLUB
Darrell Hawk, President
4702 Frank Road
Hutchinson, KS 67501

GREAT PLAINS CORVETTE ASSOC.
Bob Schoenberger
1404 Tulane
Liberal, KS 67901
*Stu Emmert Chevrolet
Liberal, KS
(316) 624-2584

KANSAS CITY CORVETTE ASSOCIATION
Jack Perry, President
13441 West 70th Terr.
Shawnee, KS 66216
*New Union Chevrolet
Raytown, MO
(816) 356-6610

MID-AMERICA CORVETTE CLUB
Rick Izard
10428 Bradshaw
Overland Park, KS 66215

SOUTH WINDS CORVETTE CLUB
Jeffrey Orr
1518 S. Clara
Wichita, KS 67209

TOPEKA CORVETTE CLUB
David Pierce
6120 N. W. North Hills Dr.
Topeka, KS 66617

TOUCH OF GLASS CORVETTE CLUB
John Hecker, President
14502 W. 92 St.
Lenexa, KS 66215

WALLBANGERS CORVETTE CLUB
Don Crockett
7120 Robinson
Overland Park, KS 66602

KENTUCKY

CENTRAL KENTUCKY CORVETTE CLUB
Robert Liter
133 Bourbon Hills Drive
Paris, KY 40361
*Burt Gross Chevrolet
Irvine, KY
(606) 723-2119

DERBY TOWN CORVETTE CLUB
Kenneth Thompson
6506 Shirley Avenue
Prospect, KY 40059

EAST KENTUCKY CORVETTE CLUB, INC.
Rodney Maynard
629 South Mayo Trail
Pikeville, KY 41501
*Johnson Motor Sales, Inc.
Pikeville, KY
(606) 432-5551

FALLS CITY CORVETTE CLUB
Butch Hume
P. O. Box 16187
Louisville, KY 40216
*Bob Hook Chevrolet
Louisville, KY
(502) 499-0800

REBEL CORVETTES OF THE BLUEGRASS
Steve Fister
P. O. Box 23401
Lexington, KY 40523
*Conrad Chevrolet
Lexington, KY
(606) 269-4321

LOUISIANA

BATON ROUGE CORVETTE CLUB, INC.
Les Tassin, President
13512 Bogwood Avenue
Baton Rouge, LA 70818
*McInnis Peterson Chevrolet, Inc.
Baton Rouge, LA
(504) 293-5500

CAJUN CORVETTE CLUB
Rick Minter
P. O. Box 1119
Gray, LA 70359

CRESCENT CITY CORVETTE CLUB
Richie Zitzmann, President
P. O. Box 50553
New Orleans, LA 70150

RIVERFRONT CORVETTE CLUB
Harry B. Donaldson
2061 Lovers Lane
Shreveport, LA 71105

S'PORT CITY CORVETTE CLUB
Philip Gatson, Governor
4056 Mayfield St.
Shreveport, LA 71109

TWIN TOWN CORVETTES
Bob Evenson, Treasurer
P. O. Box 5372
Alexandria, LA 71307
*Futrell Chevrolet, Inc.
Colfax, LA
(318) 442-0423

MARYLAND

BEL AIR CORVETTE CLUB
Cindi Gallant
1508 Amesbury Ct.
Bel Air, MD 21014

CORVETTE CLUB OF AMERICA
Will Turnbow
10400 Windfall Ct.
Damascus, MD 20872

CORVETTE CLUB OF BALTIMORE
Bill Lyberger
265 Arundel Bch. Rd.
Severna Park, MD 21146

FREE STATE CORVETTE CLUB OF MARYLAND
Nick Timmons, Secretary
15613 Dorset Road T-2
Laurel, MD 20707
*JBA Chevrolet
Glen Burnie, MD
(301) 766-6300

G-BURG 'VETTES, INC.
Steve Clipper
P. O. Box 3712
Gaithersburg, MD 20878

GLASS FORCE CORVETTE CLUB
James Downing
10604 Gay Court
Upper Marlboro, MD 20772

GLASS OF CLASS CORVETTE CLUB
P. O. Box 2792
Landover, MD 20785

METRO-VETTES CORVETTE CLUB
Robert A. Smith, President
13202 Keverton Drive
Upper Marlboro, MD 20772

SOUTHERN MARYLAND CORVETTE CLUB
Bob Sohl
Box 310
Waldorf, MD 20601
*Lowe Chevrolet
Upper Marlboro, MD
(301) 627-5700

MASSACHUSETTS

BAY STATE CORVETTE CLUB, INC.
Babe Johnson
26 Ticonderoga La.
Millis, MA 02054

BRISTOL COUNTY CORVETTES
Francis Tobia
1008 Almy Road
Somerset, MA 02726

CAPE COD CORVETTE CLUB
c/o George T. Shoner
P. O. Box 91
Toaticket, MA 02536

CLIPPER CITY CORVETTE CLUB, INC.
Clyde A. Fowler, Jr.
P. O. Box 211
Newburyport, MA 01950

CORVETTES OF BERKSHIRE
Peter Gregoire
P. O. Box 1044
Pittsfield, MA 01201

CORVETTES UNITED
Gordon Peterson, President
P. O. Box 41
Greendale Station
Worcester, MA 01606

EASTERN MASS. CORVETTE CLUB
Bill Davis
P. O. Box 531
Dover, MA 02030

NORTH SHORE CORVETTES OF MASS.
Dan Gale
398 Lowell St.
Andover, MA 01810

SILVER CITY CORVETTE CLUB
William A. Mendes
84 Lemos Street
New Bedford, MA 02740

SOUTH SHORE CORVETTE CLUB
Phil McCormack, President
Box 95
N. Weymouth, MA 02190
*DeSantis Chevrolet
Brockton, MA
(617) 586-7900

TRIBORO CORVETTE CLUB
Dennis Kern
714 N. Main St.
Attleboro, MA 02703
*Mandeville Chevrolet
N. Attleboro, MA
(617) 695-3501

MICHIGAN

BAY VALLEY CORVETTES
Ed Flores, President
381 W. Salzburg Road
Bay City, MI 48706
*Wickstrom Chevrolet
Bay City, MI
(517) 684-4411

BLUE WATER CORVETTE CLUB
Tom Ingerson
4297 Guilford Lane
Port Huron, MI 48060

CANTON CORVETTE CLUB
Don Bristow
1076 Kings Court
Canton, MI 48906

CAPITAL CITY CORVETTE CLUB
Pat Spinrad
3738 Turner
Lansing, MI 48906

CHESANING CORVETTE CLUB
Larry J. Fischer
518 S. Line St.
Chesaning, MI 48616
*La Clair Sales
Chesaning, MI
(517) 845-3057

CORVETTE CLUB OF BATTLE CREEK, INC.
Jay Farleigh
20386 Pine Lake Road
Battle Creek, MI 49017

CORVETTE CLUB OF MICHIGAN, INC.
Ken Watson
P. O. Box 2528
Livonia, MI 48151
*Les Stanford Chevrolet
Dearborn, MI
(313) 565-6000

CORVETTE CLUB OF YPSILANTI
Dave Johnson
1175 Oak Street
Ypsilanti, MI 48197
*Jack Webb Chevrolet
Ypsilanti, MI
(313) 481-0210

CORVETTE COVENTRY SW MICH
Roger Thomas
2651 Lake Bluff Terrace
St. Joseph, MI 49085

FLINT CORVETTE CLUB, INC.
Jim Harris
P. O. Box 984
Flint, MI 48501
*Vic Canever
Fenton, MI
(313) 629-1581

GMC CORVETTE SET
Hugh Patterson
1171 Barneswood Ln.
Rochester, MI 48064
*Bill Fox Chevrolet
Rochester, MI
(313) 651-7000

GRAND VALLEY CORVETTE CLUB
Maynard Van Singel
2017 Pinnacle Dr. S.W.
Wyoming, MI 49509

HURON VALLEY CORVETTE CLUB
Betty Gumtow
P. O. Box 88
Ypsilanti, MI 48197
*Rampy Chevrolet
Ann Arbor, MI
(313) 663-3321

JACKSON CORVETTE CLUB
Susan Butters, Governor
P. O. Box 931
Jackson, MI 49201
*Art Moehn Chevrolet
Jackson, MI
(517) 787-7700

KALAMAZOO CORVETTE CLUB
Jim Bartel
1404 Hardwick Dr.
Kalamazoo, MI 49002
*Mani Sorets
Chevy Town U.S.A.
Decatur, MI
(616) 423-7097

MID-MICHIGAN CORVETTE CLUB
Roger Case
723 Sparling Drive
Saginaw, MI 48603
*Martin Chevrolet
Saginaw, MI
(517) 781-4590

NATIONAL CORVETTE RESTORERS SOCIETY
Michigan Chapter
Bill Nichols
28035 Brian Hill Drive
Farmington Hills, MI 48018

NORTH OAKS CORVETTE CLUB
Jim Thatcher
2104 Shankin Drive
Walled Lake, MI 48088

ROYAL CORVETTES OF WESTERN MI
George Powell
11990 N. Maple Island Road
Fremont, MI 49412

SHIAWASEE CORVETTE CLUB
Jim Sweet
5167 East M-21
Corunna, MI 48817

STINGRAYS OF FLINT
P. O. Box 4008
Flint, MI 48504

SUPERIOR CORVETTES OF UPPER MICHIGAN
James B. King
135 Pearce Street
Gwinn, MI 49841
*Frei Chevrolet, Inc.
Marquette, MI
(906) 226-2577

TOUCH OF GLASS 'VETTE CLUB
Bill Dabney
8472 Berkshire Dr.
Ypsilanti, MI 48197

MINNESOTA

CENTRAL MINNESOTA CORVETTE ASSOC.
Jim Vos
5 Skyview Drive
Sauk Rapids, MN 56379
*Murphy Chevrolet
Foley, MN
(612) 968-6239

CLASSIC CORVETTES OF MINNESOTA
Dale Crosby
2636 MARYLAND AVE. E
ST. PAUL, MN 55119

HIAWATHALAND CORVETTE ASSOCIATION
Gail Fisher
718 17th St. S.E.
Owatonna, MN 55060

MINNESOTA VALLEY CORVETTE CLUB
Karolyn Fitzpatrick
104 South Mayfair Drive
Mankato, MN 56001

NATIONAL CORVETTE RESTORERS SOCIETY
Minnesota Chapter
Deane Parker
1673 W. County Road C-2
Roseville, MN 55113

RED RIVER VALLEY CORVETTE CLUB
Pete Pianka
2202 19th Street So.
Moorhead, MN 56560
*Gateway Chevrolet
Fargo, ND
(701) 282-5522

ST. CROIX VALLEY CORVETTE ASSOCIATION
Jim Berg
P. O. Box 104
Stillwater, MN 55082

SUBURBAN CORVETTES
Marty Weniger
6785 Yucca Lane
Maple Grove, MN 55369
*Iten Chevrolet
Brooklyn Center, MN
(612) 561-9220

MISSISSIPPI

CAPITOL CITY CORVETTE CLUB
John L. Farmer
545 Terry Road
Jackson, MS 39203

DIXIE CORVETTE ASSOCIATION
Rip Collins, President
P. O. Box 73
Pascagoula, MS 39567

MAGNOLIA CORVETTE CLUB
Cindra Duncan
P. O. Box 2624
Columbus, MS 39704

MID-MISSISSIPPI CORVETTES
Ron St. John
P. O. Box 4581
Meridian, MS 39304
*Nelson Hall Chevrolet
Meridian, MS
(601) 693-4411

MISSISSIPPI GULF COAST CORVETTE CLUB
Linda Bell
102 Ancient Oaks Cr.
Biloxi, MS 39532

MISSOURI

BOONE TRAIL CORVETTE CLUB
Stanley Eilmann
73 Park Charles Blvd. N.
St. Peters, MO 63376

CLASSIC CORVETTE CLUB
Kirk Kenton
P. O. Box 1556
Kansas City, MO 64141
*Dahmer Chevrolet
Independence, MO
(816) 836-8420

GLASS EXPRESS CORVETTE CLUB
Jim Weidmaier, Jr.
4302 Maxwell Road
St. Joseph, MO 64505

NATIONAL CORVETTE RESTORERS SOCIETY
Kansas City Chapter
Kirk Kenton
1718 Baltimore
Kansas City, MO 64108

ORIGINAL CORVETTE CLUB OF ST. LOUIS
M. C. Britz
559 Hickory Ridge Ct.
Des Peres, MO 63131
*Weber Chevrolet
St. Louis, MO
(314) 567-3300

SEDALIA CORVETTE CLUB
Bill Simon
2413 Cedar Lane Rt. 3
Sedalia, MO 65301
*Bob McEnerney Chevrolet
Sedalia, MO
(816) 826-8320

SHOW-ME CORVETTES, INC.
Bob Eyraud
1406 Sylvan Lane
Columbia, MO 65202

SHOW-ME-VETTES OF SOUTHEAST MISSOURI
Phil Ventimiglia
318 Walter
Farmington, MO 63640
*Turner Chevrolet
Farmington, MO
(314) 431-2414

ST. LOUIS CORVETTES UNLTD.
John Gaffney
8 Fernwood Drive
St. Peters, MO 63376

TOUCH OF GLASS CORVETTE CLUB
Patrick Bauer
4312 E. 10th Street
Kansas City, MO 64137

'VETTE SETTE CORVETTE CLUB OF SPRINGFIELD
Gordon Sellers, President
P. O. Box 3134
Springfield, MO 65807
*Reliable Chevrolet
Springfield, MO
(417) 887-5800

MONTANA

ELECTRIC CITY CORVETTE CLUB
Dennis Frazier
CMR Box 6043
Great Falls, MT 59406
*City Motor Co.
Great Falls, MT
(406) 761-4900

GLASS REUNION CORVETTE CLUB
Lawrence Koler
117 North 19, Apt. 5
Billings, MT 59102

HELLGATE CORVETTE CLUB
John Christensen
1825 Riverside Drive
Missoula, MT 59801

HYALITE CORVETTE CLUB OF GALLATIN COUNTY, INC.
Gene Spranget
408 Staudaher
Bozeman, MT 59715
*Don Norem Chevrolet-Buick
Bozeman, MT
(406) 587-5501

TREASURE STATE CORVETTES
Davis S. Johnson, Sec.
1921-6 Ave.
Helena, MT 59601

NEBRASKA

CLASSY GLASS CORVETTE CLUB
Keith Jurey
1590 Beverly Blfd.
Gering, NE 69341

CORNHUSKER CORVETTE CLUB LTD.
Walt Stecki
6314 S. 33 Street
Omaha, NE 68107

CROSSROADS CORVETTE CLUB
Dan Snipes
136 Ohio
York, NE 68467

FREMONT CORVETTE CLUB
Kenneth Wolter
2323 E. 10th
Fremont, NE 68025

MID-NEBRASKA CORVETTE CLUB
Pod Bosselman, Historian
Route 1 Box 109
St. Libory, NE 68872

MIDWEST EARLY CORVETTE CLUB
Dave Minniear
12818 Southdale Drive
Omaha, NE 68137

NATIONAL CORVETTE RESTORERS SOCIETY
Missouri Valley Chapter
Virgil Wipf
5619 Salt Valley View Road
Lincoln, NE 68512

NEBRASKA CITY CORVETTE CLUB
Richard D. Elmore, Vice-President
1901 Central Avenue
Nebraska City, NE 68410
*Larson Motors, Inc.
Nebraska City, NE
(402) 873-5507

NEBRASKA CORVETTE ASSOCIATION
Jim Harman
7110 Willow Avenue
Lincoln, NE 68507

PLATTE VALLEY CORVETTE CLUB
Steven L. Reed
2203 East Norfolk Avenue
Norfolk, NE 68701

'VETTE SET OF NEBRASKA
Gary Lantzer
4203 New York Avenue
Grand Island, NE 68803

NEVADA

BIGGEST LITTLE CORVETTE CLUB IN RENO
Mel Watson
4210 Inverness Drive
Reno, NV 89502

BOULDER CITY CORVETTE CLUB
Larry Bounty, President
1500 Marita Drive
Boulder City, NV 89005

CARSON CITY CORVETTES
Jack "Snoopy" Bell
3801 Lyon Lane
Carson City, NV 89701
*Dan Flammer Chevrolet
Carson City, NV
(702) 882-1343

CORVETTE COMPETITION TEAM
"Jeep" Infantino
50 Greenstonee Cr.
Reno, NV 89512

LAS VEGAS CORVETTES ASSOC.
Jerry McCorkle, President
P. O. Box 962
Las Vegas, NV 89125

RENO CORVETTES
Bill Riley
P. O. Box 2681
Sparks, NV 89432

NEW HAMPSHIRE

CORVETTES OF NEW HAMPSHIRE
Sherman Gates
3 New Boston Road
Amherst, NH 03031

GATE CITY CORVETTE CLUB, INC.
Carole Souza
Jeremy Hill Road
Pelham, NH 03076
*Talarico Chevrolet, Inc.
Milford, NH
(603) 673-3333

LAKES REGION CORVETTES
Ron Burton
P. O. Box 6362
Lakeport, NH 03246
*Fred Madore
Chev.-Pont.-Olds., Inc.
Plymouth, NH
(603) 536-2810

SEACOST 'VETTES
Jere McCarthy
36 Lone Star Avenue
Farmington, NH 03835

NEW JERSEY

BOARDWALK CORVETTES OF ATLANTIC CITY
Keith Parker
P. O. Box 5044
Atlantic City, NJ 08404

CAPITAL CITY CORVETTE CLUB
Ronald C. Young
8 Mulford Lane
Belle Mead, NJ 08502
*Towbin Chevrolet
Trenton, NJ
(609) 890-1000

CLASS GLASS CORVETTE CLUB OF BERGEN COUNTY
Joseph M. Fasano
127 La Salle Avenue
Hasbrouck Heights, NJ 07604
*Konner's Chevrolet
Paramus, NJ
(201) 261-7100

C.M.T. 'VETTES LTD. OF CENTRAL JERSEY
Roger Devlin
50 N. Finley Avenue
Basking Ridge, NJ 07920
*Headquarters Chev., Inc.
Madison, NJ
(201) 377-1230

CORVETTE EXPRESS
Greg Norton
9 Syngle Way
Englishtown, NJ 07726
*Future Chevrolet
Aberdeen, NJ
(201) 566-8000

GARDEN STATE CORVETTE CLUB
Frank Stech
P. O. Box 548
Woodbury, NJ 08096
*Martin Chevrolet
Turnersville, NJ
(609) 629-8700

SPIRITS OF '53 CORVETTE CLUB
John Datz, President
10 Halick Court
East Brunswick, NJ 08816
*Laffin Chevrolet
South River NJ
(201) 254-2120

SURF CORVETTE CLUB
Jack Russell, Vice-President
1001 Ridge Avenue
Manasquan, NJ 08736
*Surf Chevrolet
Point Pleasant, NJ
(201) 899-7400

WOODBRIDGE CORVETTE CLUB
Seymour Goldstein
P. O. Box 644
Woodbridge, NJ 07095

NEW MEXICO

EL PASO CORVETTES, INC.
Fred Hernandez
P. O. Box 414
Santa Teresa, NM 88008

NEW MEXICO CORVETTE ASSN.
David Averill
1121 Georgene N.E.
Albuquerque, New Mexico 87112
*Ed Blacks Chev. Center, Inc.
Albuquerque, New Mexico
(505) 268-2411

NEW YORK

ADIRONDACK MOUNTAIN 'VETTES
Steve Gagnier
P. O. Box 1174
Plattsburgh, NY 12901

CENTRAL NEW YORK CORVETTE CLUB
Gary F. Baechle
18 Homestead Road East
Clinton, NY 13323

CLASSIC CORVETTES OF BUFFALO
Bruce Fenwick
190 Chasewood Drive
East Amherst, NY 14051

CLASSIC CORVETTES OF LONG ISLAND
Carolyn Grasso
P. O. Box 632
Merrick, NY 11566
*Bast Chevrolet
Seaford, NY
(516) 785-4100

CORVETTE OWNERS OF WESTCHESTER, INC.
Ken Carollo
581 North State Road
Briarcliff Manor, NY 10510
*T. A. Byrne Chevrolet
Mt. Kisco, NY
(914) 241-3400

CORVETTES OF BUFFALO, INC.
Robin Kohlhagen
S. 4430 Buckingham Lane
Hamburg, NY 14075

CORVETTES UNLIMITED
Richard Bauer
P. O. Box 16252
Rochester, NY 14616

ENCHANTED MOUNTAIN CORVETTE CLUB
Mike Palmesano
38 Cameron Avenue
Hornell, NY 14843

EAST NORTHPORT CORVETTE OWNERS ASSOC.
Robert Horowitz
11 Woodsorrel Lane
East Northport, NY 11731

EMPIRE CORVETTE CLUB
Gerry Toscano
28-42 Wilson Ave.
Bellmore, NY 11710

FIVE STAR CORVETTE CLUB
Mike Sullivan
160 Albany Post Road
Hyde Park, NY 12538

FOOTHILLS CORVETTE CLUB
Bob Miller
P. O. Box 799
Glens Falls, NY 12801/

GLASS SOCIETY CORVETTE CLUB
Wayne Lewis
P. O. Box 34
Garden City, NY 11530
*Pape Chevrolet
Huntington, NY
(516) 427-0900

GLEN REGIONAL CORVETTE CLUB
Tom Markferding
P. O. Box 155
Elmira, NY 14901
*Elm Chevrolet
Elmira, NY
(607) 734-4141

JEN-O-SEE FAS-GLAS
Rex Rider
1234 West Lake Road
Conesus, NY 14435

LOCK CITY CORVETTES, INC.
David Ferris
P. O. Box 413
Lockport, NY 14094

MID-HUDSON VALLEY CORVETTE ASSOC.
John Morgan
P. O. Box 1762
Poughkeepsie, NY 12603

MOHAWK VALLEY CORVETTE CLUB
Brian Humphreys
P. O. Box 321
New Hartford, NY 13413
*Frank Gee Chevrolet, Inc.
Marcy, NY
(315) 797-8000

OSWEGO COUNTY CORVETTE CLUB
P. O. Box 346
Fulton, NY 13069
*Burritt Chevrolet
Oswego, NY
(315) 343-8948

ROCHESTER CORVETTE CLUB, INC.
Bob Frank
P. O. Box 14612
Rochester, NY 14614
*Bob Johnson Chevrolet
Rochester, NY
(716) 663-4040

SOUTHERN TIER CORVETTE CLUB
David Nixon
P. O. Box 25
Windsor, NY 13865

SOUTH SHORE CORVETTE OWNERS ASSOC.
Ellen Guerrieri
1815 Middle Country Road
Centereach, NY 11720
*Hustedt Chevrolet
Centereach, NY
(516) 585-2700

SYRACUSE CORVETTE CLUB, INC.
Edward V. Sutton
P. O. Box 2866
Syracuse, NY 13220
*Reymore Chevrolet
Central Square, NY
(315) 668-2673

TOWN AND COUNTRY CORVETTES, LTD.
William Lado
P. O. Box 551
Oneonta, NY 13820

Tri-'Vettes, Ltd.
Bob Mason, President
P. O. Box 454
East Greenbush, NY 12061
*De Nooyer Chevrolet, Inc.
Albany, NY
(518) 458-7700

'VETTES IN PERFECTION, LTD.
Joel Henebry
P. O. Box 672
Latham, NY 12110
*DePaula Chevrolet
Albany, NY
(518) 489-5551

'VETTES 'R' FUN
George Claery
142 Kings Lane
Rochester, NY 14617
*Doyle Chevrolet
Rochester, NY
(716) 671-5390

WESTCHESTER CORVETTES
Delilah Rigano
RFD 1, Box 435-Austin Rd.
Mahopac, NY 10541

WESTERN NEW YORK CORVETTE CLUB
Ken Paluch
41 Stewart Road
Buffalo, NY 14211

NORTH CAROLINA

AZALEA COAST CORVETTE CLUB
Clarence M. Kirby
933 Arnold Road
Wilmington, NC 28403

CAPITOL CITY CORVETTE CLUB
Bill Billings
6609 Glendower Road
Raleigh, NC 27612

CARO-VETTES, INC.
Jim Roddy
P. O. Box 1654
Jacksonville, NC 28540
*Marine Chevrolet/Cadillac
Jacksonville, NC
(919) 455-2121

CHEVY'S UNDER GLASS
Steve Falls
5301 Spring Lane
Shelby, NC 28150

CLASSIC GLASS CORVETTE ASSOC.
Cindy Hammitt, President
P. O. Box 293
High Point, NC 27261
*Parks Chevrolet
Kernersville, NC
(919) 993-2101

CONFEDERATE CORVETTE CLUB
Francine Spargo
341 Dublin Court
Gastonia, NC 28054

CORVETTE CLUB OF WINSTON-SALEM
David Evans, President
P. O. Box 2006
Clemmons, NC 27102
*Modern Chevrolet
Winston-Salem, NC
(919) 722-4191

CORVETTES INTERNATIONAL, INC.
Doug Motley, President
511 Colchester
Raleigh, NC 27614
*Bobby Murray Chevrolet
Raleigh, NC
(919) 834-6441

FREE WHEELING CORVETTE CLUB
Charles W. Odom
Rt. 1 Box 128
St. Paul, NC 28384

GREAT SMOKIES CORVETTES
Charles Snuffer
13 Captains Drive
Candler, NC 28715

MATTHEWS AREA CORVETTE CLUB
Harry Belk, III
7940 Greenside Court
Matthews, NC 28105

METROLINA CORVETTE CLUB
Oren Hudson
1300 Idlewood Circle
Gastonia, NC 28054

PLASTIC CARS, LTD.
Stephen Bird
366 Northwest Drive
Davidson, NC 28036

QUEEN CITY CORVETTE CLUB
Larry Gunter
10637 Fairway Ridge Rd.
Matthews, NC 28105

SOUTHERN CORVETTE CLUB
Wayne Johnson, President
c/o Ben Mynatt Chevrolet
P. O. Box 1110
Concord, NC 28025

TARHEEL CORVETTES
Tim Spradley
912 Lake Dr. W.
Thomasville, NC 27360

WESTERN CAROLINA CORVETTE ASSOC.
Dale Shelton, President
P. O. Box 5872
Asheville, NC 28813
*Frank Wood
Chevrolet-Olds, Inc.
Brevard, NC
(704) 884-2611

WILKES CORVETTE CLUB
Dick Whittington
Rt. 4, Box 170
Wilksboro, NC 28697

NORTH DAKOTA

NORTHERN PLAINS CORVETTE ASSOC.
Brenda Keller, President
1501 10th St. S.W.
Minot, ND 58701
*Jim Ryan Chevrolet
Minot, ND
(701) 852-3571

OHIO

BROOKVILLE CORVETTE CLUB
Dan Taulbee, President
P. O. Box 221
Brookville, OH 45309
*Boose Chevrolet
Brookville, OH
(513) 833-4011

BUCKEYE CORVETTES, INC.
Lynn Morrison
1957 Village St. S.E.
Canton, OH 44707
*Ewing Chevrolet
Canton, OH
(216) 454-8011

CAPITAL CITY CORVETTE CLUB
Herb Law
2845 Erickman Lane
Xenia, OH 45385

CENTRAL BUCKEYE CORVETTE ASSOCIATION
Frank Andrews
P. O. Box 28684
Columbus, OH 43228

CENTRAL OHIO CORVETTE CLUB
John Wadin
2085 Jewett Drive
Columbus, OH 43229

CINCINNATI CORVETTE CLUB
Denny Davis
2373 John Gray Road
Cincinnati, OH 45231

CLASSIC GLASS CORVETTE CLUB, INC.
Bud Rainsberg
P. O. Box 54
New Philadelphia, OH 44663
*Ferris Chevrolet, Inc.
New Philadelphia, OH
(216) 343-7761

COMPETITION CORVETTE
Jim Spoth
P. O. Box 1291
Mentor, OH 44061

CORVETTE CANTON, INC.
James Geissinger
326 Zern Avenue S.W.
Massillon, OH 44646

CORVETTE CATS
Ashton Kieselbach
19530 Story Road
Rocky River, OH 44116
*Ed Stinn
Rocky River, OH
(216) 333-8900

CORVETTE CHARDON, INC.
Dan Tagum
Box 505
Chardon, OH 44024

CORVETTE CLEVELAND, INC.
Jeff Debonis
P. O. Box 81608
Cleveland, OH 44181

CORVETTES, INC.
Bob Dorgiewicz
6718 Inglewood
Holland, OH 43528
*Dave White Chevrolet
Sylvania, OH
(419) 885-4444

CORVETTE-TROY
Tom Knick
P. O. Box 125
Troy, OH 45373
*Hopkins Chevrolet-Olds
New Carlisle, OH
(513) 849-1381

CORVETTES OF HAMILTON
Kevin Kuhl
P. O. Box 103
Hamilton, OH 45012
*Rose Chevrolet
Hamilton, OH
(513) 863-7878

CORVETTES OF LANCASTER
Steve L. Ours
133 Pierce Avenue
Lancaster, OH 43130

CORVETTES UNLIMITED
Isaac Barron III, President
27700 Bishop Park Dr. 306-S
Willoughby Hills, OH 44092

CUYAHOGA VALLEY CORVETTE CLUB
Gene Stepanik
82 Berwyn Drive
Bedford, OH 44146

DE FINESSE CORVETTE CLUB
3920 Salem Ave.
Dayton, OH 45426

FLAG CITY CORVETTES, INC.
Ron Riker
c/o La Riche Chevrolet
P. O. Box 59
Findlay, OH 45839
La Riche Chevrolet
Findlay, OH

(419) 422-1855

FOUNTAIN CITY CORVETTE CLUB
Gannon Bryant
1840 Sherwood Drive
Defiance, OH 43512
*Stan Pepple
Motor Sales, Inc.
Bryan, OH
(419) 636-1128

FUN CENTER CORVETTE CLUB, INC.
Carol Engel
Rt. 3, Stiving Road
Mansfield, OH 44903

GLAS' TREATMENT CORVETTE LTD.
Seldon Hill
102 Lyric Lane
Toledo, OH 43615

GLASS CITY CORVETTE CLUB
Doug Brainard
812 Ransom
Maumee, OH 43537
*Bob Schmidt
Maumee, OH
(419) 893-0761

GLASS CONNECTION CORVETTE CLUB
Gerald Sheaks
115 W. Clay Street
Sidney, OH 45365
*Meyer Motors, Inc.
Sidney, OH
(513) 492-6114

GLASS SOCIETY CORVETTE ASSOC., INC.
Terry Shoemaker
3033 Freyer Road
Lima, OH 45807
*Ivison Chevrolet
Lima, OH
(419) 331-0343

GREATER DAYTON CORVETTE CLUB
Bob Fahrubel, President
974 N. Lincoln St.
Wilmington, OH 45177
*Jack Huelsman Chevy-Olds
Fairborn, OH
(513) 878-3471

GREENVILLE CORVETTES, INC.
Bob Hilbert
Box 41
Greenville, OH 45331
*Schwartz Chevrolet
Greenville, OH
(513) 548-3115

INNOVATIVE 'VETTES CORVETTE CLUB
P. O. Box 22646
Beachwood, OH 44122

MEDINA CORVETTE CLUB
Pete Shaffer
6035 Wadsworth Rd.
Medina, OH 44256

MIAMI VALLEY CORVETTE CLUB
Richard Knouff
313 N. Main Street
Covington, Oh 45318

MOUND CITY CORVETTE CLUB
Gary Kosier
Box 674
Newark, OH 43055

NATIONAL CORVETTE RESTORERS SOCIETY
Gary Mortimer, V.P.
& membership
6291 Day Road
Cincinnati, OH 45247

NATIONAL CORVETTE RESTORERS SOCIETY
Lake Erie Chapter
Nancy Mastney
3069 Holly Drive
Brunswick, Oh 44212

NORTH EAST OHIO 'VETTE CLUB
Frank Arona, Governor
5315 Harper Road
Solon, OH 44139

NORTHERN OHIO CORVETTE OWNERS ASSOC.
Michelle Hopkins
P. O. Box 9137
Canton, OH 44711

SANDSTONE CITY CORVETTE CLUB
Jerry Hladek
261 Greenlawn Drive
Amherst, OH 44001

7-11 CORVETTE CLUB
P. O. Box 8095
Akron, OH 44320

SOUTHEAST OHIO CORVETTE CLUB
Jim Hill
212 East Church Street
Woodsfield, OH 43793
*Rice's
Chev.-Olds-Buick-Pontiac
Woodsfield, OH
(614) 472-1664

TIRETOWN CORVETTE CLUB
Ron Bessick
P. O. Box 331
Cuyahoga Falls, OH 44222
*Marhofer Chevrolet
Stow, OH

TRI-COUNTY CORVETTE CLUB
Gary Yoder
5697 Werkshire Terr.
Milford, OH 45150

TRI-VETTES, INC.
Jim Heck
1903 Camelot Lane
Findlay, OH 45840

ULTRA 'VETTES, INC.
Art Dickman
48 Edison Drive
Milan, OH 44846
*Dorr Chevrolet Co., Inc.
Milan, OH
(419) 499-2511

VINTAGE 'VETTES OF CINCY
J. Lee Patrick
9003 Symmesridge Lane
Loveland, OH 45140
*Bill Woeste Chevrolet
Cincinnati, OH
(513) 232-1100

WELLINGTON AREA CORVETTES
Dwight Justice
211 Woodland Street
Wellington, OH 44090

WEST OHIO OUTLAWS
Dean Beck
3436 Twp. Rd. Rt. 1
Carey, OH 43316

WES-'VETTES CORVETTE CLUB, INC.
Earnest Brown, Jr., President
3719 Cornellwood Drive
Dayton, OH 45406

OKLAHOMA

GREAT PLAINS CORVETTE ASSOC.
David Brashear
P. O. Box 2623
Lawton, OK 73505
*P-A Chevrolet
Lawton, OK
(405) 355-3280

NATIONAL CORVETTE RESTORERS SOCIETY
Oklahoma Chapter
Roy L. Sinor
7413 South First Street
Broken Arrow, OK 74011

OKLAHOMA CITY CORVETTE CLUB
Larry Phillips
P. O. Box 60573
Oklahoma City, OK 73106

SOONER CORVETTE CLUB
Jim Wheat
502 N. Forest St.
Jenks, OK 74037

TULSA 'VETTE SET, INC.
Steve Cotton
P. O. Box 470381
Tulsa, OK 74147

OREGON

CASCADE CORVETTE CLUB
Bruce Lamont
P. O. Box 363
Eugene, OR 97440
*Joe Romania Chevrolet
Eugene, OR
(503) 342-1121

CORVETTE CONNECTION
Dennis Ellexson
P. O. Box 1114
Klamath Falls, OR 97601

HIGH DESERT CORVETTE CLUB
Dave Pina
Rt. 7915 Hwy. 126
Redmond, OR 97756
*Dave Hamilton Chevy-Olds
Redmond, OR
(503) 548-1064

NATIONAL CORVETTE RESTORERS SOCIETY
Northwest Chapter
Bert Lukens
13720 N.E. Whitaker Way
Portland, OR 97230

NORTHWEST CORVETTE ASSOCIATION
John Hydorn
14224 N.E. Eugene Ct.
Portland, OR 97230

WILLAMETTE VALLEY CORVETTE ASSOC.
Patrick Taylor
1725 Juneau St. S.
Salem, OR 97302
*Capitol Chevrolet
Salem, OR 97301
(503) 585-4141

PENNSYLVANIA

ALLENTOWN AREA CORVETTE CLUB
Bob Wetherhold, President
626 W. Union Blvd.
Bethlehem, PA 18018
*Frederick Chevrolet, Inc.
Slatington, PA
(215) 767-1181

AQUARIAN CORVETTE ASSOC., INC.
Jack Hoefle
P. O. Box 101
Bristol, PA 19007

CENTRAL PENNSYLVANIA CORVETTE CLUB
Tom Kovach, President
P. O. Box 4281
Harrisburg, PA 17111

CORVETTE CLUB OF DELAWARE VALLEY
Bob Huey
P. O. Box 397
Willow Grove, PA 19090
*Bryner Chevrolet
Jenkintown, PA
(215) 886-3140

CORVETTE CLUB OF NORTH-EASTERN PENNSYLVANIA
Frank Davis, President
1702 Penn Avenue
Scranton, PA 18509

CORVETTE CLUB OF WESTERN PENNSYLVANIA
Sam Grabiak, President
Box 319
New Alexandria, PA 15670
*Grabiak Chevrolet, Inc.
New Alexandria, PA 15670
(412) 668-2231

CORVETTE ERIE LIMITED
George Lyons
3063 West 26 St.
Erie, PA 16506

COUNTY CORVETTE ASSOC.
H. John Rose
308 Larchwood Road
Westchester, PA 19382
*Frankel Chevrolet
Ardmore, PA
(215) 473-5600

CUMBERLAND VALLEY CORVETTE CLUB
Michael Filanowski, President
P. O. Box 1008
Mechanicsburg, PA 17055

EASTON AREA CORVETTE CLUB, INC.
George Rickert
P. O. Box 3027
Palmer Township, PA 18043
*William Chevrolet
Raubsville, PA
(215) 258-0400

FLOOD CITY CORVETTE CLUB
Mary Anne Seebacher
207 Karen Way
Johnstown, PA 15904
*Ron Davidson Chevrolet
Ebensburg, PA
(814) 472-7580

GREATER PHILADELPHIA CORVETTE CLUB
Hank Speer, President
P. O. Box 824
Richboro, PA 18954

KEYSTONE STATE CORVETTE CLUB
E. Wayne Holmes
176 E. Horseshoe Trail
Chester Springs, PA 19425

LANCASTER COUNTY CORVETTE CLUB
Gary Lintner
P. O. Box 4622
Lancaster, PA 17604
*Reed Chevrolet
Elizabethtown, PA
(717) 367-1189

LAUREL VALLEY CORVETTE CLUB
Larry Oldham
407 Pittsburgh St.
West Newton, PA 15089

MASON DIXON CORVETTE CLUB
Tom Martin
200 Gorman Drive
Chambersburg, PA 17201
*H & H Chevrolet
Shippensburg, PA
(717) 532-2121

NATIONAL CORVETTE RESTORERS SOCIETY
Delaware Valley Chapter
Marie McKeaney
345 Keswick Avenue
Glenside, PA 19038

PERRY COUNTY CORVETTE CLUB
Mike Shaffer
P. O. Box 183
Shermansdale, PA 17090
*Regester Chevrolet
Thompsontown, PA
(717) 535-5121

PRESQUE ISLE CORVETTE CLUB
David Devine, Secretary
P. O. Box 604
Erie, PA 16512
*Cramer Motors, Inc.
North East, PA
(814) 725-4507

SCHUYLKILL VALLEY CORVETTE CLUB
W. Lee Wehr
Beechwood Avenue
Marlin, PA 17951
*Paul Chevrolet & Olds
Ashland, PA
(717) 875-1117

SKYLINE DRIVE CORVETTES, INC.
John Catalano
Box 802
Reading, PA 19603
*T. J. Chevrolet
Reading, PA 19607
(215) 777-5000

S.U.N. CORVETTE CLUB, INC.
Denny Shaffer, President
P. O. Box 508
Lewisburg, PA 17837
*Diehl Chevrolet-Cadillac Co.
Lewisburg, PA
(717) 524-2296

TRI-STATE CORVETTE ASSOC.
Steve Meers
7327 State Road
Philadelphia PA 19136

UNITED RAYS CORVETTE CLUB
P. O. Box 99713
Pittsburgh, PA 15233

USA-1 CORVETTE CLUB
Jeff Port
105 W. Logan Street
Bellefonte, PA 16823
*MacIntyre Chevrolet
Lock Haven, PA
(718) 748-4008

YORK COUNTY CORVETTE CLUB
Bob Berkebile, President
P. O. Box 852
York, PA 17405
*Apple Chevrolet
York, PA
(717) 848-1300

RHODE ISLAND

CORVETTE CLUB OF RHODE ISLAND
Wayne King
25 Jane Lane
Bristol, RI 02809

SOUTH CAROLINA

CAROLINA CORVETTES, INC.
Wayne Punch
208 Stone Ridge Road
Greer, S.C. 29651
*Whitaker Simmons Chevrolet
Pendleton, S.C.
(803) 235-5422

COASTAL CORVETTE CLUB, INC.
Wendle Skipper
P. O. Box 181
Myrtle Beach, SC 29578

CORVETTE CHARLESTON, INC.
Skip McBride
428 Middleton Drive
Goose Creek, SC 29445

ELECTRIC CITY CORVETTE
Steve Feltman
115 W. Calhoun St.
Anderson, S.C. 29621
*Clinkscales Chevrolet
Belton, S.C.
(803) 338-7745

GREATER COLUMBIA CORVETTES
Harry Woodard
7216 Hilo Street
Columbia, SC 29209

SPARTANBURG CORVETTE CLUB, INC.
Pete Dawley
110 Holly Circle
Lyman, S.C. 29365
*M & M Chevrolet
Spartanburg, S.C.
(803) 582-5444

STINGRAYS OF GREEN-VILLE, S.C.
Rt. 4 Box 308
Simpsonville, S.C. 29681

SOUTH DAKOTA

BLACK HILLS CORVETTE CLUB
Ralph Island
315 St. Andrew
Rapid City, SD 57701
*Rapid Chevrolet
Rapid City, SD
(605) 343-1282

MIDWEST CORVETTE CLUB
Ron Hudson
P. O. Box 1335
Sioux Falls, SD 57101

SIOUX FALLS CORVETTE CLUB, INC.
Bob Schunneman
P. O. Box 90
Sioux Falls, SD 57101
*Frank Stinson Chevrolet
Sioux Falls, SD
(605) 336-1700

TENNESSEE

CHATTANOOGA GLAS
Clon Fortnor
2617 Dancing Waters
Jonesboro, GA 30263

BEALE STREET CORVETTE ASSOC.
Ben Gilbert, Governor
3006 Harris Cl
Memphis, TN 38114

CORVETTES, INC.
Larry Jones
109 Allen St.
McMinnville, TN 37110
*Shelton Chevrolet
& Cadillac, Inc.
McMinnville TN
(615) 473-1535

COUNTRY ROAD CORVETTE CLUB
Gaylen Hodges, President
2036 Dinsmore Drive
Clarksville, TN 37040

EAST TENNESSEE CORVETTE CLUB
Ross Birchfiel
801 E. Harper Avenue
Maryville, TN 37801
*Reeder Chevrolet Co.
Knoxville, TN
(615) 687-7710

GOLDEN CIRCLE CORVETTE CLUB
Jeff Garner
106 Charlesmeade
Jackson, TN 38305

MURFREESBORO CORVETTE CLUB

Carl Witty
1615 Saltlick Place
Murfreesboro, TN 37130

'VETTE SETTE
Durrel Crowley
215 Sullivan
Memphis, TN 38109

TEXAS

ABILENE CORVETTE CLUB
Connie Keaton, President
1301 Minter Lane
Abilene, TX 79603
*Larry Rigby Chevrolet
Abilene, TX
(915) 695-8800

CEN-TEX CORVETTE CLUB, INC.
James Olson
P. O. Box 3241
Waco, TX 76707
*Steakley Brothers
Chevrolet Company
Waco, TX
(817) 772-8850

CONCHO VALLEY CORVETTES
Larry Brokaw
Rt. 5 Box 5067
San Angelo, TX 76904
*Mustang Chev. Corp.
San Angelo, TX
(915) 653-4561

CORPUS CHRISTI CORVETTE CLUB
Tim Painschab
5801 Crestwood
Corpus Christi, TX 78415
*Vista Chevrolet
Corpus Christi, TX
(512) 855-2100

CORVETTE CLUB OF TEXAS
Ray Hall, President
13112 Southview
Dallas, TX 75240
*Friendly Chevrolet
Dallas, TX
(214) 526-8811

CORVETTE OWNERS ASSOCIATION OF SOUTH TEXAS
Nick Clevenger
15703 Bright Star
San Antonio, TX 78232

COWTOWN 'VETTES, INC.
Ben Gresham
205 Alexander Ct.
Irving, TX 75061

EAST TEXAS CORVETTE CLUB
Gayley Beal
600 Sunnyhill Drive
Tyler, TX 75702

GREAT SOUTHWEST CORVETTE CLUB
David Jasper
1802 Glen Brook
Irving, TX 75061

HOU-TEX 'VETTES, INC.
Chris Ronson
P. O. Box 742047
Houston, TX 77274

LONE STAR 'VETTES
Kathi Richardson
4818 Woodrow
Galveston, TX 77550

LONGHORN CORVETTE CLUB, INC.
David Doig
12801 Sherbourne St.
Austin, TX 78729
*Henna Chevrolet
Austin, TX 78752
(512) 454-2501

LOS CHRISTO RAYS
Erich Goedner
4121 Darwood
El Paso, TX 79902

MID-COAST CORVETTE CLUB
Maggie Dengler
142 Oyster Creek Dr. #37
Lake Jackson, TX 77566

MID-TEXAS CUSTOM CORVETTE ASSOCIATION
Pete Miller
1205-B Wales Drive
Killeen, TX 76542

NATIONAL CORVETTE RESTORERS SOCIETY
Texas Chapter
Sheldon Massey
3305 Winton Drive
Amarillo, TX 79121

SAN JACINTO CORVETTE CLUB
Diane Carey, President
61 Park West Dr. East
Houston, TX 77072

SUN CITIES CORVETTE CLUB
Dee Albert
10441 Adonis
El Paso, TX 79924

TEXARKANA CORVETTE CLUB
Bob Ellison, President
5805 Oak Flat
Texarkana, TX 75501
*Orr Chevrolet Co
Texarkana, TX
(214) 794-6145

TEXAS CORVETTE ASSOC.
Don Lothringer
Box 5036
Universal City, TX 78148

TEXAS OUTLAWS CORVETTE CLUB, INC.
Venita McGrath
900 Briarcliff Court
Arlington, TX 76012

TEXAS 'VETTES, INC.
Bob Pinkston
218 Molina
Sunnyvale, TX 75182

WEST TEXAS CORVETTES, INC.
Danny Knox
1108 Dover
Lubbock, TX 79416
*Modern Chevrolet
Lubbock, TX
(806) 747-3211

UTAH

CORVETTE CLUB OF UTAH
John Kennedy, President
519 North 5th West
Bountiful, UT 84010
*Gus Paulos Chevrolet
West Valley City, UT
(801) 969-8221

VERMONT

CORVETTE CLUB OF VERMONT
Jock Cowdrey
Box 204
Randolph, VT 05060
*Cody Chevrolet
Montpelier, VT
(802) 223-6337

VIRGINIA

BEACHCOMBERS CORVETTE CLUB
Len Porter
144 S. Parliament Dr.
Virginia Beach, VA 23462
*RK Chevrolet
Virginia Beach, VA
(804) 486-2222

BLUE RIDGE CORVETTE CLUB, INC.
Phillip Kania
P. O. Box 1
Stuarts Draft, VA 24477
*Hays Chevrolet, Inc.
Staunton, VA
(703) 885-1584

CAPITAL CITY 'VETTE CLUB
P. O. Box 25473
Richmond, VA 23220

CORVETTE CLUB OF RICHMOND
Roger Kisner
Box 6313
Richmond, VA 23230

HAMPTON ROADS CORVETTE CLUB
Martin Merenda
18 Sir Francis Wyatt Place
Newport News, VA 23606
*Hutchen's Chevrolet
Newport News, VA
(804) 874-8111

NATIONAL CORVETTE RESTORERS SOCIETY
Mid-Atlantic Chapter
Tom Stewart
2303 Maple Street
Virginia Beach, VA 23451

NEW RIVER VALLEY CORVETTE CLUB
Eddie Lovern
Rt. 2 Box 437A
Christiansburg, VA 24073
*Harvey's Chevrolet Corp.
Radford, VA
(703) 639-3923

NORTHERN VIRGINIA CORVETTE CLUB
Jim Bryfonski
P. O. Box 4472
Arlington, VA 22204
*Rosenthal Chevrolet
Arlington, VA
(703) 920-8700

VIRGINIA CORVETTE CLUB
Robert Anderson
P. O. Box 11292
Lynchburg, VA 24506

VOLUNTEER CORVETTE CLUB
Michael Coomer
251 Mabe Hill Drive
Bristol, VA 37620
*Looney Chevrolet-Cadillac
Kingsport, TN
(615) 246-4101

WASHINGTON

CLASSICAL GLASS CORVETTE CLUB OF TACOMA
Gary "Soupy" Campbell
33617-25th Lane S.W. J8
Federal Way, WA 98023

COLUMBIA RIVER CORVETTES
Jerry Kazeck
P. O. Box 357
Kelso, WA 98626
*Bud Clary Chevrolet, Inc.
Longview, WA
(206) 425-0407

CORVETTE MARQUE CLUB OF SEATTLE
Mike Shelly
P. O. Box 534
Kirkland, WA 98083
*Lee Johnson Chevrolet
Kirkland, WA
(206) 827-0521

CORVETTES DE OLYMPIA
Larry Johnson
P. O. Box 2154
Olympia, WA 98507

MAJESTIC GLASS
Linda Gilbert
2230 W. Parkway Drive
Mount Vernon, WA 98273
*Seaside
Chevrolet-Buick, Inc.
Anacortes, WA
(206) 293-5166

PENINSULA CORVETTE & CO.
Bill Eldridge
561 Olele Point Road
Port Ludlow, WA 98365
*Bill Koenig Chevrolet
Port Angeles, WA
(206) 457-4444

SPOKANE CORVETTE CLUB
John Wallace
P. O. Box 3032
Spokane, WA 99220
*Camp Chevrolet
Spokane, WA
(509) 456-7890

SUNLAND CORVETTE CLUB
Bettie Sartin
P. O. Box 2913
Tri Cities, WA 99302
*Bill McCurley Chev.
Pasco, WA
(509) 547-5555

VALLEY 'VETTES
Les Lennington
2105 S. 69th Avenue
Yakima, WA 98908
*Sunfair Chevrolet
Yakima, WA
(509) 248-7600

'VETTERS
Bob Lattimar
972 Industry Dr.
Seattle, WA 98188

WEST VIRGINIA

APPALACHIAN CORVETTE CLUB, LTD.
Rick Sumner
3034 East Beckley Station
Beckley, WV 25801

BLENNERHASSET CORVETTE ASSOCIATION
David G. Hefner
107 Maple Dr., Rt. 1
Williamstown, WV 26187

CENTRAL WEST VIRGINIA CORVETTE CLUB
Roger Stevens, Jr.
P. O. Box 64
Bridgeport, WV 26330
*Harry Green Chevrolet
Clarksburg, WV
(304) 624-6304

CORVETTE CLUB OF WEST VIRGINIA
Kent Pascoli
37 Willow Lane
Wheeling, WV 26003
*Paul Reilley Chevrolet
Glen Dale, WV
(304) 845-5070

KANAWHA VALLEY CORVETTE CLUB
Henry Szozda
5131 Dover Drive
Cross Lanes, WV 25313

UNIVERSITY CORVETTES
F. N. Crouch
60 S. University Avenue
Morgantown, WV 26505
*University Chev.-Cadilac
Morgantown, WV
(304) 296-4401

WISCONSIN

BADGER STATE 'VETTES, LTD.
George Griffith, President
6953 S. Phyllis Lane
Franklin, WI 53132

BLACKHAWK CORVETTE CLUB
William Kahabka
701 Alder Avenue
Delavan, WI 53115

CORVETTES LIMITED MADISON
Jim Whiteside
3741 Busse St.
Madison, WI 53714
*John Erickson Chevrolet
Verona, WI
(608) 256-6292

CORVETTES OF THE NORTH
John Bodette
151 Sarah Circle
Wisconsin Rapids, WI 54494
*Brostrom-Kickert
Chevrolet, Inc.
Wisconsin Rapids, WI
(715) 423-7020

FOND DE 'VETTES, LTD.
Mary Schnettler
Rt. 5, Box 108D
Fond Du Lac, WI 54935

CLASS GLASS CORVETTE CLUB
Kercene Day, Jr.
6503 W. Florist
Milwaukee, WI 53218

KETTLE MORAINE CORVETTE, LTD.
Earl Mondloch, Governor
338 Pioneer Road
Sheboygan, WI 53081

MUSKEGO CORVETTE CLUB
Lyle Premetz
4635 South 114th Street
Greenfield, WI 53228

OZAUKEE CORVETTE CLUB
Randy Krentz
1348 Port View Dr.
Port Washington, WI 53074
*Flaherty Chevrolet-Olds
Port Washington, WI
(414) 284-4422

SOUTHEASTERN WISCONSIN CORVETTE CLUB
Kraig Manna
4523 Harding Road
Kenosha, WI 53142
*Berman/Shaver Chevrolet
Racine, WI
(414) 886-1010

VALLEY 'VETTE, INC.
Dick Rank
P. O. Box 2555
Appleton, WI 54913
*Stromberg Chevrolet-Cadillac
Appleton, WI
(414) 733-5581

WISCONSIN CORVETTE CLUB, INC.
P. O. Box 1115
Milwaukee, WI 53201

WYOMING

CENTRAL WYOMING CORVETTE ASSOCIATION
LeRoy Engdahl
111 Primrose
Casper, WY 82604

THUNDER BASIN CORVETTES
John Schonberg
181 Independence Drive
Gillette, WY 82716
*Davis
Chevrolet-Cadillac, Inc.
Gillette, WY
(307) 682-8851

(National Council of Corvette Clubs
Nancy Sable
P. O. Box 813
Adams Basin, NY 14410
(716) 352-9188

(Western States Corvette Council)

Ted Bush
2321 Falling Water Court
Lake Santa Clara, CA 95054
(408) 988-1628

(United Council of Corvette Clubs)

Gloria Williams
315 Edington Road
Akron, OH 44313
(206) 666-2937

(Canadian Council of Corvette Clubs)

Western Region
Pat Watson
11800 Pintail Drive
Richmond, B.C.,
Canada V7E 4P5
(604) 271-4147

Eastern Region
Debbie Shadbolt
795 Sprouds Lane
Pickering, Ontario,
Canada L1V 3M2
(416) 839-6265

(National Corvette Restorers Society)

Gary Mortimer
6291 Day Road
Cincinnati, OH 45247
(513) 385-8526 (evening)

John Amgwert
P. O. Box 81663
Lincoln, NE 68501-1663
(402) 421-1953 (day)

CANADA

Canadian Council of Corvette Clubs - WESTERN REGION

British Columbia

B.C. CORVETTE CLUB
T. Osiowsy
P. O. Box 20508
Burnaby, B.C.
Canada V5H 3X9
*Courtesy Chevrolet
Burnaby, B.C.
(604) 437-8511

CENTRAL INTERIOR CORVETTE CLUB
2510 Briarwood Avenue
Kamloops, B.C. V2B 4Z9

CHILLIWACK CORVETTE CLUB
Box 14
Sardis, B.C. V2R 1A5

FRASER VALLEY CORVETTE CLUB
34933 Edgeview Place, R.R. 4
Abbotsford, B.C. V2S 4N4

ITALIAN RACING TEAM
17353 - 100 Ave., R.R. 12
Surrey, B.C. V3T 5J4

OKANAGAN CORVETTE CLUB
R.R. 5, 1544 Oswell Dr.
Kelowna, B.C. V1X 4K4

RIVERSIDE CORVETTE CLUB
11800 Pintail Dr.
Richmond, B.C. V7E 4P5

VICTORIA CORVETTE CLUB
P. O. Box 457, Station E
Victoria B.C. V8W 2N8

Alberta

CALGARY CORVETTE CLUB
Joseph Raj
223 Parkland Cres. S.E.
Calgary, Alta.,
Canada T2J 3Y4
*Jack Carter Chevrolet-Olds
Calgary, Alta., Canada
(403) 252-8171

CORVETTES UNLIMITED
12508 Lake Geneva Rd. S.E.
Calgary, Alberta T2J 2S5

EDMONTON CORVETTE CLUB
11907 - 126 St.
Edmonton, Alberta T5L 0W3

ITALIAN RACING TEAM
407, 10101 - 101 St.
Fort Saskatchewan,
Alberta T8L 3S7

NORTHERN ALBERTA CORVETTE OWNERS' CLUB
Box 29, Site 16, R.R. 2
Winterburn, Alberta T03 2N0

Saskatchewan

REGINA CORVETTE CLUB
Box 496
Regina, Saskatchewan S4P 3A2

SASKATCHEWAN CORVETTE CLUB
38 Cole Avenue
Saskatoon,
Saskatchewan S7L 4G3

Manitoba

CORVETTE CLUB OF MANITOBA
Irene Deane, President
3 Barker Boulevard
Winnipeg, Manitoba,
Canada R3R 2C8

Canadian Council of Corvette Clubs - EASTERN REGION

BRAMPTON CORVETTE CLUB
P. O. Box 415
Brampton, Ontario, Canada

CAPITAL CORVETTE CLUB
86 Tower Road
Ottawa, Ontario,
Canada K2G 2E9

CORVETTE ASSOC. OF HAMILTON
P. O. Box 3694
Hamilton, Ontario,
Canada L8H 7N1

CORVETTE CLUB OF NOVA SCOTIA
P. O. Box 3432
Dartmouth, Nova Scotia,
Canada B2W 5G3

CORVETTE CLUB OF ONTARIO
P. O. Box 1065
Adelaide St.
Toronto, Ontario,
Canada M5C 2K4

CORVETTE CLUB OF WINDSOR
P. O. Box 334
Windsor, Ontario,
Canada N9A 6K7

CORVETTES OF CENTRAL ONTARIO
P. O. Box 1022
Station C
Kitchener, Ontario, Canada
N2G 4E3

CORVETTES OF SOUTHERN ONTARIO
P. O. Box 334
Simcoe, Ontario, Canada N3Y 4G2

CORVETTES OF WESTERN ONTARIO
P. O. Box 4393
Station C
London, Ontario, Canada N5W 5J2

NATIONAL CORVETTE RESTORERS SOCIETY
Ontario Chapter
Dan Adie
409 Broad Street East
Dunnville, Ontario, Canada
N1A 1G6

NIAGARA CORVETTE CLUB
P. O. Box 462
St. Catharines, Ontario,
Canada L2R 2V9

PINE RIDGE CORVETTE CLUB
182 Church Street
Bowmanville, Ontario, Canada
L1C 1T9
*Ontario Motor Sales
Oshawa, Ontario, Canada
(416) 725-6501

QUINTE CORVETTE ASSOC. INC.
P. O. Box 808
Trenton, Ontario, Canada K8V 5R8

ROYAL CITY CORVETTES
P. O. Box 55
Guelph, Ontario, Canada N1H 6J6

'VETTES DE MONTREAL
6600 St. Urbain
Ste. 304
Montreal, Quebec, Canada
H2S 3G8

GERMANY

CORVETTE OWNERS CLUB GERMANY
Eugen Brender
Ernst-von-Beling-Strasse 3
Muenchen FRG
W. Germany D-8000

SWEDEN

CLUB CORVETTE SWEDEN
Box 2093
S-141 02
Huddinge- Sweden

SWITZERLAND

CORVETTES UNLIMITED SWITZERLAND
H. R. Stillhart
Seestrasse 50
Kilchberg ZH
Switzerland CH-8802
*Tip-Top Autowerke
Zurich, Switzerland
01/493 12 20
*Milchbuck Garagen
Zurich, Switzerland
01/362 37 21

SWISS CORVETTE CLUB
P. O. Box 127
CH 8027
Zurich, Switzerland

IDENTIFICATION NUMBERS

The VIN (vehicle identification number) is the most familiar number appearing on Corvettes. It is this number that appears on most titles (a few states have used engine numbers) and insurance policies.

A different VIN is assigned to each Corvette during assembly. Each car receives its number in sequence. The format of the number has changed over the years but the last digits always have indicated when a particular Corvette was assembled relative to others of the same year. For instance, the first 1953 Corvette VIN was E53F001001. The last was E53F001300, meaning total production for the year was 300. Note that you can determine the production quantities for each Corvette year in *Illustrated Corvette Buyer's Guide* by referring to the serial sequence at the head of each chapter. But one word of caution: Four thousand Corvette VIN tags disappeared during 1973 and these cars were never built. So while the 1973 sequence goes up to 34,464, only 30,464 were built. The missing numbers were 24,001 through 28,000.

The VIN is stamped into a plate that is attached to the body of each Corvette during manufacture. The location of the plate varies with different years. From 1953 through early 1960, the plate was attached to the driver's door post. All but early 1960 models and all 1961 and 1962 Corvettes had the plate attached to the steering column in the engine compartment. The 1963 through 1967 models had the plate attached to an instrument support brace visible below the glovebox. Starting with the 1968 models, federal law mandated that the VIN be visible through the windshield from outside the car on the driver's side; so the VIN plate of 1968 and newer Corvettes is located either on the windshield pillar or on top of the dash.

To aid in detecting stolen vehicles whose serial tags have been tampered with or switched, manufacturers also stamp the VIN into several locations on the frame. Enthusiasts often uncover these numbers during restorations and all Corvettes starting with the 1953 have them.

Starting in early 1960, the sequential portion of the VIN was stamped into the engine block on a pad just forward of the passenger-side head. Comparing the number stamped into the engine with the VIN serial tag thus enables the purchaser of a used Corvette to determine if the engine in the car is the exact one installed by the factory. When Corvette enthusiasts advertise a Corvette with the statement "numbers match" they are most often referring to the match between the number stamped into the engine block and the VIN serial plate.

Unfortunately, the importance attached to engine originality by Corvette enthusiasts has led to the counterfeiting of Corvettes with engines that are not original. Since the sequential portion of the VIN was *stamped* into the engine block, the surface can be milled and restamped. But there is another engine number you can check.

It is the date code. This will be three or four characters—a letter followed by numbers. The letter indicates the month of casting. The day is indicated by the first one or two numbers. The last number indicates the year. A date code of A122 translates to a block cast on January 12, 1962. Or 1972. Or 1982. The date code is on the top rear, passenger side of the block in Chevy small-blocks. It's forward of the starter by the freeze plug on the passenger side of the big-blocks.

The beauty of the date code is that it is part of the block casting and protrudes rather than being stamped after casting. It is very difficult to counterfeit. Attempts have been made by grinding off the original code, building up a weld bead, then shaping a new number with a pencil grinder. Extensive forgeries are rare and usually will not pass close inspection.

The reason the engine casting date is important is that it obviously must precede the assembly of the Corvette itself. There is no exact time lag and it's always a remote possibility that an engine block could get buried in inventory, but typically somewhere between a few days and two or three weeks pass between the time an engine is cast and then installed in a new Corvette.

Determining a Corvette's originality is a process of elimination. As you eliminate possible indicators of nonoriginality, the likelihood of originality increases. But neither you nor anyone else other than the original owner can ever be absolutely certain. As the stakes go up, so do the rewards of counterfeiting.

Some enthusiasts just entering the market for a used Corvette are under the impression that they can obtain a copy of the original sales invoice or window sticker from GM. Not true. You're on your own. This is why cars with original documentation are so prized.

If you are uncomfortable in any way about the originality of a Corvette that you're considering for purchase, either pass or get professional assistance.

RECOMMENDED CORVETTE BOOKS

Scores of books have been written about Corvettes. Each book has something of value, but some are more useful than others. Corvettes seem to have invited modifications and some earlier books have been criticized for showing minor and major photo inaccuracies.

Following are some personal favorites. This list is far from complete, but if you digest the information these books contain you'll hold your own in any Corvette discussion.

Adams, Noland. *The Complete Corvette Restoration & Technical Guide—Vol. 1. 1953 Through 1962.* Princeton, New Jersey: Princeton Publishing, Inc., 1980.

Antonick, M. B. *Corvette! America's Only.* Powell, Ohio: Michael Bruce Associates, Inc., 1978.

———*The Corvette Black Book.* Powell, Ohio: Michael Bruce Associates, Inc., 1978, 1980, 1984, 1985, 1986, 1987.

———*Corvette Restoration: State of the Art.* Powell, Ohio: Michael Bruce Associates, Inc., 1981.

———*Corvette! Sportscar of America.* Powell, Ohio. Michael Bruce Associates, Inc., 1980.

Dobbins, M. F. *Vette Vues Fact Book of the 1968-1972 Stingray.* Glenside, Pennsylvania: Dr. M. F. Dobbins, 1981.

———*Vette Vues Fact Book of the 1963-1967 Sting Ray*, 5th ed. Glenside, Pennsylvania: Dr. M.F. Dobbins.

Ludvigsen, Karl. *Corvette: America's Star-Spangled Sport Car: The Complete History.* 2nd ed. Princeton, New Jersey: Princeton Publishing, Inc., 1978.

CORVETTE PRICES 1953-1976

Source: *Vette Vues*, Volume Six through Volume Fourteen.

Vette Vues magazine is published monthly by Jim Prather in Sandy Springs, Georgia. It has been around since 1972 and it's the best source I know of for used Corvette and Corvette parts advertising. Just about everyone who deals in Corvette reproduction items and services advertises in *Vette Vues*, so reading it is a great way to keep tuned in to the marketplace.

The prices shown are advertised prices in *Vette Vues* for the nine-year period represented by Volumes Six through Fourteen. *Vette Vues* started in June, so the years shown run from June through May. For example, 1986's prices are those that appeared in *Vette Vues* from June 1985 through May 1986.

Remember, these were asking prices. Obviously, not all the cars sold and those that did may have brought less than advertised. No figure is shown if fewer than three ads appeared in a twelve month period for a particular year, something possible with Corvettes like the 1953 model.

A survey of this type has its flaws, but if used wisely it can be helpful. The price trend over the nine-year period will certainly be fairly accurate, as will the relative prices between years.

	High	Avg.	Low	High	Avg.	Low	High	Avg.	Low
	1953 Corvette			**1954 Corvette**			**1955 Corvette**		
1978	—	—	—	13,000	7,309	3,000	15,000	9,420	2,300
1979	35,000	20,833	7,500	17,400	10,530	5,500	16,000	13,083	2,500
1980	26,500	18,820	7,500	15,500	12,417	8,500	9,100	7,985	7,335
1981	45,000	27,160	8,800	24,000	13,000	4,500	25,000	20,817	11,900
1982	50,000	38,200	15,000	29,500	13,157	6,500	28,000	17,913	11,500
1983	35,000	29,667	24,000	28,000	18,568	8,500	39,950	20,597	5,000
1984	30,000	18,917	10,500	29,000	15,358	3,750	42,500	24,000	5,500
1985	40,000	31,188	20,000	35,000	16,331	4,500	24,500	20,600	12,900
1986	-	-	-	35,000	17,183	3,400	27,500	22,192	18,500
	1956 Corvette			**1957 Corvette**			**1958 Corvette**		
1978	10,000	4,904	2,500	17,500	7,163	2,750	15,000	6,035	2,195
1979	10,000	6,720	4,300	15,000	5,859	2,500	16,000	7,877	4,500
1980	22,000	7,715	2,900	20,000	9,858	5,000	11,500	7,731	4,600
1981	17,500	11,710	7,100	18,500	12,735	5,500	14,000	7,264	4,000
1982	18,000	12,200	6,000	37,000	14,736	6,500	15,700	9,824	5,000
1983	26,500	13,195	3,000	32,500	14,340	4,500	18,500	9,300	5,500
1984	22,000	15,225	10,000	36,500	15,832	5,500	22,500	10,238	2,500
1985	16,500	12,510	5,800	42,000	20,184	4,800	25,000	12,906	3,000
1986	27,500	18,557	4,000	40,000	18,681	4,800	13,900	9,962	3,800
	1959 Corvette			**1960 Corvette**			**1961 Corvette**		
1978	15,000	5,811	1,850	12,500	5,241	1,800	12,000	5,513	3,150
1979	9,500	7,344	4,250	11,000	7,436	2,600	11,900	6,189	2,950
1980	15,500	7,214	2,900	13,900	8,587	3,000	18,500	9,448	4,000
1981	15,900	7,826	2,900	13,000	7,494	4,000	15,500	8,799	3,000
1982	24,500	11,931	6,750	13,500	8,426	4,500	15,000	9,915	4,750
1983	18,500	11,370	6,700	16,500	11,034	4,700	18,500	9,902	4,800
1984	14,500	10,578	5,000	30,000	11,826	3,500	24,500	10,661	6,000
1985	26,000	11,815	7,500	21,000	11,475	6,000	15,900	9,839	3,000
1986	35,000	14,268	3,300	29,500	13,571	3,300	28,000	12,564	4,500

	1962 Corvette			1963 Corvette			1964 Corvette		
	High	Avg.	Low	High	Avg.	Low	High	Avg.	Low
1978	15,000	5,704	2,450	18,500	9,022	3,950	13,500	5,917	2,000
1979	17,000	9,123	3,000	19,800	8,990	3,000	15,000	8,015	3,500
1980	18,500	10,347	3,500	30,000	10,757	4,000	25,000	8,011	3,500
1981	20,000	9,939	4,500	17,600	10,264	3,500	16,000	8,614	3,400
1982	22,000	9,594	5,200	27,500	15,311	4,500	15,500	10,359	5,000
1983	32,000	10,241	3,000	25,000	13,190	4,500	20,000	10,281	4,500
1984	20,000	14,376	7,000	30,000	14,425	4,900	30,000	12,664	4,000
1985	25,000	13,672	3,000	38,500	16,045	5,000	32,000	12,418	4,000
1986	28,000	14,333	7,500	50,000	16,604	6,500	25,000	13,386	3,000

	1965 Corvette			1966 Corvette			1967 Corvette		
1978	18,000	7,080	2,900	14,500	6,524	1,750	13,500	7,018	2,100
1979	17,500	8,373	2,700	14,500	7,616	3,200	17,500	8,868	3,500
1980	18,500	9,264	3,300	17,000	8,203	3,400	20,000	9,831	3,800
1981	25,000	9,301	2,900	18,500	8,885	3,400	20,000	10,581	4,500
1982	25,000	11,032	4,950	23,900	10,669	4,500	33,000	12,834	4,800
1983	32,000	12,360	3,800	25,900	11,585	3,500	38,000	13,385	4,700
1984	32,500	13,490	4,200	27,500	12,036	4,500	32,000	15,104	4,200
1985	39,500	13,140	4,800	28,500	12,806	3,000	34,500	16,078	4,000
1986	33,500	15,337	5,800	35,000	13,920	3,000	45,000	17,248	7,500

	1968 Corvette			1969 Corvette			1970 Corvette		
1978	15,000	4,914	2,500	13,000	6,055	2,750	8,250	5,826	2,250
1979	15,000	6,233	2,500	12,000	7,317	2,895	12,000	6,322	2,895
1980	11,000	6,630	3,400	14,500	6,902	2,800	16,500	8,176	2,750
1981	20,000	7,732	3,200	22,500	8,065	2,800	13,000	7,863	4,950
1982	20,000	9,085	4,500	24,000	9,047	3,800	18,000	9,622	5,000
1983	25,000	9,591	5,200	20,000	9,736	3,900	25,000	9,107	4,500
1984	36,000	9,781	2,400	36,000	8,953	2,900	18,500	10,003	3,000
1985	25,000	12,918	3,600	18,500	11,117	5,200	30,000	12,574	4,500
1986	29,500	11,391	2,200	25,000	13,381	5,500	32,500	12,980	7,000

	1971 Corvette			1972 Corvette			1973 Corvette		
1978	10,500	6,076	3,500	12,000	6,947	3,999	15,000	6,346	3,800
1979	10,500	6,475	3,795	12,000	7,592	5,250	10,000	6,799	5,500
1980	23,500	8,228	3,850	14,900	8,265	3,750	12,900	7,366	4,650
1981	19,995	7,615	4,100	15,500	8,969	3,995	15,000	7,322	4,000
1982	19,000	10,611	5,500	16,000	9,365	5,200	10,750	8,239	6,000
1983	16,000	8,445	3,000	16,500	10,325	3,800	18,000	10,096	4,800
1984	29,800	9,849	2,500	19,500	10,034	3,600	15,900	9,061	4,500
1985	40,000	10,024	4,600	23,000	11,053	3,000	20,000	9,636	6,000
1986	20,500	11,464	3,000	16,300	11,027	5,000	18,000	10,459	4,500

	1974 Corvette			1975 Corvette			1976 Corvette		
1978	11,000	7,290	6,200	15,500	8,719	6,595	20,000	9,023	7,295
1979	15,000	8,127	5,900	15,000	9,187	6,400	11,500	9,000	7,700
1980	15,000	7,952	4,200	19,500	9,426	5,700	11,000	8,477	7,150
1981	14,000	10,255	5,900	18,000	9,912	6,500	11,500	8,638	7,000
1982	15,000	8,569	5,700	22,000	11,554	6,500	11,500	9,425	6,975
1983	15,300	9,194	4,700	25,500	11,521	4,900	18,000	10,392	6,300
1984	15,000	8,553	3,300	22,000	11,766	3,900	19,900	9,840	4,500
1985	20,000	11,167	5,900	22,500	12,400	2,500	19,500	9,471	2,500
1986	20,000	10,972	6,300	20,000	12,775	6,000	19,500	13,340	7,500